WAR, POLITICS AND RECONSTRUCTION

THE MACMILLAN COMPANY
NEW YORK · BOSTON · CHICAGO · DALLAS
ATLANTA · SAN FRANCISCO

MACMILLAN & CO., Limited
LONDON · BOMBAY · CALCUTTA
MELBOURNE

**THE MACMILLAN COMPANY
OF CANADA, Limited**
TORONTO

HENRY CLAY WARMOTH

WAR, POLITICS AND RECONSTRUCTION

STORMY DAYS IN LOUISIANA

BY

HENRY CLAY WARMOTH

NEW YORK
THE MACMILLAN COMPANY
1930

SET UP BY BROWN BROTHERS LINOTYPERS
PRINTED IN THE UNITED STATES OF AMERICA
BY THE FERRIS PRINTING COMPANY

PREFACE AND ACKNOWLEDGMENTS

IN the preparation of this work I have very largely used my notes, part of my diary, my public and private correspondence with various Federal, State, and Parish public officials, newspaper clippings, newspaper files, numerous public documents, and sundry works on Reconstruction.

The outstanding events of Reconstruction in Louisiana have been carefully set down, and where it seemed necessary for a clear understanding of the subject under discussion, elaboration and detailed explanations have been made. The entire aim has been to make the matter contained herein readable, clear, accurate, impartial, and useful. If I have succeeded in any measure in accomplishing these aims, I have already been amply rewarded.

I take very great pleasure in acknowledging my sincere gratitude to Professor A. E. Perkins, B.S., M.A., Supervising Principal in the public schools of New Orleans, for his efficient literary criticism of the entire manuscript and for valuable suggestions concerning the form, arrangement, and editing of the work.

With the hope that many may find profitable and pleasant reading in the book, I submit it to the reading public for whatever merit it may have and for whatever good it may do.

H. C. WARMOTH,
Ex-Governor of Louisiana.

FOREWORD

Reconstruction

So much has been written about the Reconstruction of the State of Louisiana after the Civil War and of the men who participated in that historic process, and so many false and vicious statements have been made and published, that it seems appropriate that one of the remaining chief actors should give a full and truthful narrative of the history of that exciting era and especially of the one man on whom the greatest responsibility rested.

Many of those who have written have hesitated at nothing; have strained their imaginations, and have stopped at no exaggeration or misrepresentation or falsehood which they thought would make their books or papers popular and salable. Everything was said that would disparage or discredit the officials. Nothing was said to explain, or justify their acts or their conduct. Pens were dipped deep into ink to blacken the characters of the men who upheld the Flag and fought for their right to live on Louisiana soil as free men.

Lies, unmitigated lies, notorious and malicious lies, have been printed and broadcast, and willing and eager readers have been glad to believe them. For example, one Chambers (Henry E. Chambers, author of a school history of the United States), who pretended to write a history of Louisiana in three volumes, perpetrated on two pages, 665 and 666, Volume I, five distinct lies. He said:

First: Warmoth was one of those who had been particularly successful in winning the confidence and blind devotion of the negroes.

Second: It is said of him that he landed in Louisiana a handsome, upstanding young fellow of twenty-six, comparatively penniless.

Third: And that one of the first of his *coups* successfully put through in his eventful life was to persuade the blacks that they should have a special representative—lobbyist, we would call him today—in Washington, to conserve their rights, and that he was the very man for the place.

Fourth: And at every poll was an extra box in which each voter would deposit 50 cents as a contribution to Warmoth's expenses.

Fifth: Needless to say, quite a little sum was thus realized by Warmoth, and he secured such a hold upon the blacks as—after they were in truth vested with the franchise—made him invincible when he ran for office.

Every one of these statements was in spirit, in intention, and in fact, false, and the man who put them in his history of Louisiana knew them to be false from beginning to end.

In the first place, I did not land in Louisiana "comparatively penniless." I had plenty of money with which to begin my new life after I left the army; and I at once entered upon a lucrative practice of law in the United States Courts, before courts-martial, military commissions, and governmental departments, which paid me large fees and a handsome income.

In the second place, I did not make an attempt to "win the blind devotion of the negroes."

In the third place, the Republican Party in Louisiana was formally organized in 1863, while I was fighting before Vicksburg, at Missionary Ridge, etc. It had a State Committee composed of twenty-six members, with the Hon. Thomas J. Durant as Chairman, which had been in existence for more than two years before it called a convention. The committee was composed almost exclusively of Union white men. There were but five colored men on the committee, only one of whom had ever been a slave. Some of them had owned slaves by inheritance from their white fathers. They were nearly white, and all were men of wealth and education. Some of them had been educated in France, others in Spain, and still others in the New England States. They were all the descendants of aristocratic white settlers (Canadians, French, and Spanish), pioneers of the province of Louisiana, and their free colored ancestors constituted one-tenth of the army that fought the British in 1815 at Chalmette under General Andrew Jackson, with credit to themselves and glory to the nation.

In the fourth place, this committee formally issued a call for a Convention which assembled in the city of New Orleans on the 27th day of September, 1865. The Convention was composed of one hundred and eleven delegates, only twenty of whom were colored men and only one of whom had ever been a slave. The Convention held four different sessions, and adopted and published its platform of principles, which was in substance as follows:

It declared that it reaffirmed the platform adopted at Baltimore in June, 1864, by the Convention which nominated Abraham Lincoln and Andrew Johnson.

That the Ordinance of Secession adopted by a Convention of the people of Louisiana was a declaration of war against the United States; that it disrupted, in fact though not in law, the relations existing between the general government and the people of this State.

That the acts of Congress declaring the inhabitants of Louisiana to be in a state of insurrection constituted them in law as enemies of the United States, and unfitted them for the functions of a State in the Union until restored by the action of Congress.

That it would be unwise to admit the inhabitants of Louisiana at once into the Union as a State; that a preliminary system of local government should be established by Congress to endure so long as might be necessary to test the fidelity of the people to the United States and to accustom the inhabitants to exercise in harmony and peace the rights and duties of self-government.

That the system of slavery heretofore existing in Louisiana had ceased to exist; and that we would protest against any and all attempts to substitute in its place a system of serfdom or forced labor in any shape.

FOREWORD

That the necessities of the government called the colored man into the public service in the most honorable of all duties, that of the soldier fighting for the integrity of his country and the security of constitutional government; this, with his loyalty, patience and prudence, was sufficient to assure Congress of the justice and safety of giving him a vote to protect his liberty.

The Convention provided for a voluntary election of a delegate to Congress to represent its view. In pursuance of this plan it nominated the Hon. Thomas J. Durant to represent the "Territory of Louisiana" in the Congress of the United States. Mr. Durant was obliged to decline the honor, and it was then, and not until then, that I was placed in nomination by the unanimous vote of the Convention.

In the fifth place, the falsehood as to my collecting a fund for my expenses was publicly denounced as false and malicious in every respect by a large mass meeting at the Orleans Theatre on November 14, 1865, which was presided over by Governor Benjamin F. Flanders, with one hundred vice-presidents on the platform. I paid my own expenses with the exception of $1,000, furnished me by the State Committee.

Everybody knew that an election was held on the 6th day of November, 1865; that I received nearly 20,000 votes; and that the Secretary of State, S. Wrotnowski, gave me a certificate with the Seal of the State affixed thereto, certifying to the fact, which I presented to the House of Representatives at Washington; and that I was welcomed by the Republican members of Congress and given the privileges of the floor of the House of Representatives.

I have gone thus minutely into all of these details, which were published in full in all of the newspapers of the time, with their comments, and consequently known to everybody, in order to show the reader the extremes to which this lying historian of Louisiana and other writers like him have gone to discredit and bring into disrepute the men who honestly strove to protect the loyal people of the South, both white and black, after the Civil War.

I cannot hope to reach the minds or the hearts of the men who approved, justified, excused or palliated the massacre of the Union men in New Orleans on the 30th of July, 1866; the assassination of Colonel Pope and Judge Chase in St. Mary Parish; the assassination of Judge T. H. Crawford and his District Attorney in Franklin Parish; the massacre of Opelousas in 1868, or the revolting massacres of Coushatta and Colfax. But I do hope to reach the minds and hearts of all just men and women of the American Union.

For some time before and up to the beginning of the Civil War, General W. T. Sherman, the great Union soldier, was at the head of the Louisiana State Seminary, known later and now as the State University. In May, 1904, at the laying of the corner stone of the Alumni Memorial Hall (erected in honor of David French Boyd, the successor of General Sherman as executive of the State Seminary), Judge A. A. Gunby, of Monroe, Louisiana, delivered an address on the life and services of David French Boyd, from which the following extract is taken:

He [Col. Boyd] had trouble enough in 1866 and 1867, but in 1868 a still darker struggle confronted him. A new Constitution had been established in Louisiana under which *more than two-thirds of the legislators were negroes;* and Article 135 of the Constitution provided that no separate school should be created for the races. This was the most malicious clause of that Constitution; it meant the complete ostracism of the Southern whites from the public schools of Louisiana. The problem that confronted Colonel Boyd was to preserve his school for the use and benefit of the young white men of the State, and yet to retain support from legislatures controlled by Carpet-baggers and negroes. To accomplish this delicate and yet tremendous task, he found that he had to take part in organizing the public school system of Louisiana. In this enterprise he had a staunch and unfaltering friend in Governor Henry Clay Warmoth, and he often declared orally and in writing that the Seminary would have perished had it not been for the friendship of Governor Warmoth, during each year of whose administration from 1868 to 1872 the support given to the institution was unfailing, generous, and ample.

Judge Gunby did me simple justice when he said that I was the "staunch and unfaltering friend" of the State Seminary, but he was led to reiterate the common charge as to the Constitution of the State Legislature: that "more than two-thirds of the legislators were negroes." Our opponents in their speeches and newspapers always took great pains to elaborate the charge that our Legislature was "a nigger Legislature." This was far from the truth. There was never a majority of negroes in either House of the Legislature during my four years of service as Governor. The Legislature elected in 1868, at the same time I was elected Governor, had but six colored men in the Senate out of its thirty-six members; and though the House of Representatives had more colored men in it than did the Senate they never constituted more than one-third of the membership.

So it was in the general election of 1870. Only six out of the thirty-six members of the Senate were colored men, and there were fewer negroes in the House of Representatives than in the House elected in 1868. Whatever legislation may have been worthy of criticism during my administration was the work of white men, in which the negro members played but a modest part.

Autobiographical

It is difficult to write autobiography satisfactorily. Modesty nearly always influences the writer to repress facts of merit concerning his own life. A full and impartial view of the events and circumstances is therefore often obscured. Many years have elapsed since those dramatic events that constitute what are generally known as the history of Reconstruction. As previously stated, it was my privilege and honor to play at times a leading part in that history. A gracious Providence has spared to me a long and somewhat eventful life. I have thus been enabled through the passing years to reflect upon and analyze calmly and dispassionately the crowded events that occurred during that period.

Neither aspiration for office nor any ambition whatsoever for new achievements could furnish any motive for me at this far-advanced period of my life. And I trust that no motives could prompt me to undertake this task, save pure patriotism, honorable self-defense, and a desire to leave to my country, my family, and posterity the truth, the whole truth, about the part I played in that stirring epoch of our State's history.

The weight of advancing years admonishes me that I cannot remain a spectator on the scene much longer. But I hope to show in the following pages that some of the excellent history that has been made by the State, and is now in process of making, owes a part of its better impulse to the earnest and patriotic accomplishments of the period known as Reconstuction. I shall tell here as briefly as possible, and as fully as is consistent with modesty, the story of my life and something of the lives of my ancestors; of the part they played in helping to build up our Republic, and of their lives as honorable and patriotic American citizens. This, in brief, is my apology for undertaking to leave an impartial account of the history of the State while I was its Governor and while I was representing it in sundry official capacities.

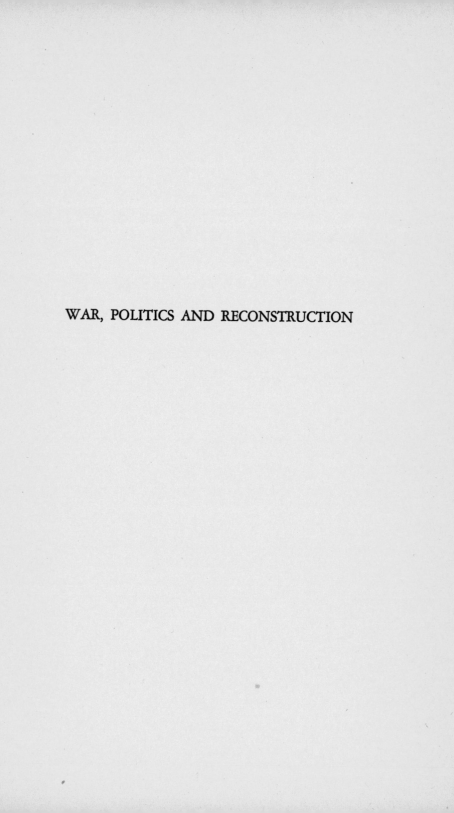

WAR, POLITICS AND RECONSTRUCTION

WAR, POLITICS AND RECONSTRUCTION

CHAPTER I

My great-grandfather, Thaddeus Hartwidge Warmoth, was born in 1761 and died December 31, 1847, being eighty-six years of age. Thomas Warmoth's name is to be found in the first census ever made in Virginia. In 1790 he had eight in his family.

When only seventeen years of age, Thaddeus enlisted in Captain Samuel Colston's Company of Colonel Thomas Gaskin's Virginia Regiment, and served through the War of the Revolution. Later he emigrated to Kentucky and settled in Garrard County, where he lived and died. His wife, Winny, our great-grandmother, died after she was sixty-eight years old. Later, on October 13, 1839, he married Mary (Polly) Bonar, when he was seventy-eight years of age. On September 21, 1818, he applied to the United States for a pension, which was granted. After his death, his widow, on February 14, 1853, when fifty years of age, applied for a pension, which was granted. She received six dollars a month during her lifetime.

My great-grandfather had five sons—Thaddeus, Jr., Thomas, Githian, Henry, and John. Henry was my grandfather. He was born in Garrard County, Kentucky, and married Margaret Sanders, a Dutch girl, who came out to Kentucky from North Carolina with her two brothers. She wore wooden shoes and could not speak English until after she was twelve years of age.

After his marriage, my grandfather moved to Bedford County,

Tennessee, and settled on Duck River, eighteen miles from Shelbyville, where my father was born.

Nathan Bedford Forrest, the great Confederate cavalry leader, was the son of a blacksmith by the name of William Forrest, a neighbor of my grandfather on Duck River, and it is not unlikely that he was my grandfather's blacksmith.

As a curiosity of the times, I have obtained a copy of the deed to forty acres of land to my grandfather, dated April 1, 1819, as follows:

ADREN ANGLE TO HENRY WORMOTH FOR 40 ACRES

This Indenture made this first day in April in the year of our Lord One thousand Eight hundred and Nineteen Between Adren Angle of the County of Bedford and State of Tennessee of the first part & Henry Wormath of the same State and County of the other part.

Witnesseth, that the said Adren Angle for and in consideration of the sum of One Hundred and fifty Dollars, the Receipt Whereof is hereby acknowledged, Hath given granted bargained and sold and by these Presents doth give grant & Sell And Convey in fee Simple unto the said Henry Wormoth his heirs and assigns forever a Certain piace or Parcel of Land Situate lying and being in the County of Bedford on the Waters of the North fork of Duck River and Bounded as follows: Beginning at a hickory William Burnett North East Corner running West Eighty four Poles To a Forked Ceder thence North fifty Eight Poles to Two Ceders in the South boundary line of a Survey in the Name of George Sanders Thence East With said line fifty one and half Poles to his South East Corner Thence North With his East boundary line forty Six Poles to a Hickory Thence East Thirty and a half Poles to a stake in Richard Trotters West boundary line thence South With said line to the Beginning Containing by Estimation forty Acres it being the Same more or Less, To Have And To Hold The aforesaid land and bargained Premises With all And Singular the rights Property imoluments and appertinances thereunto belonging or in any Wise appertaining Thereunto, To the only Proper use of him the said Henry Wormouth his heirs And Assigns forever & the said Adren Angle for himself his heirs Est And adm. doth Covenant and agree to and With the said Henry Warmoth his heirs & assigns to Warrant & forever defend The aforesaid Land & Bargain Premises

Against The Lawfull Claim or Claims of all and every Person or Persons Whatsoever In Witness Whereof the said Adren Angle Hath set his hand & affixed his Seal the Day & year above Written.

Signed Sealed and Delivered
    In Presents of
        WM. BURNETT   ADREN ANGLE   (SEAL)

(The name of Warmoth appears five times in this deed and is spelled correctly only once.)

STATE OF TENNESSEE
BEDFORD COUNTY   April Turn 1819
    I James McKisick Clerk of the Court of Pleas and quarter Sessions of the County aforesaid do hereby Certify That the Execution of the Within deed of Conveyance From Adren Angle to Henry Wormoth for 40 Acres of Land was Acknowledged in open Court by said Adren Angle And Ordered to be Certified for Registration Given under My hand at Office this 17t day of April 1819.

                                    JAS McKISICK *Clk*

Registered 25th June 1819.
    EDEN WADE *Reg*

STATE OF TENNESSEE
BEDFORD COUNTY
I, W. F. Bryant, Register of deeds for said County, do hereby certify that the above and forgoing is true and correct copy of deed from Adren Angle to Henry Warmoth, as it appears of record, in Deed Book No. k. page 233 R. O. B. C.
    Witness my hand and seal of Office at Office in Shelbyville, Tennessee, this the 9th day of August, 1922.
                    (*Signed*)   W. F. BRYANT, *Register of Bedford County.*
(SEAL)

Later, my grandfather removed to Edwards County, Illinois, and settled on a farm seven miles north of Albion, where he lived and died.

My grandparents had two sons and four daughters: John; Isaac Sanders (my father); Polly, who married David Shelby; Lucinda, who married William M. Rogers; Judy, who married Greenberry Sanders (who was killed by an explosion on a

[3]

steamboat near Dubuque, Iowa)—afterwards she married William Moore of Wabash County, Illinois; and Margaret Ann, who married John Howarton, who settled near Paducah, Kentucky, and later lived at Benton, Marshall County, Kentucky. Their granddaughter, Capitola S. Miller, is the wife of John Goodrum Miller, formerly a prominent lawyer of Kentucky and more recently a member of the New York Bar. Their great-grandson, John Goodrum Miller, Junior, one time a member of the Kentucky Legislature, is at present an active practitioner at the New York Bar.

The Warmoths or Warmouths are undoubtedly of Dutch origin. A large settlement by the name figured conspicuously in the early history of the State of New York, and furnished a lot of soldiers for the War of the Revolution. Old Peter Warmouth lived in a large brick house at Cherry Valley, New York, and at least one of his children was a victim of the Indian Chief Brant, who was allied to the British cause. Christian Warmouth was a member of the First Regiment of the Line commanded by Colonel Goose Vanschaick; William Warmouth and Peter Warmouth served in the Second Regiment under Colonel Jacob Klock and General Nicholas Herkimer.

I am glad to record that the Warmoth family, whether in New York or in Virginia, were patriots and served their country then as they did in later years.

My father was in the Mexican War and crossed the Gulf of Mexico from New Orleans to Mexico on a ship with Colonel Jefferson Davis, commanding the 2nd Mississippi Volunteers.

We read in the International Encyclopedia, Volume 20, page 296, published in 1810, that there is found in the fresh-water lakes and streams of the North a fish that bears our name. It says:

Warmouth is a small goggle-eyed fresh-water fish closely related to rock-bass of the Eastern and Central United States, which is more elongate than the sunfish, very variable in color and marking, and noted for its large mouth and great voracity. They grow to extreme weight of twenty pounds and are highly esteemed for food and are among the best, if not among the very best, game fish of the United States.

Whether our family was given the name because we were thought to be fishy, or the fish was given our name because we were game and voracious, I do not know. I have never known any of our family to be goggle-eyed or fishy, but all were game to the backbone.

My father, Isaac Sanders Warmoth, was brought up on the farm until he was fifteen years old. He was then apprenticed to a saddler by the name of Mayo, living in the town of Albion, Illinois, to learn the trade. Mr. Mayo subsequently moved to Carlinsville in Magoupin County, Illinois. After my father had completed his apprenticeship he settled in McLeansboro, Hamilton County, where he opened a shop and made saddles and harness. Later in 1840 he married my mother, who was Miss Eleanor Lane, the daughter of State Senator Levin Lane, a prosperous farmer living near the village. The young people were so popular that the neighbors turned out and built for them a log-cabin on the Court House Square, into which they moved and where I was born. Until a few years ago the house still stood facing the public square.

I was born on the 9th of May, 1842. Later my family removed to the village of Fairfield in Wayne County, some twenty-five miles distant from McLeansboro, where my father became one of the leading citizens. He was elected Justice of the Peace, and prospered in his business.

My father was, of course, the peace officer of the county. I remember that, when I was only a small boy, a bully by the name of Pea Hay attacked with his fist a respectable and quiet farmer by the name of Andrew Crews, in my father's presence. As it was my father's duty, he commanded the peace and he did it in this wise:

"I command the peace—give him 'hell,' Andy—
I command the peace—give him 'hell,' Andy—"

and Andy did give him "hell." He got his adversary down on the ground and pummeled him well; so well that when Hay was able to rise he shook himself and declared with an oath, "I have fought a hundred battles, but I have never won a victory."

My maternal grandfather, Levin Lane, was a member of a large family, the men being tall, broad-shouldered, vigorous and forceful. There were five brothers, all over six feet in height, and they were known for their strength and prowess. James Lane was the County Judge of Hamilton County for many years. Members of the family are still living in Hamilton County; among them James H. Lane, a leading attorney. He is the grandson of Lewis Lane. Thomas Lane was a Methodist preacher and settled in Peoria County, Illinois. Lemuel Lane settled somewhere in the West, and one of his sons became a prominent attorney in Missouri. My maternal grandmother was Lucinda Willis. In later years she lived with my mother and died in our home at Fairfield.

They were all Virginians, Kentuckians, or Tennesseans, and were Whigs in politics. My Grandfather Lane was on General Harrison's electoral ticket in 1840. He was also in the Black Hawk War, and the powder horn, shot-pouch and charger he used are still in existence. Judge James Lane was in the Mexican War and lived to be ninety-one years of age.

My mother was a beautiful woman. She married my father at the age of eighteen, and died when she was only thirty years of age. She bore five children in the twelve years of her married life and died when the last one was born.

Two years later, my father was married the second time, to Miss Louisa Crews, the daughter of a farmer near Fairfield, on the 30th of August, 1856. Twelve children were born to this union, three of whom are still living.

When my mother died my father had an old friend by the name of Owen, living several miles out in the country, take me for the winter. I was only ten or eleven years old. They lived in a one-story log house which had an attic. I slept up in the attic. The snow often filtered through the roof and tickled my face. I had a dog and we supplied the family with rabbit meat all winter. I had a little yoke of oxen and a sled, and my duty was to bring in the family fuel from the woods.

These good old people lived alone, the wife doing her own cooking, washing, ironing, and milking—in fact all of her housework. And no cooking was ever better in the world—and the way I got away with the food! I remember that they would finish their meal and move their chairs around by the fire, leaving me at the table, and I don't believe I ever stopped eating until from very shame I quit. Looking back at that experience, seventy-five years ago, I do not believe I have ever had a better time in my life.

My education was limited to the schools of my village and the training I was able to get as a typesetter in the local printing office. In this way I learned to spell a great many words which I did not know how to spell before.

My father was for many years a Justice of the Peace. He had a number of law books in his library of which I availed myself, and by hard study I made some progress in mastering them.

I frequented all sessions of all the courts and witnessed the trials. My associates were among members of the Bar and they seemed to like me and inspired me with an ambition to become a member of their profession. I shall never forget B. B. Smith, a partner of General I. N. Haynie, for his devotion to me. Many hours we spent together, and often for nearly whole days at a time we tramped the woods together, making speeches to each other. I am sure the trees never before nor since heard such profound arguments, or such brilliant eloquence!

I left Illinois for Missouri on April 9, 1860. I lacked one month of being eighteen years of age. I left St. Louis, Missouri, in company with Isaac Hoskinson and two other gentlemen, in a two-horse covered wagon for Springfield, Missouri. En route, running across a friend who had a farm twelve or fourteen miles from Lebanon, Missouri, I left the party and they went on. I spent a week with James Talliaferro and his family most pleasantly. He took me in his buggy to Lebanon, Laclede County, on the top of the Ozark Mountains, where I expected to take the stage the next day for Springfield, Missouri.

We arrived on a Sunday morning, stopping at the country tavern. And while I was taking my dinner alone, a strange gentleman came in and took a seat opposite me at the table. He was a man of about thirty-five years of age, large, well-built, with black hair and very black eyes. I noticed that he eyed me very closely and finally he begged my pardon and asked me where I was from. I told him that I was from Illinois, on my way to Springfield, Missouri. He asked me what my profession or business was. I told him that I was a lawyer. "Seeking a location, I suppose?" I replied in the affirmative. "Well," he said, "you don't want to go any farther, for this is the best opening right here of any place that I know of for a young, enterprising lawyer. We have only two lawyers here; one is also a doctor, and the other an opium fiend."

We talked through dinner and for several hours afterwards. He introduced me to his wife and family, and all the leading citizens of the town. He told me that if I would stop at Lebanon he would furnish me an office without expense, with himself, and that he knew everybody in the county and would help me to get any amount of business. He was such an agreeable man and offered me such excellent inducements that I finally made up my mind to accept his proposition. His name was Dr. Joseph L. Moore, a practising physician in the town of Lebanon. I moved into his office, which was on the ground floor of the tavern building; put my meagre library on his shelves, hung out my sign, "H. C. Warmoth, Attorney and Counselor-at-Law." The sign was a big one, because I knew that I did not know much law and I thought to accomplish the same purpose by as much advertising as possible. I buckled down to hard work to study the rules of practice and court procedure of the State of Missouri, of which I was entirely ignorant. I had studied the elementary principles, and knew something of the common law. I found the Missouri Code of Practice much more simple in its procedure and jurisprudence than that of the State of Illinois. I fancied that in a little while I would be able to pass an examination and be admitted to the Bar of Missouri. I was just eighteen years old, though I had the appearance of a man of about twenty-one. I confess that I did not enlighten the community with the fact that I was under age. My financial condition was such that it was necessary for me to become a bread winner. I had only a twenty-dollar gold piece in my pocket, and did not scruple at allowing the community to deceive itself as to my age. Strange as it may seem, through the influence and friendship of Dr. Moore, I soon had a respectable practice before the County Court and Justices of the Peace.

A little time afterwards, I learned that the Circuit Court of the Eighteenth Judicial District, in which I lived, would begin at Hartville, in Texas County. There were eighteen counties in this district. The Hon. Patrick Edwards was the Judge. I had never met him, as he lived in Springfield, some fifty miles away.

I determined to attend court at Hartville. It was the practice of the Bar to make the entire circuit of the eighteen counties with the Judge. It was a great treat to do so, for there were a number of jolly, bright men at the Bar of that district, and it was great fun riding from county to county, spending a week at each place holding a term of court. The members of the Bar generally put up at the same tavern and rode in a regular cavalcade on horseback from place to place with the Judge.

I arrived at Hartville alone and introduced myself to Judge Edwards and dear old Julian Frazier, the District Attorney.

They were both very polite to me, and the next day in open court I applied to the Judge for a license to practise law. He appointed a committee, composed of Julian Frazier, John S. Waddell, and Jarvis M. Barker, to examine me as to my qualifications for the profession. But, owing to the heavy docket before the court and the occupation of the attorneys, it was several days before I could get the committee together to interrogate me. But, as luck would have it, one night about eight o'clock as I was walking along the street, I met all three of these lawyers coming from a consultation.

Mr. Frazier remarked, "Here is Mr. Warmoth and we are all together—why not examine him right here?" It was at the corner of a block, a number of empty dry-goods boxes being piled upon the sidewalk. Mr. Frazier said, "Mr. Warmoth, get up on that box." And in the dark they stood around me and proceeded to examine me as to my qualifications.

I was fortunately able to answer a number of elementary questions to their satisfaction. Then Mr. Frazier proposed to me a hypothetical case. "Now, suppose this, and suppose that, and suppose again, and suppose then, and then suppose and so on," until I had not the slightest idea of what the question was—the beginning of it, the middle, or the ending of it; and finally he closed by asking, "Now, to whom does the property of the defendant belong?" I promptly replied, "To the lawyers, of course." The Committee at once agreed, "You will do. We shall take great pleasure in certifying to your capabilities as an attorney."

They did so certify, and Judge Edwards issued me a license, declaring that, "having examined me as to my character, good standing, and my learning in the law, he thereby authorized me to practise law in all the courts of the State of Missouri."

Events progressed very rapidly with me from this time on. In our little county there were many very nice people. There were a few slave-holders, but not many slaves. Only the valleys were fertile, and there were no rich people in the community. I roomed with President White, from North Carolina, who was at the head of the local academy, and Dr. Thrailkill, a young physician, at the home of Mrs. Harrison, who owned the largest residence in the town. She was the widow of the most important man in Laclede County. She was a Pennsylvanian and had two nice daughters, one of whom married Robert Fyan, later district judge and still later a congressman.

She made for us a very comfortable home. We three occupied the largest room in the house. As I recall, it must have been twenty-five feet square, with a fireplace that would take a four- or five-foot log. We had three beds in the room, each bed being in a corner. Mrs. Harrison had a nice little farm just outside of the village, and produced her own poultry, pigs, vegetables, and fruit. She had several slaves, among them an excellent cook. In my long life, I am sure that I have never had better living. The table actually groaned with good food—chicken, turkey, lamb, beef, pork, and bacon. Such bread, coffee, and tea as she served to us! Apples, peaches, pears, and all sorts of berries were in great profusion. She had our washing done for us, and furnished us with lamps and candles, fuel, and service, all for the princely sum of two dollars and fifty cents per week. Her house servants, with the exception of Adeline, who was a white woman, were slaves. There were no railroads within seventy miles of us; the public roads were rough. We had no markets, no competition, everything was cheap then; the high cost of living was certainly unknown. We were all very happy, as young people must be when so well fed and cared for; and I look back on this era as one of the happiest of my life.

I had but few diversions to take me from my law studies. I worked hard, for I realized better than anyone how little I knew, and was ambitious to succeed. A little later, I was appointed County Attorney by the County Court. I had one side of nearly every civil and criminal case in the courts of the County.

But the Presidential election soon came on. The Union men supported Bell and Everett, the Liberal Democrats supported Stephen A. Douglas, and the Extreme Southern Democrats supported Breckinridge and Lane. There were no Republicans known as such in that section of the country. I took little part in politics at that time. My closest friend was Dr. Moore and he was a red-hot Breckinridge Democrat. He was elected to the Legislature from that County. The newspaper of the County, owned and edited by Alexander McF. Hudson, was bold and outspoken in its support of the Union and the Bell-Everett ticket.

All of my brilliant prospects came to an end abruptly, as a result of the national election when Mr. Lincoln was chosen President. Many people seemed to lose their reason. The Extreme Democrats took charge of everything. They began to organize militia companies all over Southwest Missouri, and barbecues and picnics were held at which the most extreme views were expressed. Mr. Lincoln was called a low, foul-mouthed joker, a baboon, a monkey, and "negro-lover," and the audiences were asked if they wanted their daughters to take "niggers" for husbands, with the declaration that it would certainly come to pass if Lincoln and his negro-loving followers were allowed to control the Government. Dr. Wood announced in his speeches that the Union was only a rope of sand to be dissolved by a little water, or, if need be, a little blood. It was declared that one Southern man could whip a dozen Yankees; that the mudsills of the North would not fight; that all were low, groveling cowards. One of the most extreme and violent Secessionists in the community was a New Hampshire Yankee who had settled in Lebanon years before and married the daughter of a slave-holder. The little community seemed to have been turned upside-down within a night. All of the girls were singing *Dixie,* and cutting the acquaintance of those of us who were suspected of being friendly to the Union. We were denounced as Abolitionists and "negro-lovers." The Union men stood aghast. They were almost speechless. They predicted that the hysteria might pass after a little time, but they were woefully mistaken. They did not begin to realize the situation until they saw the old starry flag hauled down from the village staff, all the stars torn from it except one, and then raised again as "the flag of the Sovereign State of Missouri, and to hell with the Union!"

South Carolina seceded. The Legislature of Missouri ordered a State Convention with the purpose of following South Carolina. Arms were distributed, with powder and shot. Camp Jackson was organized in the suburbs of St. Louis, with the intention of taking possession of the city. The loyal men of St. Louis became aroused. They were organized secretly in the United States Arsenal by Captain Lyon, who marched out one day to Camp Jackson and captured the entire force, thus opening the eyes of the people to a full realization of the question. Even before this, however, the Union men of Laclede County began to take notice. We organized six hundred Union men armed with shotguns and rifles, or any kind of weapon. A number of us had been notified to leave the County within ten days. We marched with the six hundred men into Lebanon one day, took down the Lone Star flag of Missouri, raised Old Glory with its full constellation, and went into camp; and we held the fort until General Franz Siegel and his loyal Germans came to our rescue, and until after the battle of Wilson Creek, a few miles below Springfield, Missouri, where General Lyon was whipped and killed, and we had to fall back. Then we gathered up our people and withdrew to Rolla on the railroad, seventy miles away. We all had to surrender our farms, our homes, and everything to the advancing army of General Sterling Price and Governor Claiborne F. Jackson.

To the surprise of Governor Jackson and his secession Legislature, the State Convention which he called to follow South Carolina was composed of a majority of Union delegates, and when it convened at Jefferson City, Governor Jackson had already taken the field with General Sterling Price. The Convention at once proceeded to declare for the Union. It deposed Governor Jackson and chose Hamilton R. Gamble, an outstanding Union man, to be the Governor of the State. President Lincoln promptly recognized Governor Gamble, and the status of Missouri was made clear and unequivocal. I had been appointed Circuit Attorney for the Eighteenth Judicial District on the first day of February, 1861, and Hon. John S. Waddell had been appointed Judge of the Circuit Court; but war was on, and we did not attempt to hold court in the District. The Governor appointed me on July 28, 1861, a Colonel of Militia; in October following he appointed me a Brigadier-General of Militia.

General Frank P. Blair was authorized by President Lincoln to organize a brigade of infantry. He gave me authority on August 2, 1861, to raise a regiment for his brigade to be numbered the 36th Missouri Infantry. When I had enrolled seven hundred and sixty men at Rolla, we were ordered to St. Louis, where we were consolidated with another fragment and mustered into the service as the 32nd Missouri. Frank H. Manter, a soldier of some experience, was made Colonel, I was appointed Lieutenant-Colonel, and A. J. Seay was appointed Major.

The details of my service and experiences in the War are given in my daily journal.

On November 30, 1862, our regiment was mustered into the United States service for three years or during the War, at Benton Barracks in St. Louis.

On December 16th following, without drill or even full
equipment, we were ordered to the front, and on December
29th, less than thirty days after having been mustered into
service, we were engaged in attacking the enemy, who was well
intrenched behind Chickasaw Bayou, on General Joseph E.
Johnson's plantation twenty miles up on the Yazoo River,
above Vicksburg, Mississippi; in which battle we were repulsed
with heavy loss of life and some were taken prisoners. This was
one of General William T. Sherman's battles for which he was
mercilessly criticized. The press suggested that he was "crazy
and ought to be put into a lunatic asylum."

After this repulse, Major-General McClernand arrived and,
being Sherman's senior in rank, assumed the command of our
defeated and dispirited Army. He took it up the Arkansas
River, and captured Fort Hindman with General Churchill and
seven thousand Confederate prisoners, together with a lot of
artillery and other war materials. After this brilliant victory,
General McClernand returned down to the Mississippi River
where he met General Grant, who assumed command at once.
General Grant then organized his Army into three corps, assigning General McClernand to the command of the 13th, General
Sherman to the 15th, and General McPherson to the 17th. On
January 29th, 1863, I was detached from my regiment and
assigned to duty on the staff of Major-General McClernand commanding the 13th Army Corps. The Army of General Grant
and the fleet of Admiral Porter were scattered along the Mississippi River from Young's Point opposite Vicksburg to Milliken's
Bend. The object of the campaign was the capture of Vicksburg, which seemed to be impregnable, having been fortified by
General Pemberton, a distinguished engineer of the Old Army.
The country demanded the capture of Vicksburg and the opening of the Mississippi River to the Gulf of Mexico, and inci-
dentally the splitting of the Confederacy into two parts. General Grant found Vicksburg impregnable from the front.

Admiral Porter from above and Admiral Farragut from below with their fleets were unable to silence the Vicksburg guns, or to pass up or down the river without certain destruction to their vessels.

General Grant then conceived the idea of digging a canal across Young's Point, out of range of the Vicksburg guns, large enough for the Navy and his transports to pass and repass. He spent nearly the whole winter in digging this canal, but finally had to give it up. He then determined to move his Army below Vicksburg through Louisiana, and to attempt to cross it into the State of Mississippi under the protection of the Navy, and to take his chances of getting his gunboats and transports below by running by Vicksburg in the nighttime.

This movement was successful, though necessarily slow and tedious. The Louisiana side was flooded by the waters of the Mississippi River, and we had to move our troops on barges, flatboats, and skiffs. The 13th Army Corps, under General McClernand, led the advance, and we had to supply the transportation and to move the troops. I was assigned to this special duty by General McClernand, and we got all of our troops and material down to a point opposite Bruinsburg, Mississippi, where we met the gunboats of Admiral Porter's fleet and the transports which had run the batteries of Vicksburg under the cover of night as planned by General Grant.

We at once crossed the troops of our Corps over the Mississippi at Bruinsburg, and rushed rapidly into the interior. We fought the first battle on May 1st, and captured Port Gibson. We then pushed forward and fought the battles of Champion Hills and Big Black, and captured every foot of ground till we had invested Vicksburg in the rear on the 19th of May, 1863. Sherman and McPherson with their corps followed us, and after getting into line, General Grant attempted to storm Vicksburg on the 19th of May, but was repulsed with considerable loss.

General Grant made up his mind to make a second assault

on the 22nd of May. General Sherman's Corps occupied the right of our line; General McPherson's Corps occupied the center; and our Corps, the 13th, occupied the left. The attack was made at 10 A.M. all along the line. Our Corps captured one of the enemy forts with a number of prisoners, and we held it until 7 P.M.

General McClernand promptly reported his progress to General Grant at 11 A.M., and asked for a division of troops to reinforce him, saying that if he could get support at once he thought he could go into Vicksburg. The troops did not arrive till 7 P.M. In the meantime, as General Stephen D. Lee told me personally after the War, he had so strengthened his line on our front that when we attacked late in the evening, he was able to repulse us. I was severely wounded in this attack.

After General Grant's failure on the 22nd of May, he found it necessary to begin a siege of Vicksburg, which lasted from May 22nd till July 4th—forty-four days.

There was sore disappointment at the failure of General Grant to support promptly General McClernand's call for reinforcements on the 22nd of May. Because of General Sherman's jealousy and hatred of General McClernand, and his influence with General Grant, it finally resulted in General McClernand's being relieved of his command and sent home but a few days before the surrender of Vicksburg; and Major-General E. O. C. Ord was placed in command of the 13th Army Corps. On account of my wound, I was sent home to recover. My first leave of absence was for twenty days. It became necessary for me to have my leave extended twice.

On my return to the Army I made a full report of my absence, enclosing with it surgeons' certificates approved by the Medical Director of the Department of Missouri, accounting for every day of my absence. General Ord returned my report with his endorsement, "entirely satisfactory." A few days after my return to duty, I received an order from the War Department, "dishonorably dismissing me from the service for absence without leave, and for circulating false reports about the Army with which I was serving." I at once called upon General Grant at his headquarters in Vicksburg, and showed him the order. He told me to step across the hall to Major Bowers' office—that the Major would give me a copy of the papers. I did so, and asked Major Bowers for copies of the papers, which he offensively refused to give me. I stepped back to General Grant's table and reported to him the conduct of Major Bowers; he at once arose from his table and walked with me over to Major Bowers and told him to give me copies of all of the papers in the matter, which he did.

On examining the papers, I found that Lt.-Col. J. H. Wilson, Aide-de-camp and Inspector on General Grant's staff, had made an official report that he had inspected the staff of the 13th Army Corps, and had found that Lt.-Col. H. C. Warmoth had been absent from duty three weeks without leave. On the back of this report General Grant had written, "This officer on receiving a slight wound on the 22nd of May immediately availed himself of a leave of absence, and while on his way north circulated the report that our losses at Vicksburg on the 22nd of May were from ten to twenty thousand, thereby producing undue excitement in the North and encouraging the hopes of the enemy."

With this paper I at once proceeded to prepare my case. I did not ask any favors of General Grant, but went at once to Springfield, Illinois, and showed my order of dismissal to General McClernand. General McClernand gave me a letter to President Lincoln, in which he gave a full history of my having been wounded by his side on the evening of the 22nd of May; of his giving me a leave of absence on the certificate of the Chief Surgeon of the 13th Army Corps; and of his entire satisfaction with my services as an officer on his staff; adding that my dismissal from the Army was inspired by the hatred of General Grant and his clique for himself, General McClernand.

Now, fortunately for me, I had been among the first officers of the Army to arrive at Cairo, Illinois, from the front, after the battles around Vicksburg, and the two attacks on its works. I had found the air full of rumors of General Grant's defeat, and the greatest alarm prevailing over his disaster. Being an officer of a Missouri regiment, I had been sought out by the correspondents of *The Republican* and *The Democrat,* the two leading papers of the city of St. Louis, to whom I gave elaborate interviews, which were published the following morning in both newspapers. In these I gave a full account of the brilliant campaign through Louisiana, of the crossing of our troops over the Mississippi River, of our campaign through Mississippi, and of the battles we fought, including the two assaults on the works of Vicksburg. I spoke of the confidence of the Army that Vicksburg would soon be in our hands, I spoke of General Grant in most respectful terms. Now, all of this fully answered the charge that I had "exaggerated our losses and produced undue excitement in the North, and encouraged the hopes of the enemy."

With General McClernand's letter to the President, and copies of these two newspapers, together with a number of most complimentary letters from Division, Brigade, and Regimental Commanders in our Army as to my services, I proceeded to Washington. I arrived in Washington on the night of August 29, 1863, stopping at Willard's Hotel.

I was a stranger in Washington. I knew nobody connected with the Government. But early the next morning, I went directly to the White House, and was told that the President would receive only cabinet officers and members of Congress until 3 P.M., when he would receive the public. I then took a stroll over the streets of the City, and put in my time until the hour I expected to be received by the President.

August 30th, I called on the President and was received by him with the general public after 3 P.M. I was all alone, in disgrace and, as may be supposed, very much depressed. There must have been at least fifty men and women in the reception room waiting to see the President on all sorts of matters. I let everybody go in ahead of me, and when anybody else would come in I let him have my place. We were all drawn up in line and I determined to have my interview with the President alone. I heard several of the conversations between the different people and the President, and I found that there were several other officers of the Army in much the same predicament in which I found myself; and I heard the President say to each one who asked for a court-martial or a military commission to give him a chance to vindicate himself: "Now, my dear friend, we are in the midst of war and we cannot stop to hold courts-martial or military commissions now; but you come to me after the war is over and I will give you a court-martial or a military commission and every opportunity to vindicate yourself." You can well imagine my feelings when I heard what I supposed to be my death-knell repeated several times.

Finally everybody had been heard and had withdrawn, and I was there alone with the President. I began my conversation by saying, *"Mr. President, I cannot wait until the war is over for my vindication. I must have justice now. I cannot stand being put off."* I told him who I was, that I was on General McClernand's staff; and I presented General McClernand's letter and handed him my other letters and papers. After patiently looking over my letter from General McClernand, and some of the other papers, the President said to me, "Colonel, I cannot give you a court-martial or a military commission, but I'll tell you what I will do—I will refer your papers and your case to General Joseph Holt, the Judge-Advocate General of the Army, for his report, and I will act on that." I told him that would be entirely satisfactory to me.

So he took all of my papers, folded them up, and put them into a large envelope, wrote an endorsement referring the letters and papers to General Holt for report, and told me to take them to General Holt myself. I thanked him very much and took the papers to the Judge-Advocate's office. I was introduced to Major William Winthrop (Assistant Judge-Advocate General to General Holt). He told me that General Holt was absent at that time and would be for some days; but that he would take up the matter himself, examine the case and have a report ready for General Holt on his return. In talking over the matter and in looking over the papers, I found that one important paper was missing. I told Major Winthrop that I must have left it on the President's table. I went immediately to the White House, and at the foot of the great stairs I met the President coming down. I told him that I must have left the paper on his desk. He said, "Was it a *Missouri Republican?*" I said "Yes, sir." And the President turned around and walked up that great, long flight of stairs with me to his room. He found the paper on his desk and handed it to me.

We then walked down the stairs together and I promised to bring the paper the next morning to the Judge-Advocate's office. I walked with the President down to the Treasury Department and through it to my hotel, the Willard. The President was in excellent humor. While we were walking together I said, "Mr. President, you know in the olden times the people used to go out on a great plain and select their tallest man for their leader. Don't you think I would have run you a pretty good race in those days and under those circumstances?" He replied, "Do you think so?" And with that he began to straighten up, and when he had gotten thoroughly straightened up I said, "No, no, Mr. President, I would not have stood any chance with you." He laughed heartily. It seemed to me that he rose seven feet high, as he towered so much above me with his tall hat. We passed into the Treasury Department Building and he left me, turning into a corridor and saying he was going to see Mr. Chase (the Secretary of the Treasury) and bade me good-day.

The next morning I called at the Judge-Advocate General's office, and gave Major Winthrop the paper I had left on the President's table. Major Winthrop, who was a highly educated, sincere and earnest man, took great interest in my case. General Holt did not return for several days, but in the meantime Major Winthrop had examined the whole matter and prepared an elaborate report fully vindicating me and ending his report with the following recommendation:

It is believed that few young men in the service can present a fairer or more honorable record, and in view of the manifest injustice which has been done Lt. Colonel Warmoth, and of his evident value to the service, it is recommended that the special order dismissing him from the service be at once revoked so that he be placed as to pay, and rank, etc., in precisely the position which he would have occupied had he not been dismissed.

General Holt, after signing my report, congratulated me on my vindication. He handed me the report and asked me to take it to the President, which I lost no time in doing. I gave it to Colonel John Hay, the President's private secretary; he laid it on the desk of the President, who a little later approved it and ordered my restoration; and he permitted me to take it to the War Department with a note of introduction from Colonel Hay. The next day I received the order restoring me to my rank, and departed at once for my regiment, which was still stationed at Vicksburg, Mississippi.

In passing down the river, September 26th, at a point a little below Helena, Arkansas, I passed a fleet of steamboats with troops, on one of which I recognized my regiment. I signaled the next steamer and was transferred in a skiff to the steamer "John J. Roe," having the Fourth Iowa Infantry, Colonel Williamson, on board. The next day we arrived at Memphis, Tennessee, and I at once reported to General Charles R. Woods for duty; he put me in command of my regiment, Colonel Manter having been killed. General Osterhouse commanded our Division. We were headed for Chattanooga, Tennessee, to aid General Grant in capturing Lookout Mountain and Missionary Ridge, and to secure Chattanooga as a base of operations.

After a long march over awful roads, and with some skirmishing but no heavy fighting, we reached the valley facing Lookout Mountain on November 23rd. General Joe Hooker with the 11th Corps held the right wing of the Army. He passed us down on the left of his line. I met General Hooker, who told me that the attack had been delayed for our arrival, that the enemy was all packed and ready to go, and that we would attack the next morning. We made the assault and captured Lookout Mountain without much fighting. It was a spectacular affair. My regiment was the extreme left of Hooker's line. The next day our Army moved by the left flank, which put my command in the lead. We crossed the valley and assaulted Rossville Gap, forcing our way through it to the left and rear of Bragg's Army, and were soon fighting on the top of Missionary Ridge, which we captured in fine style. It was a brilliant performance, resulting in the occupation of Chattanooga and all of that part of Tennessee.

We were a little later ordered back to Stephenson, Alabama, and were soon put into winter quarters. On December 8th I was detailed with a few officers of my regiment to go to Missouri to recruit for our regiment. Our efforts to obtain recruits failed, for about everybody was in the Army on one side or the other. On closing my recruiting station at Louisiana, Missouri, on January 28, 1864, I went to Springfield, Illinois, to call on my old commander, General McClernand, who had just been restored to the command of his 13th Army Corps, then in the Department of the Gulf with headquarters at New Orleans, Louisiana. General McClernand was glad to see me and urged me to go with him again on his staff. I went at once to St. Louis, Missouri, to close my accounts, and found General Grant in the city visiting friends. I called on him at his family residence and told him that General McClernand wanted me to accompany him south as a member of his staff. He seemed to be surprised at General McClernand's restoration to his command, and asked me a number of questions about it; and finally told me that I might go with General McClernand, and that my order of detail would follow me to New Orleans.

We arrived in New Orleans on February 15th, and reported to Major-General Banks, commanding the Department of the Gulf.

On March 8th, we found ourselves at Matagorda Bay in command of the troops along the Texas coast to Brownsville. We held this command until April 17th when we received orders from General Banks to reinforce him speedily after his fatal battle at Mansfield, Louisiana, where he was badly whipped. We immediately loaded our transports and arrived at Alexander on the 26th of April. We reinforced General Banks none too soon, for his Army was very much discouraged and needed our help. On the 28th of April, I was sent to New Orleans to gather and hurry up all of our scattered troops. I was on this duty until General Banks came out of the Red River with his Army. General McClernand arrived in New Orleans on May 16th, dreadfully ill. We first took him to a hospital, but later to a private residence, and obtained the services of the eminent Dr. D. C. Holliday, who saved his life after a protracted illness.

On May 31st General McClernand, still being ill, received a letter from General Banks, asking that I might be ordered to report to him to serve as Judge of the Provost Court for the Department of the Gulf at New Orleans. General McClernand, having found it necessary to return home on account of his extreme illness, and after conferring with me, consented to the detail, and on June 1st ordered me to report to General Banks for duty. On June 8th, General McClernand departed for his home in Springfield, Illinois, and did no further service during the War. I served as Judge of this Court for some time, during which I became acquainted with all the members of the Bar and a great many of the residents of the city of New Orleans, and established a fondness for it and them which I have since maintained.

I later asked for and received orders to return to my regiment then at Chattanooga, Tennessee. When I arrived at Louisville, Kentucky, on November 15th, I found that my regiment had become so decimated that it was necessary to consolidate it with two or three other Missouri regiments, and I, being absent at the time and there being other field officers present, had been left out in the consolidation. This ended my military service. I then returned to the city of New Orleans, and opened a law office early in 1865. It was not long before I had a lucrative practice before courts-martial, military commissions and government departments, and in the United States Courts.

I was in the city of Washington on important legal business, and witnessed the second inauguration of President Lincoln on March 4th, 1865. I attended the President's reception at the White House and stood near Mr. Lincoln during the whole ceremony.

Through the influence of my friend, James Harlan, Secretary of the Interior in Mr. Lincoln's Cabinet, I was given, together with a gentleman by the name of Herbert, a young lawyer of the city of Washington, a pass to visit the city of Richmond. We left Washington on the government boat "Dictator" at 3 P.M. on April 5th. The only other passengers were Vice-President Andrew Johnson and Ex-Senator Preston King of New York. We four were together all evening, and spent the whole time discussing the War and public affairs. Mr. Johnson was very bitter against the rebel leaders, and declared that they should be severely punished. My friend, Herbert, made bold to say that he did not believe Mr. Lincoln would punish the chief leaders of the Rebellion. Mr. Johnson rebuked Mr. Herbert severely for expressing such an opinion. In a tone almost angry he told Mr. Herbert that he should not talk that way, that that was the way public opinion was made. He should say that every one of the rebel leaders should be severely punished, and that "treason must be made odious."

At the Spottswoode House in Richmond, we met Charles A. Dana, Assistant Secretary of War, with whom Mr. Johnson had an earnest conversation, an account of which Mr. Dana prints in his book entitled *Recollections of the Civil War*. He says on page 269:

"One day, after the meeting of this Committee, I was in the large room downstairs in the Spottswoode Hotel, when my name was called, and I turned around to see Andrew Johnson, the new Vice-President of the United States. He took me aside and spoke with great earnestness about the necessity of not taking the Confederates back without some conditions or without some punishment. He insisted that their sins had been enormous, and that if they were let back into the Union without any punishment the effect would be very bad. He said they might be very dangerous in the future. The Vice-President talked to me in this strain for fully twenty minutes, I should think—an impassioned, earnest speech on the subject of punishing rebels. Finally, when he paused, and I got a chance to reply, I said:

"'Why, Mr. Johnson, I have no power in this case. Your remarks are very striking, very impressive, and certainly worthy of the most serious consideration, but it does not seem to me necessary that they should be addressed to me. They ought to be addressed to the President and to the Members of Congress, to those who have authority in the case and who will finally have to decide this question which you raise.'

" 'Mr. Dana,' said he, 'I feel it to be my duty to say these things to every man whom I meet, whom I know to have any influence. Any man whose thoughts are considered by others, or whose judgment is going to weigh in the case, I must speak to, so that the weight of opinion in favor of the view of the question which I offer may possibly become preponderating and decisive.'

"That was in April. When Mr. Johnson became President, not long after, he soon came to take entirely the view which he condemned so earnestly in this conversation with me."

After spending a few days in Richmond with old Army friends, I returned to Washington and was there when General Lee surrendered his Army, with eighty-two Generals and about 35,000 men. I heard Mr. Lincoln's speech from the upper window of the White House on the night of April 11th. I met General Grant in the lunchroom of the Hotel Willard on the night of April 14th, upon his arrival after the surrender, shook hands with him and congratulated him upon his grand success. That same night Mr. Lincoln was assassinated at Ford's Theatre by John Wilkes Booth. I attended a meeting called by Senator Yates of Illinois to make arrangements for the funeral of the President, participated in all the ceremonies, and accompanied the funeral cortège as far as New York City.

I was present in the parlor of the Kirkwood Hotel when Chief Justice Chase administered to Mr. Johnson the oath of office as President of the United States. There were not more than a dozen people present; my friend, General Dwight, afterwards for many years a Judge at Auburn, N. Y., being one of them.

Of course everything was delayed for a time in Washington. I did not conclude my business and return to New Orleans until May 6th, but was successful in what had called me to Washington, and for which I received a large fee.

CHAPTER II

As related before, Richmond surrendered on April 3, 1865. General Lee surrendered his Army on the 9th of April; Johnston on April 26th; and Jefferson Davis was captured on the 10th day of May. General Sterling Price surrendered the Western Army on the 25th day of May, and the War was at an end so far as fighting in the field was concerned.

The Confederate soldiers soon began to return in great numbers to their homes in New Orleans and the State of Louisiana. They were a seedy lot of fellows, much worn by long and hard service. They appeared to be delighted that the War was over, that they could be with their loved ones again, and were free from the rigors of military discipline and the hardships of war. They surely did enjoy new and clean clothes and good food, not to say something good to drink. They had not had much of any of these for four years. It was before the day of artificial ice, and I doubt if the Confederate soldier had seen commercial ice during his whole term of service. Sugar and coffee were almost equally scarce, and it was a delight to see the rebel boys revel in the good things at Moreau's, Victor's, Antoine's, and Madame Pelerine's restaurants.

The ex-Union soldiers located in New Orleans (there were many of us here then) received the "Johnnies" with open arms. Many were the good dinners, lunches, and breakfasts that we served to them—our late enemies but newly made friends. Long and delightful were the reminiscences of the march, the campaigning, and the battles in which we had been engaged on opposite sides in different sections of the South.

My regiment fought Colonel Bill Forrest, brother of General

Forrest, at Decatur, Alabama, and one of my men shot him through the hips. He spent some time in New Orleans after the War and he well remembered our contests and the incidents of the battles which we fought. There was a pretty girl living near Cherokee Station. We fought and drove each other to and fro by this girl's home day after day for a week. She said that Colonel Forrest was her "Rebel Sweetheart" and that I was her "Yankee Sweetheart." She sang for us and played the piano; she gave me a pretty handkerchief. It was a great pleasure to tell her that I had won her, because we had shot her "Rebel Sweetheart" at Decatur, Alabama. But I guess the Colonel won her at last, for I have not seen nor heard of her since that campaign.

I remember well General James Longstreet, General Dick Taylor, E. D. White, Frank B. Jonas, Captain C. H. Slocumb, General Harry T. Hayes, General Frank B. Armstrong, Major Penn Mason, Governor P. O. Hebert, General Dan Adams, Colonel W. J. Behan, Major Andrew S. Herron, Colonel J. D. Hill, Frank Zachary, Captain H. Dudley Coleman, J. O. Nixon, Colonel J. B. Walton, Eugene Waggaman, General Stephen D. Lee, E. John Ellis, Frank H. Hatch, General Gibson, General M. J. Thompson, General G. T. Beauregard, Colonel Davidson B. Penn, Colonel Jack Wharton, dear old Colonel Dan Wilson, J. B. Eustis, Tom Ocheltree, C. C. Duson, Captain J. B. Donnelly, Tom Bynum, C. C. Cordill, and a host of others who returned at the end of the War. I can see them now after sixty-two years have elapsed: fine, spirited, handsome fellows with crowns of glory for duty earnestly and gallantly performed. We lent some of them money and helped many of them in many ways. Later I appointed a number of them to office while Governor of the State.

The returned Confederates found a lot of Union officers and soldiers located, or locating, in their beloved city and State. General Frank P. Blair, my old brigade, division, and corps commander, engaged in cotton-planting in Madison Parish. It will be recalled that General Blair was the Democratic candidate for Vice-President of the United States on the ticket with Governor Horatio Seymour of New York, in 1868, against General Grant and Schuyler Colfax.

My friend, Whitelaw Reid, afterwards Editor of *The New York Tribune,* and later Ambassador of the United States to Great Britain, engaged in a similar enterprise in Madison Parish. Captain Hiram R. Steele, Captain Edward N. Whitney and Captain Abram N. Gould engaged in cotton-planting in Tensas Parish; John Foose, Lewis Clarke, James Barnett, Daniel Thompson and J. B. Lyon engaged in sugar-planting in St. Mary Parish; General Lionel Sheldon, Colonel Don A. Pardee, Major William Grant, Major W. W. Howe and Major J. D. Rouse took to the law; while General W. L. McMillan, General J. Hale Sypher, Captain George A. Sheridan, Colonel William Pitt Kellogg, John Lynch, General Frank J. Herron, General W. B. Benton, Captain Charles W. Lowell, John F. Deane, C. W. Keating, D. A. Reese, Captain A. S. Badger, General Cyrus Bussey, Captain Thomas A. Woodward, Pearl Wight, Colonel Jack Williamson, H. C. Dibble, Dr. M. A. Southworth, Captain S. B. Packard, Colonel James F. Casey, General James B. Steedman, General James McCleary, Colonel Charles B. Dillingham, L. J. Higby, Colonel H. H. Pope, and hundreds, if not thousands, of other ex-Union soldiers and northern friends scattered themselves over the State.

Some were cotton planters; some sugar planters; some merchants, manufacturers, lawyers, doctors, and speculators; while others held important Federal offices. All of us were soon up to our eyes in politics, made so by conditions which none of us could control.

I regret to have to say that it was not very long after the end of the War until the enthusiastic, cordial and even affectionate relations which had sprung up between the ex-Union and the returned Confederate soldiers began to show evidences of cooling off. The Union men here were generally men of means. They were successful in business and usually prosperous. They stood well with the officers and men in the Army of Occupation. They had money and good credit in the North, and but few of the Confederates had either.

Many things occurred to estrange these newly made friends: the assassination of President Lincoln, for instance, and the attempt of President Johnson to connect the Southern leaders with the crime. President Johnson offered large rewards for the arrest of Jefferson Davis and other leaders, directly charging them with the crime of killing President Lincoln. On May the 2nd, within seventeen days after his accession to the Presidency, he officially charged "Jefferson Davis, Jacob Thompson, Clement C. Clay, Beverly Tucker, George M. Sanders, William C. Cleary and other rebels and traitors against the Government of the United States" with the murder of Mr. Lincoln. He offered "$100,000 reward for the arrest of Jefferson Davis, $25,000 for the arrest of Clement C. Clay, $25,000 for the arrest of Jacob Thompson, $25,000 for the arrest of George M. Sanders, $25,000 for the arrest of Beverly Tucker, and $10,000 for the arrest of William C. Cleary, late clerk of Clement C. Clay."

Then there were other acts of the national administration which were deemed harsh; among them the order to shackle and closely confine Jefferson Davis in Fortress Monroe, and the arrest and detention of many other Confederate leaders. There were reports of uprisings of freedmen against the whites in many localities. The atmosphere became charged with rumors, suspicions and individual acts which tended to keep the people in a state of the wildest suspicion and excitement.

The insolence of a refractory house servant was reported in the press and charged "to the outrage of freeing the slaves," and all sorts of things were predicted from "this revolutionary act of Mr. Lincoln." The newly freed population realized the great change that had taken place in their relation to their old masters, and some of them were not slow in showing it. It might be said that they "felt their oats," and the returned Confederates declared that their "niggers were putting on airs," all of which was intolerable to the high-spirited Southerners.

Three colored men, said to be natives of San Domingo, published a daily newspaper in New Orleans, *The New Orleans Tribune,* which held out to the colored people the hope of making Louisiana a "Negro State." There were also many free negroes in the State who had immigrated from the North.

In Charles Gayarre's *History of Louisiana,* he calls attention to the annual message of Governor Robert C. Wickliffe to the Legislature in 1857. He says (speaking of Governor Wickliffe):

He also informed the Legislature that the immigration of free negroes from other States of the Union into Louisiana had been steadily increasing for years; that it was a source of great evil, and demanded legislative action. "Public policy dictates," he observed, "the interest of the people requires, that immediate steps should be taken at this time to remove all free negroes who are now in the State, when such removal can be effected without violation of law. Their example and associations have a most pernicious effect upon our slave population."

Many Confederates had real or fancied grievances against the Yankees which soon developed in their hearts. General Butler and his administration became a theme of discussion: his supposed brutality; his "wanton imprisonment" of citizens who had remained within his lines and who had shown hostility to the Union Army. The organization of negro troops was bitterly condemned, also his celebrated woman order; and hundreds of other acts of Union soldiers were recalled by the returned Confederates.

It was not long before the reaction came, and the men who had been civil and even cordial at the end of the War were passing each other in the streets with a bare recognition, and later on with "dead cuts." No more dinners—no more breakfasts— no more convivial intercourse. The social clubs closed their doors in our faces. Young ladies of the city, who had been happy to receive us before, passed us on the streets without recognition, or were "not in" when we called. I was personally insulted and driven from the door of a gentleman with whom I had formerly been on most intimate terms.

The Union people who remained at home and fraternized with the Union Army, who attended the balls and receptions of the military commanders and participated in the social life of the times, were especial objects of the resentment of the returned Confederates. Especially were the families of those men who had entered the Union Army subjected to ostracism and persecution. Five thousand Louisiana white men had enlisted in the Union Army.

General Butler's administration was thought to be harsh. It is probable that he had to do some harsh things, as the mob of New Orleans assaulted Union men, tore down the United States flag, and offered him and his troops every insult possible. Some women actually spat in the faces of Union officers and emptied filth on soldiers and sailors from the windows as they paraded in the streets. A man by the name of Mumford led a mob and tore down the Union flag over the United States Mint, placed there by Admiral Farragut.

General Butler felt obliged, in order to protect his officers and men from insult, to issue the following order:

Headquarters, Dept. of the Gulf, New Orleans,

May 15th, 1862.

General Order No. 28.

As the Officers and Soldiers of the United States have been subject to repeated insults from the women (calling themselves Ladies) of New Orleans, in return for the most scrupulous non-interference and courtesy on our part, it is ordered that hereafter when any female shall by word, gesture, or movement, insult or show contempt for any officer or soldier of the United States, she shall be regarded and held liable to be treated as a woman of the town plying her vocation.

        By command of   MAJOR-GENERAL BUTLER.
GEORGE C. STRONG, A. G., *Chief of Staff*.

It is said that no further insults were offered officers and soldiers by women after the publication of this order. General Butler arrested and tried Mumford for his crime by a military commission which found him guilty, and he hanged him right under the staff of the flag he had pulled down in front of the United States Mint. From that day New Orleans was the most peaceable city in the nation.

General Banks soon afterwards succeeded General Butler in command, and tried to restore good will; he tried to induce the people to resume their peaceful vocations, encouraged them to reopen their factories and renew the cultivation of their farms and their sugar, rice, and cotton plantations. He organized the colored labor and induced them to remain at their homes and cultivate their fields. He fixed a low rate of wages for plantation hands; fixed the hours of field work; and provided that the laborers should have three good meals each day, and that half of the wages should be retained by the employer until the end of the crops, in order to encourage the laborers to remain on their plantations. He held an election for Congressmen. Michael Hahn and Benjamin F. Flanders were elected from the First and Second Districts of New Orleans, and they were seated in the House of Representatives.

He put everybody to work who wanted work, and he fed the poor and helpless men, women and children out of the supplies of his Army. Later, he thought to turn the civil government over to the people of the State. He ordered an election for a Civil Governor and State Officers under the old State Constitution. This election was held on the 22nd of February, 1864, and Michael Hahn, a native of the State, was chosen Governor, and James Madison Wells, a large cotton planter of Rapides

Parish, also a native of the State, Lieutenant-Governor, with a full complement of State Officers and a Legislature, all of whom were natives or life-long citizens of the State. Only free white males over twenty-one years of age were allowed to vote at this election or participate in the Government.

General Banks' plan was not approved by all of the Union men of the State, and many abstained from participation in it. The Civil War was in full blast and General Banks' plan was regarded by many Union men in the State as premature. Thomas Jefferson Durant, Benjamin F. Flanders, Rufus Waples, and a large number of other prominent Union men opposed the movement on that account. The result was that but a very small vote was polled at the election. Nevertheless, Governor Hahn with his State Government was inaugurated in Lafayette Square in New Orleans on the 4th day of March, 1864, with great pomp and splendor, amid the firing of cannon, the singing of patriotic songs, and the great applause of the assembled multitude. I witnessed the inauguration as a soldier of the United States.

It should not be forgotten that a majority of the people of the State of Louisiana were not in favor of secession. This was shown by the vote at the presidential election in 1860. Although not one single vote was polled for Mr. Lincoln, Breckinridge and Lane, the extreme Democratic candidates, received but 22,680 votes; while Bell and Everett, the avowed Union candidates, received 20,204 votes, and Douglas and Johnson received 7,625 votes. It is well known that there were no more earnest Union men than the Douglas Democrats. It is therefore safe to say that these 27,829 voters, or a majority of 5,148, who cast their votes for Bell and Douglas were opposed to secession.

It is further shown by the fact that 17,296 votes were cast against secession at the election of delegates to the secession convention, while only 20,448 votes were cast for the secession delegates. The majority for secession in the city of New

Orleans was only 400. The Parish of St. James, which elected ex-Governor Roman a delegate to the Convention, cast but 73 votes for secession and gave 509 votes against it. (Fortier— Vol. 4, page 23.)

These facts show that the people of Louisiana were dragooned into secession by the extreme Democratic politicians of that day. This condition existed at the time General Butler and Admiral Farragut arrived in the city of New Orleans. The forces of the United States were received with cordiality by the Union men and women, although the streets were filled with a hostile, howling mob of thugs and ruffians, led by Mayor John T. Monroe of New Orleans and his murderous police.

On March 28th following, Governor Hahn's Legislature ordered an election for delegates to a Constitutional Convention "to revise and amend" the State Constitution, but it proceeded to form a new Constitution for the State, which it submitted to the people for the ratification. *It did not enfranchise any colored citizen,* although Mr. Lincoln suggested it.

President Lincoln wrote Governor Hahn a personal letter as follows:

I barely suggest for your private consideration whether some of the colored people may not be let in; as, for instance, the very intelligent, and those who have fought gallantly in our ranks. . . . But this is only a suggestion, not for the public, but to you alone.

A. LINCOLN.

The newly formed constitution received but 4,684 votes, while 789 votes were cast against its ratification. Nevertheless President Lincoln, on the advice of General Banks, recognized the new State Government, and it proceeded to administer the laws. The Legislature that was chosen met on October 3, 1864, and a full Civil Government was in power in all of that part of the State within the lines of the Union Army, but it was only a small part of the State.

Exactly one year later the legislature elected Governor

Michael Hahn to the United States Senate, whereupon he resigned as Governor on March 4, 1865, and Lieutenant-Governor James Madison Wells became Governor of the State. One month later (April 14) Mr. Lincoln was assassinated, and Vice-President Johnson became President of the United States. Richmond, the Capital of the Confederacy, had already been captured, and General Lee had surrendered his Army at Appomattox to General Grant on the 9th of April, 1865.

The Confederate Armies having surrendered, the War, so far as fighting was concerned, was at an end. Reconstruction became the all-engrossing question for the nation. A new Congress had just been elected to serve for two years. A conflict arose at once between President Johnson and Congress as to the terms and conditions on which the rebellious States were to be allowed to resume their political relations with the Union.

Congress assumed the position that the Constitution of the United States should be amended in several particulars: among others things, that slavery should be abolished; that Confederate War claims should never be paid; that no discrimination should be made against citizens on account of race, color, or previous condition of servitude; and that none of the rebellious States should be admitted to representation in Congress until they should ratify the 13th, 14th and 15th Amendments to the Constitution of the United States.

Certainly the State of Louisiana had formally withdrawn from the Union, as the Ordinance * adopted by a convention of the people on January 28, 1861, will show.

The Congress of the United States had solemnly declared that the inhabitants of the Confederate States were in a state of insurrection against the authority of the United States. This declaration was approved by President Lincoln, and the Judiciary Committee of the United States Senate had unani-

* See Appendix A.

mously declared that the two Senators, Hahn and Cutler, claiming seats from Louisiana under the General Banks program of 1864, could not be admitted to seats in that body "till some joint action of both houses shall, by some recognition of the existing State Government acting in harmony with the Government of the United States and recognizing its authority, should be adopted." This report was signed by all of the members of the Judiciary Committee of the Senate, including the great Democratic Senators Reverdy Johnson of Maryland and Thomas C. Hendricks of Indiana.

Therefore, the appointment of provisional Governors by President Johnson to reorganize the rebellious States under their old Constitutions was a gross usurpation by the President, and it was resented by an overwhelming majority of the people of the loyal States, as shown by the Congressional Election of 1866.

The attitude of the President was so in conflict with the opinions of Congress that the fiercest political struggle in the history of the nation occurred. Mr. Johnson was totally devoid of tact, and as stubborn and as arbitrary as he was tactless. He reasoned that he had four years to serve, and he was induced to believe that "his policy," as he called it, would be crystallized and completed in that time, and that the people of the nation, when they should come to elect the new Congress, would be obliged to accept "his policy." So he proceeded to "reorganize" the rebellious States along the lines that he had laid down. Notwithstanding all of these facts, and within two months after the surrender of the Confederate Armies, President Johnson appointed Provisional Governors in each of the rebellious States without consulting Congress, and authorized these Provisional Governors to order elections for State Officers, Legislatures, and Members of Congress in their respective States under their old State Constitutions. In the State of Louisiana the President found that J. Madison Wells was acting Governor of that State under the election ordered by General Banks, but which had been specifically and unanimously repudiated by the United States Senate in refusing to seat the Senators elected by its Legislature.

Governor Wells visited the President at Washington and declared himself in favor of Mr. Johnson's "policy," and the President recognized him as Governor like the other Provisional Governors appointed by him. The Governor at once ordered an election for State, Parish, and Congressional Offices, and also for Members of the Legislature.

There were at this time three political parties in the State of Louisiana: the "National Republican Party," headed by the Hon. Thomas J. Durant, ex-Governor B. F. Flanders, Rufus Waples, Charles P. Horner, and others; the "Conservative Union Party," headed by Governor J. Madison Wells, Judge James G. Taliaferro, George S. Lacey, Cuthbert Bullett, and others, all Union men; and the "Democratic Party," headed by Judge H. D. Ogden, ex-Governor Robert C. Wickliffe, Albert Voorhies, James B. Eustis, Andrew S. Herron, and others, all returned Confederates.

The Democratic Party held a State Convention in the city of New Orleans and adopted a platform of principles from which the following is extracted:

First, Resolved, That we emphatically approve of the views of President Johnson with regard to the reorganization of the State Governments of the South.

Resolved, That we hold this to be a Government of White People, made and to be perpetuated for the exclusive political benefit of the White Race, and in accordance with the constant adjudication of the United States Supreme Court, that the people of African descent cannot be considered as citizens of the United States, and that there can in no event nor under any circumstances be any equality between the White and other Races.

The Democratic Convention nominated J. Madison Wells as

its candidate for Governor, and Albert Voorhies, who declared himself "to be still a Rebel," for Lieutenant-Governor. The Conservative Union Party, also, nominated J. Madison Wells for Governor with James G. Taliaferro, a staunch old Union man, for Lieutenant-Governor. Each party filled its ticket with its own members. The Conservative Union Party was overwhelmed everywhere at the election, and the Confederate (or Democratic) State and Legislative ticket was elected by an immense majority. The Legislature was almost unanimously made up of ex-Confederates.

The Republican Party formally refused to participate in the reorganization scheme of President Johnson, and therefore put no State, Congressional, or other ticket in the field.

At the First Session of the Legislature, and within a few days of its first meeting, it adopted a resolution declaring that the Constitution of 1864 under which Governor Wells held office was the "creation of fraud, violence, and corruption, and did not in any manner represent the people of the State of Louisiana." The Legislature also adopted a resolution protesting against the seating in the United States Senate of Michael Hahn and R. K. Cutler, who was elected by the former Legislature and whose credentials were signed by Governor J. Madison Wells. The spirit shown by this Legislature was one of intense and violent hostility to everything that had been done in Louisiana by Union men during the War.

Encouraged by President Johnson, matters proceeded very rapidly. Impatient to possess themselves of all power and all offices of the State, the Legislature passed a bill providing for the election of a mayor and muncipal officers for the city of New Orleans.

This bill was vetoed by Governor Wells,* who claimed that further guarantees and amendments to the city charter, with

* See Appendix B for an extract from his veto.

a radical revision of the registry and election laws, should first be adopted.

For confirmation of Governor Wells's statement regarding pre-War conditions in Louisiana, I would call attention to such records as the veto message of Governor Paul O. Hebert in 1856, the message of Governor Robert C. Wickliffe to the Legislature in 1857, and the *New Orleans Delta* of May 6, 1860—all describing the amazing orgies of lawlessness and the anarchy prevailing at that period; a reign of "force and fraud, of the knife, of the sling-shot and brass knuckles"—while orderly and decent government was paralyzed and prostrate.*

But the bill for a city election was passed over the Governor's veto, and became a law. The New Orleans city election was held under it, and John T. Monroe was elected Mayor. It was this same John T. Monroe who was the master spirit of these "Know-Nothing" murders; who led the mobs of ruffians in 1854 and again in 1856; who had taken possession of the streets of New Orleans on election day; whose violences and murders and outrages had been the subject of the messages to the Legislature by two different Governors of the State, and of the editorial just referred to (see Appendices C, D, E); and whom General Butler was obliged to confine in Fort Jackson and later to expel from the Union lines. After his election as Mayor, he at once proceeded to restore his old gang of thugs, ruffians, and murderers to power in New Orleans.

Being now possessed of all power in the State, and in all the Parish and Municipal Governments throughout the State, the returned Confederate politicians lost no opportunity to show their aversion and hostility to all classes of Union men, and especially to the recently emancipated negro population.

All Union men were made to feel the heavy hand politically,

* See extracts in Appendices C, D, and E.

commercially, and socially. The old Union men were denounced as "renegades, scallawags, and traitors to the South" during the Civil War. The thousands who had remained loyal to the Union were insulted and assaulted on every occasion, and were made to feel that they were outcasts in their own homes. The new men, ex-officers and soldiers of the Union Army and many Northern citizens who had settled in the States were called "Yankees," "Carpet-baggers," and "Adventurers," and subjected to all sorts of ostracism and indignities.

It looked as if all of these classes of Union citizens were to be compelled either to surrender their self-respect and give up everything and leave, or to organize and to fight for their rights to live in the State. We young men proposed to fight, and we accepted any and all legitimate allies.

Organized violence was common throughout the State. Personal difficulties growing out of the issues were common everywhere. The greatest sufferers of all, however, were the newly emancipated slaves. They were whipped and scourged and killed mercilessly. No one was punished for killing negroes. Ingenious laws, ordinances and rules were at once adopted by the new Legislature and by local authorities, which practically restored slavery.

Any reader doubting this statement—that virtual re-establishment of slavery by State law and municipal regulation was attempted in Louisiana—may refer to copies of the ordinances of the towns of Opelousas and Franklin, and of the Act of the Legislature of Louisiana within fifteen days after it convened in 1865, and of extracts from slightly later Acts at the same session.* Not only did these laws violate the constitutional provision prohibiting slavery or *involuntary servitude,* and arbitrarily discriminate against colored people generally: they forbade the negro to sell or barter personal property or even to

* See Appendices F, G, H, and I.

reside in certain towns, and gave the mayors thereof the power to dictate how the negro should worship God therein.

All of these acts of the Legislature and municipal regulations meant the practical re-establishment of slavery in the State of Louisiana. The Acts were passed within the first fifteen days of its first session. This legislation and the various instances of widespread wanton violence and ostracism aroused the Union men of the State and the nation, and they determined to organize for their own protection and for the protection of the freedmen and the old free negroes before the War.

On September 27, 1865, a Convention of the Republican Party was held in New Orleans, over which the Hon. Thomas Jefferson Durant presided. Mr. Durant was one of the eminent lawyers of the State and a leading Douglas Democrat before the War. He had been United States District Attorney for Louisiana, under President Polk.

A State Committee was formed, which proceeded to organize the Union Republican Party of the State of Louisiana. I participated in this Convention and was made the corresponding secretary of the State Committee. There was a small number of intelligent old-time free men of color in this Convention, and several of them were placed on the State Committee. They had never been slaves; some of them were slave-holders; most of them were nearly white. They were large property-owners and among our best citizens. Their colored ancestors had been soldiers under Governor Claiborne, and under General Jackson in 1815. They paid taxes on over fifteen million dollars' worth of property in the city of New Orleans.

The Convention adopted the following resolutions as the party platform, and issued an address to the people of the State:

(1) *Resolved*—That this body shall be styled the Convention of the Republican Party in Louisiana, and does hereby reaffirm the platform

of principles adopted at Baltimore, in June, 1864, by the Convention which nominated Abraham Lincoln and Andrew Johnson.

(2) *Resolved*—That the Ordinance of Secession adopted by a Convention of the people of Louisiana, called by an Act of the Legislature, was a declaration of war against the United States; it disrupted in fact though not in law the relations existing between the General Government and the people of this State, and rendered the latter incapable of exercising the privileges of citizens of the United States.

(3) *Resolved*—In addition, that the acts of Congress of the United States, declaring the inhabitants of Louisiana to be in a state of insurrection, constituted them, in law, enemies of the United States, and unfitted them for the functions of a State in the Union until restored by the action of Congress.

(4) *Resolved*—That loyal State Governments are essential to the Government of the United States, without which it can not operate; that the rebellion was carried on by insurgent States, therefore it is the duty of the United States, at the earliest possible moment consistent with the general welfare to establish by act of Congress a Republican Government in Louisiana.

(5) *Resolved*—That this duty is imposed by the Constitution on "the United States," and not on any military commander or Executive officer; but must be performed by the United States, represented by the President and both houses of Congress.

(6) *Resolved*—That the system of slavery heretofore existing in Louisiana, and the laws and ordinances passed from time to time to support it, have ceased to exist; and we protest against any and all attempts to substitute in their place a system of serfdom, or forced labor in any shape.

(7) *Resolved*—That the necessities of the nation called the colored men into the public service in the most honorable of all duties—that of the soldier fighting for the integrity of his country and the security of the Constitutional Government; this, with his loyalty, patience and prudence, is sufficient to assure Congress of the justice and safety of giving him a vote to protect his liberty.

(8) *Resolved*—That it would be unwise to admit the inhabitants of Louisiana at once into the Union as a State. A preliminary system of local government should be established by Congress to endure so long as may be necessary, to test the fidelity of the people to the United States, and to accustom the inhabitants to exercise in harmony and peace the rights and duties of self-government.

(9) *Resolved*—That this Convention reaffirms the principles set forth in the Declaration of American Independence in 1776:—That all men were created equal, and that republican and just governments require the consent of the governed; and deem this a fitting occasion to repeat and reaffirm our convictions in these great truths, from the peculiar circumstances in which our loyal fellow-citizens of African descent are placed, though equal in numbers to the white race; denied all political rights and governed without their consent; subjected to taxation without representation, and subjected to trials by courts and juries; and denied all participation in their organization and administration.

(10) *Resolved*—That this convention adopts, as the basis of its political organization, universal suffrage, liberty and the equality of all men before the law.

(11) *Resolved*—That under existing circumstances, this Convention considers it inexpedient to nominate candidates for State Officers.

In order to represent the views of the Union men of Louisiana to Congress, it was determined to hold a voluntary election for a delegate to represent the "Territory" of Louisiana in Congress. The Hon. Thomas J. Durant was nominated by acclamation, but he declined the honor; after which I was nominated by the Convention as such delegate, and a voluntary election was held on the 6th of November, 1865. I received 19,396 votes in thirteen Parishes of the State. My credentials were signed by the Secretary of the State, with the seal of the State attached.

I spent several months in Washington during the next session of Congress. I was accorded a seat on the floor of the House of Representatives, while the Senators and Representatives elected by the Johnson-Wells State Government had to be contented with seats in the Galleries.

The Legislature proposed to take the sense of the people on the 7th day of April, 1866, on the question of calling a Convention to make a new Constitution for the State. Governor Wells vetoed the Bill. The Legislature in the meantime, and among its first acts, adopted a joint resolution protesting against the seating of Michael Hahn and R. King Cutler, who were in Washington claiming seats as Senators elected by the former Legislature with credentials signed by Governor Wells. It proceeded to elect two others as such Senators, the Hon. Randall Hunt and the Hon. Henry Boyce.

The proposed Act of the Legislature providing for a Convention to make a new constitution in the place of the Constitution of 1864, under which Governor Wells had been first elected, declared that said Constitution of 1864 was "the creature of fraud, violence, and corruption, and did not in any manner represent the people of the State." But before taking final action on the Governor's veto, the Speaker of the House—the Hon. Duncan S. Cage—and Hons. James B. Eustis and W. E. Eagan, Members of the House, were sent to Washington to confer with President Johnson. After their conference with the President, these gentlemen united in a telegram to the Legislature advising against the calling of the Convention, for the reason "that it might seriously embarrass the President's Reconstruction Policy." The telegram read as follows:

Washington, March 8th, 1866
To Hon. Albert Voorhies, President of the Senate,
    and Hon. J. B. Elam, Speaker *pro tem.* House of Representatives:
We have had a long and agreeable interview with the President today, which was evidently pleasing to him likewise. Our coming here was opportune, and may avert great embarrassment. We also had an interesting interview with the Secretary of the State, and are to have another interview with the President on Saturday, by appointment.

(*Signed*)   W. E. EAGAN
            D. S. CAGE
            J. B. EUSTIS

The following telegram was also sent to a Member of the House of Representatives:

Washington, March 8th, 1866
To Hon. A. L. Tucker, House of Representatives:
After interviews with the President and Secretary Seward, we are

[46]

thoroughly convinced that further agitation of the Convention question will seriously embarrass the President's reconstruction policy.

(*Signed*) D. S. CAGE
J. B. EUSTIS
W. E. EAGAN

So the Bill for the Convention was laid aside. These events and this condition in Louisiana and in Washington produced a bitter feud between Governor Wells and his newly made friends, the extreme Democratic politicians, who controlled the State Legislature of Louisiana and the municipality of the city of New Orleans.

Governor Wells became desperate, and denounced his late supporters as being guilty of the greatest ingratitude; he expressed his regret at having been the means of bringing them into power, and sought for any opportunity to overthrow them.

It appears that before adjournment of the Constitutional Convention of 1864, it had, by resolution, authorized the President of the Convention "for any reason he might think proper" to reconvene the Convention.

Notwithstanding the Convention had been dead for over two years, Governor Wells in his desperation conceived the plan to have this Convention reconvene, and he induced a member— though not the President of the Convention—as required by the resolution, to issue a call for its reassembling, and in furtherance of the scheme, Governor Wells issued a proclamation authorizing the election of delegates to fill vacancies in the Convention that might have taken place since the adjournment. The election was fixed for the third of September following, but the first meeting of the Convention was fixed for the 30th of July.

According to the call, the Convention was to meet on the 30th of July, 1866. Governor Wells called on me and asked for my co-operation in this movement. But our friends took the ground that the Convention of 1864 was dead and could not be revived, and that Congress only could control the situation. We strenuously opposed President Johnson's plan of Reconstruction as well as Governor Wells' program.

But it appears that the movement had the approval of ex-Governor and Senator-elect Hahn, and the men who participated with him in the organization of the State Government of 1864. This is shown by the fact that a mass meeting was held in the city of New Orleans soon after the call for the Convention had been issued, over which ex-Governor Hahn presided and at which he made a speech favoring the call. Dr. Dostse and others made violent speeches which tended to increase the bitterness of the factions.

Mayor Monroe, who had but recently been elected and installed Mayor of the city of New Orleans, announced his determination to break up the Convention if it attempted to hold a session. He wrote a letter to General Baird, commanding the United States Army, dated July 25, 1866, in which he repeated his determination to break up the Convention "unless it was supported by United States troops." General Baird replied protesting against any resort to violence.

Only a small number of members answered the call—not nearly enough to constitute a quorum—and if they had been left alone the whole proceedings would have been regarded as a farce. But the spirit of tumult and violence was still in the hearts of the Confederate politicians and they did not hesitate to resort to violence and bloodshed to carry out their purposes.

The night before the date fixed for the meeting of the Convention, Mayor Monroe armed his police and a large number of his followers and sympathizers with the purpose of carrying out his threat to break up the Convention. I stood on the gallery of a friend's house on Canal Street and saw the police and mob gather. The police were in uniform, but the mob was distinguished by shirt sleeves and white handkerchiefs around their necks.

A signal shot was fired and the mob deployed across the head of Dryades Street, moved upon the State House, and shot down the people who were in the hall. Forty-eight were killed outright, sixty-eight were severely wounded, and ninety-eight slightly wounded in the hall and on the streets. Mayor Monroe's threat to break up the Convention succeeded completely and, but for the appearance of General Baird with United States troops later, the killing would undoubtedly have been much greater than it was.

After this affair, a number of Union men left the State never to return, among them being the Hon. Thomas J. Durant, the leader of the Republican Party in Louisiana. His residence was at the corner of Canal Street and University Place, and he and his family had been obliged to witness the massacre of the Union men on that day. It was more than they could endure.

Conditions in the South became such that Southern loyalists felt it necessary to call a Convention to meet in Philadelphia on the 3rd of September, 1866. Every Southern and "Border" State was largely represented, except South Carolina. The delegates were all white men with two exceptions and these were from Louisiana.

This Convention presented to the people of the nation all the facts and demanded that Congress should take measures to protect the Union men of the South against the organized Confederate elements. I was Chairman of the Committee on Reconstruction and read the report. The report concluded with these words:

There can be no safety for the country against the fell spirit of slavery, now organized in the form of serfdom, unless the Government by national and appropriate legislation, enforced by national authority, shall confer on every citizen in the States we represent the American birthright of impartial suffrage and equality before the law.

In discussing the question of Negro Suffrage in the South, Governor Wm. G. Brownlow of Tennessee said:

Some gentlemen, from a mistaken view of my character, said they were afraid of Negro Suffrage, and wanted to dodge it. I have never dodged any subject, nor have I ever been found on both sides of any subject. While I am satisfied with everything done here, I would go further. I am an advocate of Negro Suffrage, and impartial suffrage. I would rather be elected by loyal Negroes than by disloyal white men. I would rather associate with loyal Negroes than with disloyal white men. I would rather be buried in a Negro graveyard than in a Rebel graveyard; and after death I would sooner go to a Negro heaven than a White Rebel's hell.

A Congressional election was to be held in November following. Together with ex-Governor A. J. Hamilton of Texas and a number of other delegates, I made a canvass of the Northern States. We spoke in the New England States, New York, Ohio, and Indiana, and ended at Springfield, Illinois, only a few days before the election. The Congressional election went overwhelmingly for the Union Republican Party.

The newly elected Congress repudiated President Johnson's policy of Reconstruction. It proposed the 14th and 15th Amendments to the Constitution of the United States. It adopted measures for the Reconstruction of the ex-Confederate States. It provided that there should be no discrimination of voters on account of race, color, or previous condition of servitude. It disfranchised certain classes of Confederates, and put the details of Reconstruction in the hands of General Grant. President Johnson vetoed all of these measures, but Congress passed them over his head.

Major-General P. H. Sheridan was appointed in command of the Fifth Military District, in which was the State of Louisiana. His headquarters were at New Orleans. He first ordered a registration of all legal voters. Later he called a Convention to form a State Constitution, which prepared and submitted to the people a constitution for their ratification; an election was ordered for State Congressional, Parish and Legislative Officers to take place at the same time.

About this time we began the organization of the Grand Army of the Republic in Louisiana. At an encampment held at the Mechanic's Institute at 7 P. M., on January 11, 1868, the following officers were unanimously elected:

Grand Commander, General H. C. Warmoth. Senior Vice-Commander, Captain L. A. Snaer. Junior Vice-Commander, Captain S. B. Packard. Asst. Adj. General, Colonel George E. Yarrington. Quartermaster-General, Major W. W. Howe. Council of Administration: General L. A. Sheldon, Captain George Gresham, Captain J. B. Cooper, Sergeant J. A. Heall and Captain J. A. Raynal. Delegates to Philadelphia Grand Army: General L. A. Sheldon, Captain S. B. Packard, Dr. J. B. Cooper, and Captain J. A. Raynal.

The following resolution was adopted:

RESOLVED: That the Grand Army of the Republic of Louisiana stand by and support the plan of Reconstruction proposed by the Congress of the United States.

After the Convention had formed a new Constitution and General Sheridan had ordered an election, the Republican State Committee called a Convention to meet in the city of New Orleans on January 14, 1868, to nominate a State ticket.

At this time there were two distinct factions in the State Republican Party in the State of Louisiana. One of them called itself the "Pure Radicals" and was led by three San Domingo negroes who owned and published the *New Orleans Tribune,* and who urged the negroes of Louisiana to assert themselves and follow Hayti, San Domingo, and Liberia, and to make Louisiana an African State.

The "Pure Radicals," led by the *New Orleans Tribune,* began their campaign to Africanize the State as early as October 23, 1867.

WAR, POLITICS AND RECONSTRUCTION

On October 23, 1867, this paper published an editorial on the coming Constitutional Convention. It said:

This Convention, elected by a mass of 80,000 voters among whom there were not 8,000 white men, will be composed of a small majority of Caucasian delegates—showing thereby that no selfish design, no exclusive view, guided the colored masses.

There will be in that Convention two parties, the "Pure Radicals" and the "Compromising Republicans." Efforts will be made by parties outside of the Convention to secure the ascendency of the compromising section. But such efforts are doomed to fail.

On October 30, 1867, this paper published an article entitled "The White Man's Party and the Radical Party," in which it said:

There will be in the coming Convention a "White Man's Party" which is already organizing in the vain hope of controlling the future Government of the State. . . . We are in a situation to be just to ourselves and to elect our fellow-men. Let us do it.

But [white men] must understand how the time has changed. We now have the ballot, to use it in our own behalf. We have more than the ballot: we compose a majority in the State, and with *the help of our Radical white friends,* we compose a majority in the Convention . . . the colored masses are the masters of the field. Everything depends on the colored vote.

These extracts from the editorials of this influential newspaper among the colored people clearly indicate the purpose of those leaders. Encouraged by the protection that they expected from the United States Army, and realizing the helplessness of the formerly ruling white people, they thought to establish an *African State Government.*

This is more clearly indicated by an editorial in the *Tribune* under date of December 26, 1867, in which it said:

There are by this day three Governments among civilized nations entirely in the hands of men of the African race. There are the Dominican Republic, Hayti, and Liberia. All of these are Republican in form. Liberia, though the youngest of the three, has taken the lead as far as true Republican institutions and industrial development are concerned. That little Republic was created like a new territory in the United States on a virgin soil, whereon the fabric of society could be built according to the will and pattern of the founders. The hindrance of an old and cumbering state of things was not met there. None of the prejudices left by monarchical rule was encountered on that new soil. Liberia was free from the sense of inequality and the love of social distinctions which Hayti inherited from French monarchical rule and from the teachings of the Roman Church.

Even as early as October 25, 1867, this paper published an article entitled "Political Bearing," which urged the colored men of the Convention that each and every choice to be made by the Convention for its officers should be dictated by racial considerations. It said:

From the President down to the doorkeeper, and from the clerk and the chief reporter down to the printer, the choices should be made so as to convince the people of the State that the supremacy of a privileged class will be no longer fostered and the time has come when the representatives of the colored race can find favor as well as white men. It is to be demonstrated that long services and unfaltering devotion to the cause of Radicalism shall obtain the reward, irrespective of color or race, and to that effect it is important to choose officers from among both populations.

But there is something more. It is important to show that the oppressed race will not be overlooked; that from this time forward the rights of the neglected race will be recognized, to share in all departments of our State Government. The Convention will have many things to do to break the spell under which we were laboring. The choice of officers will, therefore, have a political bearing, and cannot be dictated by fitness only.

The Convention will meet under very peculiar circumstances—circumstances of originality and grandeur. It will be the first constitutional assembly, the first official body, ever convened in the United States without distinction of race or color. It will be the first mixed assemblage, clothed with a public character. As such this Convention has to take a position in immediate contradiction with the old assemblies of the *white man's government*. They will have to show that a new order will succeed the former order of things, and that the long-neglected race will, at last, effectually share in the Government of the State. . . .

Let our friends be bold and go to the point, as far as the application of the principle of equal rights and equal share is concerned.

When the time came to nominate candidates for Governor and other State officers, this "Pure Radical" faction insisted that the candidate of the Republican Party for the office of Governor should be a negro.

The other faction, named by the *Tribune* and its Pure Radical faction the "Compromising, or White Republicans" faction, was composed of the mass of white and colored Republicans who saw the danger of following the extreme views of the *New Orleans Tribune,* and its Pure Radicals.

When the Convention came to select its candidate for Governor, five gentlemen were proposed by their respective friends. Major Francis E. Dumas, colored, was proposed by the Pure Radicals as their candidate. Mr. P. B. S. Pinchback, colored, was also proposed, but Mr. Pinchback withdrew his name, declaring that he "did not believe it to be a wise thing to nominate a colored man for the office of Governor at this time." Major Dumas' name was not withdrawn.

The contest was a spirited one, and it resulted in the success of the so-called "Compromising" faction by a close vote on the second ballot, H. C. Warmoth receiving 45, and F. E. Dumas 43 votes. Major Dumas was tendered the nomination for Lieutenant-Governor by a vote of 57 as against W. J. Blackburn, an old white Union man, who received 27 votes. But Major Dumas declined the nomination on our ticket the next day in the following letter:

New Orleans, La., January 14, 1868

To The Honorable Members of the Republican Convention.
Gentlemen:

With the expression of my thanks for the honor conferred upon me by the Nominating Convention for Lieutenant-Governor of Louisiana, I beg leave to state that I decline being placed in that capacity on the Radical Republican Ticket. I authorized no one to bring my name forward for that position in the Nominating Convention.

I remain, Gentlemen,

Your obedient servant,

(*Signed*)   FRANCIS E. DUMAS

On motion of Colonel Don A. Pardee, the resignation was accepted and the Convention proceeded to the selection of a candidate for the office of Lieutenant-Governor.

First Ballot

Whole number of votes cast 88
Necessary for a choice 45
O. J. Dunn received 38
W. J. Blackburn 23
L. A. Snaer 13
C. C. Antoine 8
G. W. Reagan 3

Second Ballot

O. J. Dunn Received 54
W. J. Blackburn 27

The nomination of Mr. Dunn was made unanimous.

The Convention proceeded to nominate Antoine Dubuclet for Treasurer; George E. Bovee for Secretary of State; George M. Wickliffe for Auditor; Simeon Beldon for Attorney-General, and T. W. Conway for Superintendent of Education. Five white men and two colored men constituted the ticket.

Resolutions were adopted, among which was the following:

RESOLVED: That we believe in and shall endeavor to carry out the great and immutable principles of equal rights for all men, irrespective of race, color, or previous condition.

(*Signed*)   JAMES H. INGRAHAM, *Chairman*

J. V. NOBLE

L. A. SNAER

DON A. PARDEE

Adjourned *sine die.*

The Republican Convention that nominated me for Governor, together with a full State ticket, was composed mainly of delegates to the Constitutional Convention who were elected by the people under the Act of Congress of 1867.

These delegates were composed of several different elements of our people. There were, first, many of the old original Union white men of the State who had remained loyal during the War. Then there was a small number of ex-officers of the Union Army and Navy, together with a number of other Northern business men who had settled in Louisiana during or immediately after the end of the War. Also there was a number of free men of color who were descendants of the original French, Spanish, and Canadian immigrants who had cohabited with their slave women, some of whom, at least, had been educated in France or Spain, and who at the death of their white fathers inherited a part, if not all, of their fathers' estates. This element was important on the arrival of Governor Claiborne in 1803; so much so that their recognition by him and his organization of them into the Territorial Militia was the cause of serious criticism and controversy by the ancient Louisianians, who had no good feeling for Governor Claiborne or General Wilkinson, or, in fact, for the United States, until some time after the Battle of New Orleans.

General Jackson recognized this mulatto or free-men-of-color corps. He encouraged it; he inspected it; he issued an address to it; he flattered it for its good soldierly appearance, and at the end of the War he complimented it most highly for its gallant and useful service in the battle of the 27th of December, 1814, and the great battle of the 8th of January, 1815.

This element of colored people had greatly increased in numbers, wealth, intelligence, and importance by 1867. Many of them were owners of slaves, and some of them were actually in the Confederate Army, but not registered as negroes. On November 23, 1861, the Confederate Grand Parade took place in New Orleans, and it was estimated to be seven miles long. One feature of this review was a regiment of free men of color, 1,400 in number. The *Picayune* speaks as follows of another review on February 9, 1862:

We must pay deserved compliment to the companies of free men of color, all well-dressed, well-drilled, and comfortably uniformed. Most of these companies have provided themselves with arms unaided by the administration.

They were planters, merchants, brokers, and mechanics of various trades. They paid taxes on over $15,000,000 of property in New Orleans alone.

As related before, there were a number of free negroes who had come to Louisiana from the North before the War. They were the subject of a message, as formerly stated, to the State Legislature by Governor R. C. Wickliffe in 1856, who said that they had been steadily increasing for years, and that this was a source of great evil and demanded legislative action. He demanded that all free negroes be removed from the State.

So the reader will see that the race question obtruded itself early in our Republican politics. There was a class of colored people in Louisiana who really hoped and believed that the change in affairs would result in the Africanization of the State. These three San Domingo refugees (colored) by the names of Roudanez, who had located in the State of Louisiana, had brought with them their Dominican and Haytian predilections. One of these men was a physician of eminence; all of them were men of intelligence. They were the publishers of the daily newspaper in the city of New Orleans already referred to, called the *New Orleans Tribune*. They led in the insistence that the Republican Convention should nominate a colored man for Governor. They were responsible for the naming of F. E. Dumas as this nominee. Mr. Dumas was a very respectable and wealthy colored man, and I was nominated over him by only two votes' majority. These men were so dissatisfied with their failure to nominate a colored man for Governor that they would not allow Major Dumas to accept the nomination on our ticket for Lieutenant-Governor. They forced him to decline our nomination.

So dissatisfied were these Pure Radicals with our ticket that they brought forward an opposition ticket headed by Judge Taliaferro for Governor, with Major Francis E. Dumas for Lieutenant-Governor, making a full ticket mostly composed of members of the Constitutional Convention. But the great mass of people supported our ticket. In fact, out of 86 Republican members of the Constitutional Convention 78 members signed a declaration declaring themselves in favor of our ticket, notwithstanding that Judge Taliaferro, the President of the Constitutional Convention, was the candidate of the bolters for Governor. Only four white delegates of the Constitutional Convention followed Judge Taliaferro in the bolt, all of whom were candidates on his State Ticket. The Pure Radical or bolting ticket was wholly inspired by the faction led by the *New Orleans Tribune,* which was sorely disappointed by their failure to nominate a negro candidate for Governor.

The State Executive Committee, composed of 140 members, with the greatest unanimity adopted on January 23rd the following resolutions:

(1) RESOLVED: That we cordially endorse and earnestly support the candidate nominated by the Radical Republican State Convention, headed by the General Henry C. Warmoth.

(2) RESOLVED: That we condemn and denounce any effort to get up another ticket as an attempt to defeat our party and defeat Reconstruction and the success of our principles.

(3) All members of the Central Executive Committee of the Radical Republican Party of Louisiana, who oppose the nomination of the State Convention of our party, shall be regarded as disorganizers and their seats be declared vacant.

(4) WHEREAS, *The New Orleans Tribune* has ceased to represent the principles and views of the Republican Party of Louisiana:

(5) THEREFORE, RESOLVED, That we hereby repudiate it as

the organ of the party and of this Committee, and appoint *The New Orleans Republican* the organ of our party.

(*Signed*)   SETH W. LEWIS, *President State Central Committee.*
(*Signed*)   WM. VIGERS, *Secretary*
        S. B. PACKARD, *Chairman, Campaign Committee*
        DENNIS BURREL, *Secretary.*

Under the second resolution, Chas. Smith, O. Voiche, L. Rodriguez, J. S. Soude, W. R. Crane, J. L. Monthieu, and three others were unanimously expelled.

The canvass and election passed off quietly. It was conducted by officers of election, selected by General Sheridan. The Pure Radical ticket, headed by Judge Taliaferro and Major Dumas and supported by the *New Orleans Tribune,* received 38,046 votes, while our ticket received 64,941 votes, a majority of 26,895. Ex-Governor Henry W. Allen, late Confederate Governor, received 9,000 votes, although he was a refugee in the City of Mexico at the time.

I was regarded as leading the Conservative or Compromise element, as it was termed by the radical *New Orleans Tribune,* and Judge Taliaferro and Major Dumas were regarded as the leaders of the Pure Radical or Extreme Faction.

I have reason to believe that a large number of conservative white men of the State supported me, while only the extreme radicals, or "negro factions," supported Judge Taliaferro and the *New Orleans Tribune.*

I was inaugurated in the State House in the city of New Orleans on July 13th, 1868, at a time when the whole South was in a state of turmoil. The extreme political leaders of both parties exerted every influence to inflame the people, and to embarrass, hamper, and destroy the new Government.

The following is my inaugural address:

Mr. President and Gentlemen of the Senate and House of Repre-
    sentatives:

I am deeply impressed with the grave and peculiar significance of this occasion, and the magnitude of the responsibility which I am this day to assume. I trust the hearts of all of us are moved and pervaded by a realizing sense of the new and serious duties we have been called upon to discharge. Before me is the first Legislature as an equal member of the American Union, that has sat for seven years, so full of startling and wonderful as well as painful and terrible events— so pregnant with momentous issues, so productive of great and glorious results. Nor do I deem it expedient at this time to trace the chain of causes which led to these events and produced these results, or to discuss the questions of who have been most culpable and responsible for whatever has been wrong or mistaken in the past, and who are most deserving of credit for whatever is good in the present. We have here met not to speculate upon the past, nor to brood and quarrel over its ashes, but rather to meet the great living issues of the present, and the duties which it imposes upon us. We stand amid the ruins of an old order of things; it should be ours to work wisely and manfully for the establishment of a new and better order of things upon the foundation which even seven years have established. So long as time is spent in futile and irritating discussions upon the realness and probable permanency of those foundations, or persistent and perhaps turbulent efforts to unsettle and upheave them, so long will the public peace, order, and tranquillity refuse to be restored, and so long will the restoration and development of all the great interests of the State be delayed and endangered.

Gentlemen, the corner-stone of these foundations laid and fixed forever by a great war, sealed as I firmly believe by the hand of God Himself, and recognized by that organic law under which we have assembled, and which I am here to swear to support and defend, is the equality before the law and the enjoyment of every political right of all the citizens of the State, regardless of race, color, or previous condition; and only when this grand distinctive feature of the new Constitution shall be stamped on every act of legislation, and when such legislation shall find approval and support in that general public sentiment which gives to law its vitality, will our State fairly enter upon that career of greatness and prosperity which the Almighty designed for her. It would be idle to deny that while a large majority of our people have testified in the strongest manner to their approval of that feature of the Constitution of which I have spoken, there is still a minority, not wanting in intelligence and virtue, who are strenuously opposed to it. Much is to be hoped from the good sense, the discretion and inherent love of justice of the American people for the

gradual wearing-away of the prejudices upon which alone this opposition is founded. Meantime, let our course, while resolute and manly,
be also moderate and discreet. Let legislation be kept as much as
possible in harmony with the sentiments of the whole people. It is
better that the course of legislation should rather fall behind than
to outstrip the popular wishes and demands. Let everything consistent with right and justice be done to bring back the era of good
feeling, and to wash from the memories of all everything that tends
to alienate one class or one party from another.

I refrain at this time from entering into any discussion of measures
which I may deem of importance. In future I will discharge the
duty imposed upon me by giving to the General Assembly information respecting the condition of the State, and recommending to its
consideration such legislation as may seem expedient. I venture, however, to urge immediate measures for the repression of lawlessness and
disorder now rife in many parts of the State. From many parishes we
have almost daily accounts of violence and outrage—in many cases
most brutal and revolting murders—without any effort on the part
of the people to prevent or punish them.

We want peace and order; without it we can have no prosperity.
Such measures must be adopted to secure life and property as may be
necessary. If the taxpayers prefer to support a strong constabulary
force to doing their duty as citizens by helping the officers—yes, by
making the officers of the law keep the peace and protect the life of
every man, however poor—then the responsibility will be upon them,
and not the State administration. Everybody knows that the strong
men, the property-holders, and those who claim and command the
respect of their parishes, could make it as peaceable and safe throughout the State as in any part of the Union.

The hands of the courts must be strengthened and upheld—the
peace officers must do their duty—the good people must rise up and
vindicate the law. The press, too vindictive and partisan, should
unite with the government in denouncing crime, and aid in the establishment of a healthy public sentiment which of itself would protect the
peace by its frowns upon evil-doers. You should drive those drones
upon society who eat but do not work, who consume and produce
nothing, more dangerous to peace and prosperity than famine or pes-
tilence, to go to work or find another country than this to curse.

I appear before you today not as a partisan, but to take the oath
of office prescribed for those who are chosen by the people to dis-

charge the duties of the office of Governor of our State. My object will be to enforce the law, protect the people and aid in advancing the social, material, and political interests of the whole people. I believe the epoch has the smiles of Providence. Cursed for our sins with war, scourged with the epidemic, our crops blighted for a succession of years, our fair State overflowed by the torrents of the Mississippi, commerce paralyzed, the people impoverished—the event of my inauguration is welcomed by the full restoration of civil government and readmission into the Union, the fairest prospect for crops, receding floods, and improving credit. Let us vie with each other in seeing who of us shall receive most blessings for good and faithful services rendered the State.

Referring to my inauguration, the *New Orleans Times* said:

Governor Warmoth, in his inaugural address yesterday, assumed a tone far more moderate and conciliatory than had been expected. He expresses a determination to perform the duties of his office, not as a partisan, but as the chief magistrate of the State and people. Though we are well aware that lip service is cheap, yet we cannot withhold our approval of the recommendation that "legislation be kept as much as possible in harmony with the sentiments of the whole people." While recognizing the rights of a "minority not wanting in intelligence and virtue," the Governor thinks that "the course of legislation should rather fall behind than outstrip the popular wishes and demands." Though we are not without prejudices against the man who utters those fine sentiments, yet our invariable rule is to give even the devil his due. If Governor Warmoth keeps up to the promise of the programme which he has marked out for himself he will greatly improve his reputation among us, and we may add that he will disappoint a great many,—not only of his political friends, but of his political enemies. (July 14, 1868.)

The *Crescent* had the following to say:

Governor Warmoth's Inaugural

The inaugural delivered yesterday by Governor Warmoth is in some respects a remarkable document. In point of compendiousness and brevity it is almost a model. Many of our citizens will be surprised at its well-pondered and carefully guarded phraseology, and at its studiously moderate and conciliatory tone. It affords evidence that

Governor Warmoth does not wish to be classed with the rash and headlong men of his party; that he is penetrated with some wholesome convictions regarding the exigencies of the situation; and that he has not been indifferent to the advice of the *Crescent* and other conservative papers that he should address himself frankly to the interests of the State and to the common good of all her people, if he would improve his own position and prospects, either as a political leader or as a private citizen.

It is to be regretted that Governor Warmoth did not take this occasion to join the friends of universal amnesty and the removal of all political disabilities for political causes. While expressing his earnest wish for the revival of prosperity and of a healthy public sentiment, he should not have forgotten how much a policy of political vindictiveness and proscription makes against both of those objects.

"We want peace and order; without it we can have no prosperity," says Governor Warmoth. He may be assured that there is not one in the one hundred thousand of those to whom he is politically opposed who is not prepared to second him heartily in any measures which will unite the true conditions of peace and order and prosperity, security of life and property and substantial service to the State. "Let legislation be kept in harmony as much as possible with the sentiments of the whole people." Will the partisan majority in the Legislature have the wisdom or the liberality to act upon this advice?

In its issue of July 15, 1868, *The Bulletin* had the following to say:

Whatever may be our opinion of the mode in which this government has been adopted, it is our duty to extract from it as much public good as possible. It professes in every department the most conservative intentions. Why should they not be carried into effect? The Governor and Legislature have been elected against the opposition of those who hold most of the property in the city and country. These authorities cannot be displaced. It is natural they should wish to conciliate the opposition. The credit of the State, the payment of taxes, the social peace of the State, may depend on the confidence of the capital and enterprise among the minority in numbers. The colored people are content with the extraordinary stride made in their political rights. They are not vindictive. They are satisfied and do not impel the authorities to go further.

We draw these inferences of moderation from the message of Governor Warmoth, which is eminently conservative. He says:

"Let our course, while resolute and manly, be also moderate and discreet. Let legislation be kept as much as possible in harmony with the sentiments of the whole people. It is better that the course of legislation should rather fall behind than outstrip the popular wishes and demands. Let everything consistent with right and justice be done to bring back the era of good feeling, and to wash from the memories of all everything that tends to alienate one class or one party from another."

His object is declared to be "to enforce the law, protect the people, and aid in advancing the social, material and political interests of the whole people."

From these declarations comes, as a corollary, that he does not wish to see the exasperation of forcing social amalgamation in the schools or elsewhere. But if there were any doubt upon this special subject, the Republican organ, speaking of his speech to the colored people made after his inauguration, says:

"It was to a large group of these that Governor Warmoth, in the course of proceedings in his room, addressed himself as follows: 'My friends, this is a great day for the colored men of Louisiana. It is full of good for you if my hopes and expectations in your favor are well founded. If you are honest, industrious and peaceable, you will have millions of friends who will stand by you, and see that you are protected in all the political rights which they themselves enjoy. You do not wish to intrude yourselves socially upon those who do not want your society, any more than you want other people to obtrude themselves upon you without your consent. The contest from which we are emerging has not been for social equality, but for civil and political equality. This last you now have, and it will be my duty to see that you are protected in it, and, if I am not mistaken in my opinion of your race, it will be cheerfully accorded to you very soon by everybody; and remember that the roads that lead to prosperity for every man, whether white or black, are those of virtue and education, of honesty and sobriety, of industry and obedience to law.'"

CHAPTER III

UNFORTUNATELY for our State government, which was inaugurated in July, we were confronted by the Presidential election of November, 1868. The new government had less than five months in which to organize the machinery for conducting the election and to demonstrate its capacity to conduct the Commonwealth. Both national parties made Reconstruction the paramount issue of the campaign. The Republican Party denounced President Johnson and his policy of Reconstruction, and the Democratic Party denounced the Congressional policy of Reconstruction, and organized to overthrow it. There never was such bitterness displayed before or since by political parties anywhere in the nation. It was believed by both parties that the whole question of Reconstruction was to be settled by the result of this Presidential election.

General U. S. Grant, the hero of the War, was nominated by the Republicans for President, and Schuyler Colfax, Speaker of the House of Representatives, was nominated for Vice-President. Governor Horatio Seymour of New York was nominated by the Democrats for President, and my personal friend and former brigade, division and corps commander, General Frank P. Blair of Missouri, was nominated for Vice-President.

The whole South was in a blaze of tumultuous excitement. Every Confederate sympathizer put on his armor. Tremendous and frequent meetings were held in every city and parish in the State of Louisiana; nobody talked of anything but politics and what was to happen to the South as the result of the election. It is a mild statement to make that the Republican Party in Louisiana was paralyzed by the violence of the opposition demonstrated in this campaign. Semi-military organizations (mostly secret) sprang up everywhere. Republican meetings and processions in the city of New Orleans were broken up by rioters. Republican clubrooms were raided and destroyed and threats of violence appalled the people.

The opposition were told, and believed, that if they could elect Seymour and Blair President and Vice-President, with a majority in Congress, they would be able to overthrow Reconstruction and establish their party in power for a lifetime. President Johnson and his administration strongly supported their ticket. We believed that if Grant and Colfax should win, with a Republican majority in Congress, we would be able to maintain our Government and that peace and prosperity would ultimately follow. It was, therefore, a life-and-death struggle, and the opposition had the better of us if they resorted to violence, which they did to the very limit.

The Democratic State Committee began its campaign with an address, or circular letter, which was printed by the press. It ended with the following words:

CIRCULAR OF THE DEMOCRATIC CENTRAL COMMITTEE

And we would earnestly declare to our fellow-citizens our opinion that even the most implacable and ill-disposed of the Negro population, those who show the worst spirit toward the White people, are not half as much deserving our aversion and non-intercourse with them as the debased Whites who encourage and aid them, and who become through their votes the office-holding oppressors of the people. Whatever resentment you have should be felt toward the latter, and not against the colored men; but in no case should you permit this resentment to go further than to withdraw from them all *countenance, association,* and *patronage,* and thwart every effort they may make to maintain a business and social foothold among you.

> (*Signed*) THOMAS L. MACON,
> *Pres. State Central Committee*
> J. E. AUSTIN
> A. B. BACON
> THEO. F. THEINEMAN
> I. H. HALSEY
> COMMITTEE.

STORMY DAYS IN LOUISIANA

On September 28, 1868, a riot occurred in the Parish of St. Landry, one of the largest and most populous parishes of the State. It was brought about by an assault on Mr. Emerson Bentley, an ex-Union soldier and the editor of a Republican newspaper called *The St. Landry Progress*. Judge James R. Dickinson, with two other prominent Democrats, committed the assault. Mr. Bentley was very badly beaten up; the assailants said it was because of an article published in his newspaper. In the excitement, the report went out that Mr. Bentley had been killed; and the Republicans, white and colored, rushed to town, and of course the Democrats rushed to town, and the result was that 3,000 Democrats killed and wounded over 200 Republicans. They jailed eight Republicans who later at night were taken out of jail and killed.

Mr. Bentley escaped through the swamps to New Orleans. He was twenty days accomplishing it. His printing press was destroyed and St. Landry Parish, which gave me 2,200 votes for Governor in April, did not give Grant and Colfax one single vote in November. As an evidence of the tone of the opposition press at this period, I give below a few extracts from a paper published at Franklin in the Parish of St. Mary, one of the richest and most progressive parishes of the State. This paper was edited by a New Hampshire Yankee who had settled in this parish as a school-teacher some thirty years before the War. His name was Daniel Dennett.

In his issue of August 15, 1868, he said:

Old Thad Stevens Dead

The prayers of the righteous have at last removed the Congressional curse! May old Brownlow, Butler, and all such political monsters, soon follow the example of their illustrious predecessor! May his new iron works wean him from earth, and may the fires of his new furnace never go out! The Devil will get on a big bender now. With Thad Stevens in his Cabinet, and Butler in Washington, he can manage things in both Kingdoms to his liking. Lucky Devil!

A little later, on September 12, 1868, Mr. Dennett said:

[67]

WAR, POLITICS AND RECONSTRUCTION

We are opposed to running after Negroes, to talk to them. If they join the Democrats honestly, let us treat them with the utmost kindness and fairness. But to those who prefer the sneaking, thieving Carpet-bagger to an honest Southern man, we say "Stay where you are, and follow those miserable rascals to your ruin. If you want the honest white men of the South as your enemies, follow our enemies, and we will put a mark on you as distinct as that which was stamped on Cain."

Another article:

If the Government refuses protection against the depredations of unconvicted criminals and unhung convicts, Vigilance Committee thugs, Klu-Kluxes, and assassins will spring up all over the South and take the law into their own hands.

Again on October 10, 1868:

We hear nothing from St. Landry. The negroes all over the Parish have been disarmed, and have gone to work briskly. Their loyal league clubs have been broken up, the scallawags have turned Democrats, and the carpet-baggers have run off, and their carpet-bag press and type and office have been destroyed. St. Landry is quiet for the first time since the War.

Again in the same issue:

The people generally are well satisfied with the result of the St. Landry riot, only they regret that the Carpet-Baggers escaped. The editor escaped; and a hundred dead negroes, and perhaps a hundred more wounded and crippled, a dead white Radical, a dead Democrat, and three or four wounded Democrats are the upshot of the business.

Later, on October 17, 1868, he said:

The recent disasters of the Radicals in St. Landry have had a terrible effect on the little rat Pope [the sheriff of the Parish and but lately a Colonel of a Regiment in the Union Army]. He has a complication of diseases, his liver don't act, he has the colic, the toothache, and the yellow jaundice, and don't feel very well himself. If he dies, the shell of an English walnut would make a good sarcophagus in which to convey his precious remains to his Northern friends, . . . and be buried at low-water mark when the tide ebbs and flows in twenty-four hours.

[68]

On the night of this last issue of Mr. Dennett's *Planter's Banner,* five men disguised themselves in a saloon nearby and proceeded to O'Neill's Hotel in the town of Franklin, where Colonel H. H. Pope and his wife resided. On the gallery of the hotel they found Colonel Pope and Judge Chase in conversation. They killed Colonel Pope in the presence of his wife, and also Judge Chase, using both pistols and knives under the most shocking circumstances.

Judge Chase was an old citizen of the Parish and a Union man. He was connected with some of the very best people of the Parish, and was an excellent citizen. His only offense was that he was a Union man and had been elected to the office of Parish Judge by the Republicans.

Colonel Henry H. Pope was a native of Ogdensburg, New York. He was a school-teacher. He enlisted in the United States Army on the 16th day of August, 1861, and was mustered into the service as Captain of Company D of the 33rd Illinois Volunteer Infantry for a period of three years, on the 28th of August, 1861. He was promoted to Major on October 26, 1864, and Lieutenant-Colonel on November 24, 1865, at Vicksburg, Mississippi.

After the War Colonel Pope settled in the Parish of St. Mary and was elected sheriff of the Parish by the Republicans.

On October 31, only a few days before the Presidential Election, *The Planter's Banner* had this to say:

Since the shocking event of the night of the 17th, all parts of our Parish have been diligently patrolled by armed police every night. We have reports that the colored people are settling down quietly to business and labor, and becoming thoroughly disgusted with the men who have been humbugging them with lying promises and deceitful words.

Most of the negroes now show a disposition to vote the Democratic ticket, and live on friendly terms with the white people of the Parish.

In the same issue, it printed the following:

WAR, POLITICS AND RECONSTRUCTION

The Last Chance

Next Tuesday let us take a Democratic Ticket in one hand, and a Radical Ticket in the other, and say to each negro voter, "Choose today whether you take the Southern White Man or the Carpetbagger for your future friend. If you choose the men who have been raising the devil in this Parish since the War, look for no more favors from us. We allow you to vote for our enemies but you must be treated as our enemies if you vote for men whose aim is to rob and ruin us."

These articles demonstrate the character and spirit with which the Presidential campaign was carried on throughout the State of Louisiana by the Democratic Party, when General Grant was elected President of the United States.

The city press of New Orleans, especially *The Commercial Bulletin, The Crescent* and *The Bee,* was equally violent. The *Nachitoches Vindicator,* edited by J. H. Cosgrove; *The Shreveport Times,* edited by H. J. Hersey; *The Monroe Telegraph,* edited by Geo. W. McCrany, and other country papers, were, if possible, more violent and extreme in their assault upon the Republicans.

The consequence was that secret Democratic organizations were formed, and all armed. We had "The Knights of the White Camellia," "The Ku-Klux Klan," and an Italian organization called "The Innocents," who nightly paraded the streets of New Orleans and the roads in the country Parishes, producing terror among the Republicans.

Our dear old friend, Captain James Dinkins of New Orleans, now eighty-six years of age, is still in buoyant health and spirits; he and his darling wife are favorites of the people of the South. Captain Dinkins was one of the dashing leaders of General N. B. Forrest's Confederate cavalry during the Civil War. He loves to tell how the Ku-Klux Klan originated, and he has lately published a letter over his own signature from which I extract the following:

"In the midst of the distress in the South, there was a frolic by four young men who had been officers in Forrest's Cavalry. Captain John W. Morton, chief of Forrest's Artillery; Sam Donaldson and William Forrest, Jr., members of the General's Staff; and William Rains, who had commanded the Provost Guard of Chalmers's Division. They were attending school at Pulaski, Tennessee, to prepare themselves for entering college. After study hours, on a sultry August night, Sam Donaldson proposed that they go out and have some fun. It was agreed, and they used the sheets of their beds to wrap around themselves. They sallied forth and marched into a meeting in a negro church. The preacher had been exhorting his congregation to repent, and announced that some dreadful punishment would be sent upon them unless they did. Just at this time, the four 'ghosts' entered the church. The congregation climbed out of the windows and the back door.

"A few days afterwards, Captain Morton visited Memphis, and related the incident to General Forrest, and then and there the Ku-Klux Klan saw the light. General Forrest summoned a number of his former soldiers to Memphis, and they returned to their homes with instructions to organise Klans for the invincible Army.

"The Order grew throughout the South, and proved to be the most successful Army that ever entered the field. The queer costumes, the great secrecy, and the weird mystery operated upon the minds of the ignorant and vicious negroes and the undesirable whites.

"The Ku-Klux Klan was composed of the best citizens of our Country. Their mission was to protect the weak and oppressed, negroes as well as the whites.

"The writer of these lines was the Grand Monk of Klan Number 14 of Madison County, Mississippi, and is the sole survivor of that Klan. We went forth always after midnight; our horses were covered with white canvas; the robes we wore were black with a red cross on the breast and a white circle around the eyehole. Negroes often said, 'De horses is bigger dan sho' nuf horses, and I seed dem folks drink three buckets of water at one time.'

"The history of the Ku-Klux Klan is a priceless heritage. It was a creation born of necessitous times, of pure and patriotic impulses. It was organized to protect the women of the South, who were the noblest, loveliest, best women in the world. And although the ladies made the robes, there never was one who ever mentioned it.

"The Ku-Klux Klan preserved the Union. The carpet-baggers were as much alarmed as the negroes."

Such is the story of the creation of the Ku-Klux Klan, as told by one who knows. The Klan extended over the entire South. A record of the conduct and the doings of that patriotic organization, so loudly praised by our good friend Captain Dinkins, is to be found in the Congressional Reports, made after full investigation; it will live for future generations to read.

It was not Charles Sumner, Thaddeus Stevens and Ben Butler that gave the emancipated slaves the ballot; it was our own Southern brothers who made it necessary to save the negroes from extermination.

The Ku-Klux Klan seemed to enjoy reading of their antics in the newspapers, as exemplified in *The Planter's Banner* of May 23, 1868:

MR. EDITOR: There is much excitement among the negroes, and even some of the white folks all over Attakapas, about the Ku-Kluxes that have lately appeared in this country. I am not superstitious, and will not tell you what I believe about these strange, ghostly appearances, but will give you some general items and rumors.

The negroes have entirely deserted one prairie in Attakapas. The negroes of Lafayette Parish were lately nearly all of them preparing to leave, the K.K.K.'s having frightened them every night, and carried off a carpet-bagger from Illinois. One negro, a big-talking radical somewhere in the Parish of St. Martin, was lately carried off by these Confederate ghosts at night, and has never been heard of since.

A night traveler called at the negro quarters, somewhere in Atta-kapas, and asked for water. After he had drunk three buckets full of good cistern-water, at which the negro was much astonished, he thanked the colored man and told him he was very thirsty, that he had travelled nearly a thousand miles in twenty-four hours, and that was the best drink of water he had had since he was killed at the Battle of Shiloh. The negro dropped the bucket, tumbled over two chairs and a table, escaped through a back window; and has not been heard from since. He was a radical negro.

White men on white horses have lately been sailing through the air at midnight at Pattersonville, Jeanerette, and various places all over the southern part of this state. If negroes attempt to run away from the K.K.K.'s, these spirits always follow them and catch them, and no living man ever hears from them again.

The leader of this new order is said to be perfectly terrible. He is ten feet high, and his horse is fifteen. He carries a lance and a shield like those of Goliath of the Philistines. The last troop of the Confederate spirits informed a friendly negro that they had left Nashville about twelve hours before, and when they returned they were going to evaporate old Brownlow. They would have done it before, but the Devil was not prepared to receive the Governor of Tennessee and Thad Stevens, so they had to wait.

Some suppose the mysterious appearances in Attakapas to be the spirits of the Federal dead that have lately been unearthed by the Government grave-diggers all through this country; but that cannot be, since they are all friendly to the white people of this country, particularly to the women and children and good negroes. Only one Federal spirit has been discovered since the excitement began. At midnight, by the grave of a Federal soldier who had been a convict before he left the North, and who had done many wrongs to the people of the South, his bones having been boxed up and sent North by the grave-diggers, the spirit sat and in mournful strains sang the following:

"Who burst the barriers of my peaceful grave?
  Ah! cruel death, that could no longer save,
    But grudged me e'en that narrow, dark abode,
    And thrust me out into the wrath of God;

Where shrieks and chains,
And all the dreadful eloquence of pains,
My only song, black, fierce, malignant light,
The sole refreshment of my blasted sight!"

A few nights ago a K.K.K. alighted in front of some cabin, and gave four raps on the door. The colored head of the family made his appearance.

"Any carpet-baggers in this neighborhood?" said the frowning ghost.

"No, sah," said the negro.

"Any yellow tickets in this cabin?"

"No, sah," was the reply.

Taking off his head, and handing it to the colored gentleman, he said: "Please hold my head while I tighten this cork leg; I lost one leg when I was killed at Shiloh."

The negro fainted, and has not yet come to his senses!

One of the K.K.K.'s lately dismounted at the door of a clubroom where some carpet-baggers were giving bad advice to a houseful of negroes. Rapping loudly at the door with the butt of his whip, he was admitted. The carpet-baggers were paralyzed. "Hold on a minute," said the ghost, "till I turn this screw and let a little more power into this steam arm, and I will clean out these white devils who are giving you black people bad advice, and will not leave a bone unbroken in their bodies." The carpet-baggers went out like chimney-swallows, and scaled the fences like chicken-thieves.

(Signed) K.K.K.'s.

Attakapas, May 20, 1868

Our Democratic friends in the Presidential campaign had great fun importing a big black negro down to Louisiana from Mississippi to make speeches for the Seymour-and-Blair ticket. His name was Willis Rollins and he made many Democratic speeches during his campaign. He told a lot of good stories and not a few bad ones. He abused me for being a carpet-bagger, and said he had known me for many years and that I was a bad lot. I can't recall his speeches, but I remember that our Democratic friends enjoyed them immensely. He was spied on Canal Street one day by a bunch of colored people and they ran into a Democratic clubroom, where an immense crowd of colored people soon assembled to hoot and jeer at him. He was afraid to come out or show himself. The clubroom was just around in Canal Street from the State House, and Colonel J. B. Walton and Major Ned Austin, two leading Democrats, fearing a riot, came to the State House to get me to go out and see if I could not protect their colored orator. I readily consented and found Canal Street full of colored people, shouting and hooting at Rollins. They wanted to lynch him, and I fear they would have done so but for my timely arrival at the scene of excitement.

Messrs. Walton and Austin took me up into the rooms of this club, and as soon as I appeared in the gallery a big shout and cheers went up for me. After the cheering I spoke as follows:

FELLOW CITIZENS: *I* know you will stand by me in protecting this black man in his right to be a Democrat, as we want him and these white gentlemen to protect us in our right to be Republicans. I have enjoyed reading the speeches of this black Democrat very much because I know that all of our Democratic friends have been delighted with them. He has been quite severe in his criticism of General Grant and especially so as to my public and private character. But he has been no worse than some of his white associates. I will try to bear his funny speeches with equanimity.

But I have come here to impress upon you, my colored fellow-citizens, that this man has a perfect right to be a Democrat if he wants to be one, the same as you and I have a right to be Republicans. We don't care what his motives are; that is none of our business. I only wish that our Democratic friends could find it in their hearts to be more generous to your race and to make it to your interest for more of you to be members of their political party. Race conflicts are sure to ensue if party lines are based on race. Your safety and the safety of the white people and their prosperity depend largely on the willingness of the white race to accord you equality of rights with themselves. The more negroes becoming Democrats will bring more white men into the Republican Party and in that is the safety of the Republic and the prosperity of the people.

So, my dear Republican friends, I urge you all to go peaceably to your homes and let our Democratic friends enjoy the oratory of their black companion. (Loud cheers, and the street was soon clear.)

All the newsboys that evening sold lots of papers. They cried out, "Here is the evening *Times!*" "Here is the evening *Crescent!*" "Here is the evening *Picayune—all about Governor Warmoth's great Democratic speech!*"

These K.K.K. Democratic organizations took possession of the State and city. They destroyed Republican newspaper offices; attacked Republican processions; broke up Republican meetings; raided and destroyed Republican clubrooms and inaugurated a reign of terror everywhere. Sixteen Republicans were killed in the streets of New Orleans the week before the election.

Affairs became so desperate that I was forced to address the following letter to Major-General Rousseau:

Executive Department, State of Louisiana, Oct. 25, 1868.
Major-General L. H. Rousseau,
    Commanding Department of Louisiana.
    General:—The evidence is conclusive that the civil authorities in the Parishes of Orleans, Jefferson, and St. Bernard are unable to preserve order and protect lives and property of the people.
    The Act of Congress prohibiting the organization of Militia in this State strips me of all power to sustain them in the discharge of their duties, and I am compelled to appeal to you to take charge of the peace of these Parishes and to use your forces to that end.
    If you respond favorably to my request, I will at once order the sheriffs and police forces to report to you for orders.
    Very respectfully your obedient servant,
                                    H. C. WARMOTH
                                    Governor of Louisiana.

In doing this, I had no intention of avoiding responsibility but I was determined that no question of authority should be raised by the Military Commandant. General Rousseau telegraphed my letter to the Secretary of War, endorsing what I stated, and received the following reply:

STORMY DAYS IN LOUISIANA

War Department, Washington, Oct. 26, 1868.
Brevet-Major General L. H. Rousseau,
 Commanding Department of Louisiana, New Orleans:
 Your despatch of the 26th, forwarding a message from the Governor of Louisiana and asking instructions, has been received. You are authorized and expected to take such action as may be necessary to preserve the peace and good order, and to protect the lives and prosperity of citizens.

(Signed)   J. M. SCHOFIELD
Secretary of War

Upon receipt of this order from the Secretary of War, and with my consent, General Rousseau selected General J. B. Steedman (a distinguished ex-Union officer from Ohio, though a Democrat, who happened to be stationed at New Orleans by President Johnson, as Collector of Internal Revenue) for Superintendent of Police for the Metropolitan District, comprising the Parishes of Orleans, St. Bernard, and Jefferson.

General Rousseau thereupon issued the following address to the people of New Orleans:

Headquarters Department of Louisiana
(States of Louisiana and Arkansas)
New Orleans, La., October 28, 1868

To the People of New Orleans:
 Fellow-Citizens, I have received instructions from the authorities at Washington to take such action as may be necessary to preserve peace and good order and to protect the lives and property of citizens. As the City is quiet to-day, I think it a proper time to make the above announcement, and to call upon all law-abiding citizens to aid me hereafter in carrying out these instructions, and to that end they are earnestly *requested* to refrain from assembling in large bodies on the streets, to avoid exciting conversation and other causes of irritation and excitement, and to pursue their ordinary vocations as usual. The police force of the City has been reorganized, and inefficient members have been dropped from the rolls and others appointed in their places; and General J. B. Steedman is appointed Chief of Police, *pro tempore,* by the Board of Police Commissioners. General Steedman and his police force will be supported by the Military; and assurance is given

[77]

alike to the peaceful and the lawless that everything at my command
and to the utmost of my ability will be used in the endeavor to obey
these instructions.

For the present, political processions and patrolling the streets by
armed men is prohibited.

LOVELL H. ROUSSEAU
Brevet-Major General U. S. A., Commanding Department

General Rousseau was a fine fellow, and a brilliant soldier
in the Union Army during the Civil War; but he was also a
Kentucky Democrat, with all of the prejudices against Reconstruction, and a supporter of President Johnson's policy. He
was sent to Louisiana to help carry the State for Seymour and
Blair, and the result was as President Johnson liked it.

General Rousseau, being a Democrat, was taken up by the
leaders of the Democratic Party upon his arrival in New
Orleans; and it is said that he actually visited and made a
speech at one of the Democratic clubs.

I believe that General Steedman honestly tried to preserve
order, but he soon found that he could not do it even with
General Rousseau and his troops at his back, and he resigned
his post two days before the election. The result was that
Republican clubrooms and processions were again raided, and
Seymour and Blair received 88,225 votes, while Grant and Colfax received but 34,859 in the State. But 276 Republican votes
were polled in the city of New Orleans out of a Republican
registration of 21,000 voters.

By contrasting the vote polled not quite six months before,
for the Republican State ticket and the ratification of the State
Constitution with the vote for General Grant, it may be seen
with what absolutism the Democratic Party ruled the election
in November. Out of 48 Parishes in the State, seven, to-wit:
De Soto, Lafayette, St. Landry, Vermillion, Franklin, Jackson,
and Washington, polled for me, as Governor, 4,707 votes in
April, but they did not give General Grant a single vote. Eight

other Parishes, to-wit: Bienville, Bossier, Caddo, Claiborne, Morehouse, Union, St. Bernard, and Sabine, gave me 5,520 votes in April, but cast only ten votes for General Grant in November. Twenty-one Parishes, casting 26,814 votes in April for the Republican State ticket and the new Constitution, gave General Grant only 501 votes in November; and the whole State, polling 61,152 votes for the Republican State ticket, or a majority of 17,413, in April, gave General Grant only 34,859 votes. Seymour and Blair were given 88,225 votes, but Grant and Colfax received 214 votes in the Electoral College while Seymour and Blair received but 80 votes.

I was but twenty-six years of age and was conscious of my want of experience and fitness for the tremendous responsibility that I was to assume. I found the State and the city of New Orleans bankrupt. Interest on the State and City bonds had been in default for years; the assessed property taxable in the State had fallen in value from $470,164,963.00 in 1860 to $250,063,359.63 in 1870; taxes for the years 1860, 1861, 1862, 1863, 1864, 1865, 1866, and 1867 were in arrears. The City and State were flooded with State and City shinplasters, which had been issued to meet current expenses. Among the first acts of the new Legislature was one to postpone the collection of all back taxes, and later they were postponed indefinitely.

Our public roads were mere mud trails; there was not a hard-surfaced road in the whole state. There was but one canal, that from the center of the city of New Orleans to Lake Pontchartrain, six miles long. There were no telephones then, and the telegraph was very limited. The United States mails were generally carried on horse or mule-back. The city of New Orleans had but four paved streets, and they were made of large blocks of stone imported before the Civil War from Belgium at enormous cost. The rest of the streets were at times impassable. There were no cottonmills nor other industries in the State or city.

New Orleans had no wharves, a few warehouses, and but two hospitals. It had but few lines of street railway, and the street cars were drawn by small single mules, with a little tinkling bell. The only drainage consisted of open ditches. Our best mechanics worked for from $2.00 to $2.50 a day. Our field hands got only 50¢ to 75¢ a day. One of the richest and most progressive men in the State of Louisiana to-day cut cane on my Magnolia plantation in 1877 for 75¢ a day.

The amount of the State and City debt was unknown, the securities for which were selling at from 22¢ to 25¢ on the dollar. There was no money in either treasury. The people drank either water caught in cisterns from the dirty roofs of their houses or the dirty unfiltered water of the Mississippi River. Epidemics of yellow and malarial fevers prevailed nearly every year. Houses were unscreened and mosquitoes were as common as the flies that filled the air.

The slaughter-houses were so located that all of their offal and filth were poured into the Mississippi River, just above the mains that supplied the people with their drinking-water.

New Orleans was a dirty, impoverished, and hopeless city, with a mixed, ignorant, corrupt, and bloodthirsty gang in control. It was flooded with lotteries, gambling dens, and licensed brothels. Many of the city officials, as well as the police force, were thugs and murderers. Violence was rampant, and hardly a day passed that some one was not shot, out under the Oaks, in defense of his honor.

The levees of the Mississippi, Ouachita, and Atchafalaya rivers were in a deplorable condition, having been cut in many places by both Armies for military purposes, and neglected for the past five years, flooding great areas of the State.

The sugar, cotton, and rice planters were without money or

credit, and their lands and buildings, having been neglected for four years, were in a state of dilapidation; their labor was disorganized; their mules and horses were gone, and implements scattered. The people were almost without hope.

Before the War there had been only four short pieces of railroad in the whole State. The Opelousas Railroad from New Orleans to Morgan City was but sixty miles in length, and the New Orleans and Great Jackson Railroad but fifty miles in length; while the short road from Baton Rouge to Grossetête and another short road from Vicksburg to Monroe were practically destroyed by the War and by the recurring waters from the broken levees, and abandoned.

Here was a situation; conditions that required most capable and earnest consideration. I needed the advice, help, and friendly co-operation of the ablest men of the State. I looked around to find them. I did not want politicians seeking for power and place, but men of affairs and experience in business. I found them in Dr. W. Newton Mercer, Joseph H. Oglesby, General Richard Taylor, Duncan F. Kenner, and John G. Gaines. They advised with me and helped me as no other men in the State did at that time.

There was a demand by the progressive business men of Louisiana for more railroads. Everybody joined in a movement to get more transportation, especially from the city of New Orleans, to connect at Shreveport with Houston, Texas, and the Northwest.

A company was formed in the city of New York, headed by ex-Governor E. D. Morgan; ex-Governor Griswold; the great bankers Morton-Bliss & Company and Seligman Brothers; and the great builders of the Pacific Railroad (Oakes Ames & Company of Boston) and other capitalists, who applied to our Legislature for a charter to build a railroad from the city of Mobile, Alabama, through New Orleans to Houston, Texas, with a branch to Shreveport. The press of the city of New Orleans, the Chamber of Commerce, and all other commercial bodies united in favor of the enterprise.

The charter was granted by the Legislature, together with State aid in large amounts to expedite the construction. The State aid was most liberal, possibly too liberal. But when we remember that hitherto every railroad in this State had been built by the issuance of State and City bonds, also by direct taxes on the people; when we know that the State of Illinois gave millions of acres of land to aid the construction of the Illinois Central Railroad; that the United States Government gave millions of acres of land—in fact, almost an empire—in aid of the construction of the great Pacific railroads; and that the people of Cincinnati had but recently voted ten millions of dollars for a railroad to Chattanooga, Tennessee, we may regard as insignificant the aid which we gave this railroad, in view of its transcending importance. When we bear in mind the great advantages which were to accrue to the people of Louisiana and especially to the city of New Orleans by the construction of this great artery of transportation, we can but express our surprise that there should have been any criticism of our legislation.

We aided the reconstruction of the short railroad from Vicksburg to Monroe, which was speedily rebuilt.

Of course, our political enemies howled at these "extravagances" and condemned me, but they would not have failed to do this if I had induced the Legislature to pass a bill to re-enact the Ten Commandments or the Lord's Prayer.

We struggled through the first two sessions of this Legislature, which at its end had possibly done some unwise things, but certainly had enacted much good and necessary legislation as well.

But no sooner had the Legislature adopted measures to construct the great railroad from New Orleans to Houston, Texas, and to Shreveport in northwest Louisiana, and granted a subsidy and subscription to its stock, than a great war was begun by a rival railroad and steamship corporation headed by Charles Morgan of New York.

Mr. Charles Morgan had recently become the owner of the short line of railroad—sixty miles long—which connected the city of New Orleans with Morgan City. Mr. Morgan owned and operated a line of steamships from Morgan City to Galveston and other Texas ports. He held a complete monopoly of this trade, and wanted no rival; so he set to work to embarrass the newly chartered company and to destroy its credit. One of his weapons was the attempt to show that the State of Louisiana was bankrupt and would not be able to meet the obligations it had granted to this competing railroad enterprise. To this end he had his lawyer prepare the following circular:

TO THE PUBLIC
New Orleans, March 18th, 1871.

The undersigned property-owners and taxpayers of the city of New Orleans, satisfied that the State Legislature has, at its late session, exceeded its power in the loans, endorsements and other obligations and grants authorized on the part of the State, the total amount of which is limited, by the recent amendment of the Constitution, to $25,000,000 (already incurred), as shown by the annexed official statement of the Auditor, take this early opportunity of notifying bankers, brokers, and dealers in securities, of this country and Europe, that they consider all such loans, endorsements, and pledges as null and of no value; that they will sustain the authorities in resisting their issue, and, if issued, will by every legal means endeavor to prevent the payment of any interest or principal, or of any tax levied for that purpose. They only recognize the State debt proper as amounting to $25,021,-734.40, as shown by the accompanying exhibit of the Auditor, and they class the "accruing debt" with the illegal legislation previously referred to.

This paper was signed by several hundred names; it was printed in French, German and English, and copies were sent abroad and to New York, and distributed in every banking-house in this country and Europe.

A syndicate had already been formed in Frankfort, Germany, to take the whole issue of this Railroad Company—the first mortgage, the second mortgage bonds, and the State bonds—but this circular stopped all negotiations; and finally the syndicate withdrew its proposition, the negotiations failed, and the work ceased. It was too heavy a load even for this wealthy corporation to carry, in addition to the seven millions that they had already spent on the road from Mobile to the city of New Orleans.

The result in the end was that Mr. Charles Morgan forced the new company to take him in, and after going through the throes of the worst panic ever known in the country, the road was finally built after a delay of nearly four years.

So urgent were the people for railroads that the Democratic Legislature of 1878, ten years later, passed a bill granting $2,000,000 of bonds to aid in the building of a branch road to Shreveport, Louisiana. This bill was signed by Governor Francis T. Nichols ten years after the legislation which I approved and for which I was so much criticized.

As stated before, when I was inaugurated, we found the finances of the State in a woeful condition. Taxes had been collected only in that part of the State which was within the lines of the Federal Army, and but imperfectly there. The Hahn-Wells State Government, set up by General Banks, recognized the situation by Act No. 12 of the Legislature, approved April 4th, 1865, by extending the time for the payment of taxes of the years 1861, 1862, 1863. The city of New Orleans had to issue bonds to the amount of $3,000,000 to take up what was known as City Notes. The State had to borrow money to pay the interest on its bonded debt (Act 48, 1869). By Act No. 1, approved January 4th, 1869, tax-collectors were required to receive, in payment of taxes due the State, warrants issued by the Auditor of Public Accounts, which were then selling at twenty cents on the dollar.

By Act 41 of 1870, taxes due for the years 1865 to 1868 were extended without interest or penalty.

We were obliged to issue $3,000,000 of bonds to take up the floating debt and unpaid coupons (March 16th, 1870).

Taxes of 1862, 1863, and 1864 were indefinitely postponed by Act 101, approved December 30, 1870.

The payment of taxes in Auditor's warrants and back coupons left the treasury empty of cash, and we had to struggle along the best way we could.

Early in 1869, the State Auditor (George M. Wickliffe) was detected in reselling on the market Auditor's warrants and coupons that had been paid into the treasury for taxes, and when the Chairman of the State Senate Committee on Finance accused him of his crimes and showed him the proof, he admitted his guilt. I at once suspended him from his office and appointed in his place a competent and highly respected old citizen of New Orleans.

The grand jury submitted fourteen indictments against the Auditor. He was tried before a jury of the city of New Orleans, which degenerated into a political campaign. The opposition press and the Auditor's friends and his attorneys ignored the facts, and claimed that the prosecution by Governor Warmoth was merely a personal controversy, and that Warmoth merely wanted to get possession of the Auditor's office for his own purposes; strange to say, the jury took the same view and acquitted the defendant. A few days later Wickliffe was tried again before another jury for a second offense, for which he had been indicted, and he was again acquitted. But the act of the jury was so outrageous that the Judge of the Court (Edmund Abell) dismissed the jury with a reprimand.

I called upon the Judge and District Attorney and urged them to continue trying the Auditor on the other twelve indictments that the grand jury had found against him. But the Democratic District Attorney declared that it was useless to involve the State in further expense and that public opinion was entirely in sympathy with the Auditor; he proceeded to enter a *nolle pros* on all of the other twelve indictments, and I was obliged to put this thieving scoundrel back into his office.

As soon as the Legislature met I sent a message detailing the offenses of the Auditor. The House of Representatives appointed a Committee to investigate the charges and promptly preferred articles of impeachment against him. He was arraigned before the Senate, the Chief Justice of the State presiding, and he was tried and convicted by a unanimous vote of the Senate. He tried to resign, but the Senate ignored his resignation and convicted him, so he could not hold another office in the State of Louisiana. He left the State and was never heard of again.

CHAPTER IV

AFTER the dreadful experiences of the Presidential election of 1868, Captain S. B. Packard, Chairman of the Republican State Committee, concluded to ask the Legislature to change the old election and registration laws; it seemed to be necessary. So the committee proposed a new registration and election law which they thought would protect the voters from a repetition of the recent outrages. The new law, approved March 16, 1870, conferred great power and responsibility on the Executive of the State. The Governor was authorized to appoint a chief election officer who should conduct a full registration and all elections. He was authorized to appoint the registrar of voters in each of the parishes on the recommendation of the chief election officer. The parish registrars were empowered to fix the polling places in each parish for each election, to appoint the commissioners of election at each poll, and to provide for the election and make the returns of the result to the Governor of the State.

The law also provided for a Returning Board before which the Governor was required to lay all of the election returns, and this board was authorized to examine all reports or protests of election as to violence, irregularities or frauds; and the board was authorized to throw out any poll, precinct, or parish that might appear to have been carried by violence or fraud.

The Returning Board provided by the law was composed of the Governor, the Lieutenant-Governor, the Secretary of State, and the two State Senators named in the law—Senator Thomas C. Anderson and Senator John Lynch.

This was an extraordinary law—it was a dangerous law; for

if the Governor and Returning Board should abuse their powers and act in a partisan spirit they could control absolutely any election held in the State.

But the violence and outrages of the Presidential election of 1868 were pointed to as the reason—or the excuse, at least—for this legislation. Of course, it met with the most violent opposition from the Democratic Party, and the Governor of the State had to stand the most vituperative denunciations for having approved it. There was no limit to the language used by the opposition.

In the meantime, I was exerting all of my power to develop the State, encourage the people, harmonize the races, and advance their material interests, and at the same time to hold down expenditures as far as possible. I sought to bring about me the best men in the State. I had many appointments of officers to make. I sought the most representative and capable men I could find. I did not confine my appointments to my own political party, but in the appointments of judges of the courts and district attorneys, I consulted the Bar; and in appointing parish officers I consulted the taxpayers and the leading conservative citizens. I did not ignore colored men, and when I could find respectable and competent persons of color I gave them the fullest consideration.

For the appointment of men of color I was denounced by the opposition as trying to Africanize the State; and for the appointment of conservative white men I was denounced by the "Pure Radicals" as trying to sell out the Republican Party to the Democrats.

After nearly two years, when I began to feel that I had gotten my government into fairly good shape and the people had begun to settle down and accept the situation, it was discovered that we had a serious factional controversy in our own party.

I had tried to administer the government on the conservative lines laid down in my inaugural address, which were so cordially approved of by the leaders of my party and by the press of the city of New Orleans at that time.

I had antagonized the colored Lieutenant-Governor, the radical *New Orleans Tribune,* and many of their supporters, by making a number of appointments of conservative white men to office, all of whom they declared to be Democrats. The spirit of "San Domingo" showed itself. They criticised my personal associates and alleged that I was trying to get into "high society."

For example, a dinner was given for me by Doctor W. Newton Mercer, who was perhaps the first man in social life in the city of New Orleans, and whose palatial residence of that time is now the Boston Club. There were twenty-five or thirty of the leading men of the State present, including General Richard Taylor (son of Zachary Taylor, once a citizen of Louisiana and President of the United States, and brother-in-law of Jefferson Davis), ex-Governor P. O. Hebert, General Dan Adams, Mr. S. H. Kennedy, Honorable Duncan F. Kenner, Alexander Walker, Effingham Lawrence, Christian Roselius, Cuthbert H. Slocumb, Albert Baldwin, Thomas J. Semmes, J. H. Oglesby, and others. The dinner was purely personal and social. I had known Dr. Mercer for some time while I was stationed in New Orleans in the Army. This dinner seemed to be most offensive to the colored Lieutenant-Governor and the radical white men who affiliated with him, many of whom I had been obliged to offend or disappoint in various ways, especially in vetoing bills passed by the Legislature in which they had large financial interests.

Among the first appointments of General Grant after he became President—in fact, in the month of his inauguration— was that of his (or rather, Mrs. Grant's) brother-in-law, James F. Casey, to be Collector of Customs at the port of New Orleans. This appointment was offensive to the colored Lieutenant-Governor, O. J. Dunn, to W. P. Kellogg and John S. Harris, who represented Louisiana in the United States Senate, and to several members of Congress from the State; and through them a movement was inaugurated by the Lieutenant-Governor and Captain S. B. Packard, Chairman of the Republican State Committee, to defeat Collector Casey's confirmation by the Senate. But it failed, and he was eventually confirmed.

Some months later, a much stronger movement was inaugurated in Louisiana to force General Grant to remove his brother-in-law. It likewise was headed by Lieutenant-Governor Dunn, Chairman Packard, Speaker Charles W. Lowell, and the two United States Senators—Kellogg and Harris. They charged that Casey did not make appointments in the Custom House to suit them; he was too slow in changing his employees, and he had "ignored negroes."

I was not consulted by these gentlemen, and knew nothing of the movement to remove Collector Casey until one night I was visited at my residence by Collector Casey and his chief deputy, State Senator P. F. Herwig, who told me of it, and said it had become so strong that they feared that it would succeed, unless they could get my help. The result of the interview was that I wrote a friendly letter to the President in Collector Casey's behalf.

When the Senators and Congressmen made their final visit to the President, he asked them whether the Republican leaders in Louisiana were a unit in favor of Casey's removal. They assured the President that every Republican leader in Louisiana desired his removal. The President then asked them, "How does Governor Warmoth stand in the matter?" They assured him that Governor Warmoth, more than any other of the leaders, desired the removal; whereupon the President opened a drawer and put my letter in their hands. The result was that these gentlemen left the President without Collector Casey's scalp, but with "red blood in their eyes for Governor Warmoth." Lieutenant-Governor Dunn and Chairman Packard never forgave me.

In the meantime, I had been obliged to suspend the Secretary of State, George E. Bovee, for having published in the newspapers (but not in the official journal) a pretended Act of the Legislature which took from the city of New Orleans its waterworks and gave them into the hands of a private corporation; it bore his official signature and had the seal of the State affixed, certifying that the Act had become a law, even without my signature and merely through the lapse of time, although in fact he knew that the bill was in my safe and that I was going to veto it at the next meeting of the Legislature. This, of course, caused a row.

My friend, the Chairman of the Republican State Committee, Captain S. B. Packard, the United States Marshal for the Eastern District of Louisiana, became offended with me because I felt obliged to veto a bill which he had passed through the Legislature, providing for the paving of St. Charles Avenue (New Orleans) with wooden blocks under the Nicholson patent, and appropriating $1,500,000 of the State's money to pay for it.

I had offended Speaker Lowell, also a member of the Republican State Committee, because I had vetoed his Ship Island Canal Bill, which proposed to take away from the city of New Orleans the control of its drainage system, and give it to a corporation, in which he was largely interested financially.

I had been obliged to veto more than thirty-nine bills that were passed by the Legislature, so I had piled up against me a lot of active enemies by this time.

The Legislature of 1869 passed an Act entitled: "An Act to enforce the Thirteenth Article of the State Constitution and to regulate licenses mentioned in said Thirteenth Article." This Act was intended to enforce the Article, which provided that all people, without regard to race or color, should have equal rights in all licensed business; and to secure to admittance of colored people to all railway cars, street cars, steamboats, stage-coaches, omnibuses or other vehicles.

Section 2 was intended to secure the free admittance of colored people to all places of entertainment and amusement, all public inns, hotels, or places of resort within the State. A refusal subjected the proprietor to a forfeiture of his license and the closure of his place of business, as well as to a suit for damages by the party aggrieved.

This Act I signed, as it was strictly in accord with the State Constitution, and it became a law on the 23rd of February, 1869. The law, of course, was a dead letter; colored men and women never attempted to avail themselves of its provisions. Public sentiment was strongly opposed to it, and the colored people were too wise to undertake to force themselves upon white people who did not want them. But the "Pure Radical" politicians held me responsible for not enforcing the law.

Later on, at the session of 1870, some colored and white Radical politicians determined to "put me in a hole," as they termed it, and thus to consolidate the entire colored race against me. So they passed a bill through both houses of the Legislature which made it a *criminal offense* for any person to refuse accommodations to a colored person on a railroad, steamboat, or street car, or in a hotel, theatre, or any other place of entertainment; and it went so far as to require the police to arrest the offender, and to direct the courts to fine and imprison him.

The bill came to me near the end of the session of 1870 and I had, under the Constitution, until the beginning of the next session of the Legislature, January 1, 1871, to act on it. But it was well understood that I would veto the bill, as I finally did. (See Journal of the House, my Veto Message and the vote sustaining the veto, especially that of the colored members.)

The Constitution provided that all residents of the State should be admitted to all public schools, colleges, and seminaries, of whatever nature soever, whether literary, legal, medical, theological, or industrial, authorized by the Legislature and under the control of the State, without distinction of race, color, or previous condition.

No attempt was made to enforce this article of the State Constitution. The white people were opposed to mixed schools. The masses of the colored people loved their children and knew too well what would happen to them if any of them should attempt to force themselves into white schools. But the "Pure Radical" or Dunn-Packard Custom-House Faction used this non-enforcement for all it was worth to prejudice me in the eyes of the colored people. They held me responsible for the non-enforcement of the law.

But the matter that aroused the most hostility against me and the most bitter resentment among these "Pure Radical" gentlemen was that the Legislature had, with the unanimous vote of both houses, submitted an amendment to the State Constitution, striking out Article 50, which made the Governor ineligible to election for a succeeding term. These "Pure Radical" politicians could not stand this. It was too much. It "broke the camel's back."

So, when the time came for the meeting of a Republican State Convention in August, 1870, to nominate candidates to fill the offices of Auditor (made vacant by the impeachment and removal of G. M. Wickliffe) and of the State Treasurer (whose term would expire under the Constitution) together with a new Legislature; the Mayor and city government of the city of New Orleans; five congressmen and all of the officers of all of the Parishes of the State, and to act on this constitutional amendment—by this time there had developed quite an opposition to me personally in my own party.

The Legislature at its January session of 1870 proposed four amendments to the State Constitution to be voted on at the November election following:

First: To make any defaulting tax collector ineligible to office until all of his defalcations should be made good to the State.

Second: Limiting the State debt to $25,000,000.

Third: Enfranchising all Confederates who had been disfranchised by the Constitution.

Fourth: Striking out Article 50 of the State Constitution, which made the Governor ineligible to reëlection for a succeeding term (this last amendment submitted by the Legislature with a unanimous vote of both houses).

As may be expected, the fourth amendment met with fierce opposition from a number of ambitious Republican politicians, each of whom aspired to be my successor. The colored Lieutenant-Governor, Oscar J. Dunn, was one of these aspirants. Captain S. B. Packard, Chairman of the Republican State Committee and United States Marshal, was another aspirant, and it is safe to say that the woods were full of other aspirants who would have liked to succeed me.

As stated before, the Republican State Convention was called to meet in August. Neither my political friend and ally at this time, Collector Casey, nor I paid any particular attention to the selection of delegates to this Convention, although I was sent as a delegate from my district; and when it assembled we found to our surprise that over four-fifths of the Convention was composed of negroes. When it came to the organization of the Convention, both my name and that of the black Lieutenant-Governor were proposed for the presidency; the Lieutenant-Governor was elected. He received 54 votes to my 43. All of the officers of the Convention were negroes, and so were a large majority of the members of all of the committees appointed by the President. It was certainly a negro convention. The "Pure Radicals" had been on the job.

During the session a resolution was introduced censuring me for not having signed the Negro Civil Rights Bill, which had been passed by the late Legislature. This provoked a long and bitter debate. But after I had spoken and shown the unwisdom of the proposed legislation, the resolution was withdrawn. It was clear to everybody that it had been introduced for the sole purpose of injuring me in the estimation of the colored people, *and to make sure of the defeat of the proposed amendment to the Constitution making me eligible to re-election as Governor.*

The negro President of the Convention was given authority to appoint a large part of the State Committee. In doing so he did not appoint a single friend of either Collector Casey or me. Collector Casey asked for a place on the State Committee but was refused. But the President of the Convention was made a member of the State Committee by special resolution, and the Convention by direct vote refused to allow "any increase in the membership of the Committee" under any circumstances.

Aside from this evident hostility to Collector Casey and me, all was harmonious in the Convention. Both Collector Casey and I, as well as all of our friends, united in the cordial support of the nominees of the Convention for State officers. There was no bolting ticket, but it was clear to Collector Casey and me that we had a fight on our hands to ratify the Constitutional Amendment making the Governor eligible for re-election. And having been ignored by the President of the Convention in the appointment of any of our friends on the State Committee, Collector Casey and I concluded to organize an Auxiliary Committee to aid in the conduct of the State campaign and the election of the ticket, and to which our pecuniary contributions could be made.

Lieutenant-Governor Dunn and Chairman S. B. Packard pretended to take great umbrage at the organization of this Auxiliary Committee, and harped upon their grievances ever afterward. They did everything they could to defeat the proposed amendment to the Constitution, making the Governor eligible for a succeeding term.

General George A. Sheridan and I took the stump and canvassed the State in favor of all of the nominees of the Republican Party and also the ratification of the four amendments to the Constitution submitted by the Legislature. We had immense meetings through the State. Our enemies controlling the Democratic press were most abusive in their criticisms of my administration and of me especially. They advised their people "to remain at home and protect their property from these two 'carpet-baggers,' Warmoth and Sheridan, who were liable to steal everything we had if we should give them a chance." The effect of these diatribes was to give us most valuable advertising—so much so that it seemed to us that everybody was attracted to our meetings. Wherever we went we invited leading local attorneys and conspicuous men to join us in a discussion of the political issues, and nearly everywhere we found ambitious gentlemen anxious to meet us.

I would usually speak first and explain the situation and the issues to the people, and tell them what I had already accomplished for the people and what I hoped to do in the future. I showed them that I wanted to limit the State debt to $25,000,000, that I wanted to keep every tax collector who might be a defaulter from holding any office until he made good his defalcation, that I wanted to enfranchise every ex-Rebel in the State, and that I desired, if my administration should be so satisfactory to the people as to cause them to wish to retain my services as Governor of the State, that they should not be debarred from that great privilege by any Constitutional provision limiting them in their right. After I finished my speech, the ambitious Democrat would follow me; and while he criticised me for many things, real or imaginary, he could not but approve of every one of the four constitutional amendments proposed by the Legislature, the ratification of which I advocated; and he generally ended with some complimentary remarks about the strange young man who had so recently settled in their State and had attained such high official position. Then my friend General Sheridan, who was, I believe, one of the most accomplished orators I have ever known, followed him. He never failed to convulse his audience with his wit and irony, or bring tears to their eyes by his pathos and sympathy.

After canvassing northern Louisiana and ending in Claiborne Parish, one morning just at daylight we reached the Red River, opposite the city of Shreveport. We drove our carriage on to the ferry boat and crossed the river; and in passing up to the hotel we noticed that every window and gallery of the houses we passed was hung in black. We had read the Shreveport newspapers during our campaign and were prepared for almost any hostile demonstration, but this seemed to be quite unusual— beyond anything we had encountered, and we looked at each other inquiringly. So when we got to the hotel and registered our names and were sent up to our rooms with a little black boy who carried our bags, we closed the door and whisperingly inquired of him as to what all of this meant. He said in reply, "Didn't you know that General Lee died last night?" Sheridan looked at me, and I looked at Sheridan, and we both felt great regret at the death of General Lee; but we were much relieved to find that it was "not our funeral."

After breakfast, General McCleary, our candidate for Congress in that district, and a number of other friends, called upon us. They told us that they had arranged to hold our meeting out about two miles from the city. We told General McCleary and the committee that we would not go out of the town to speak; that we came there to talk to all of the people and that they must find some way of holding the meeting in the city of Shreveport. As it happened, an old friend, Dr. Joseph L. Moore, called on me. I had known Dr. Moore at Lebanon, Laclede County, Missouri, before the Civil War; in fact, it was he who had induced me to locate in his county, and who had been my earliest and best friend, but from whom I had been obliged to separate on the breaking out of the War; he joining the Confederate Army and going South, and I joining the Union Army and fighting on the other side.

At the end of the War he became a resident of Shreveport. We had a most cordial and affectionate reunion. I later told him of our difficulty about finding a place to hold our meeting. "Why," he said, "I will arrange all of that for you. We have a great big platform in front of the market house where we hold our political meetings, and I will get that for you." And he did.

Our friends could not get a brass band in town to play for us, but it happened that old John Robinson of Cincinnati was holding a circus in Shreveport at the time, and our friends gave him $500 to postpone his circus that day and let us have his brass band of seven or eight pieces.

I think I never saw such a big place in my life. There must have been two hundred chairs on the platform, and every one was empty except those occupied by the brass band, General McCleary, General Sheridan, and myself. There were certainly three thousand people standing in front of us. Away over to the left was a little bunch of colored men who did not seem to have spirit enough to declare that their souls were their own. But right in the midst of the great audience—in front of the speakers—was my old friend, Dr. Moore, looking up at me with the kindliest eyes. I spoke for an hour and had most respectful attention. I began my speech my saying:

You have in your midst a highly respected citizen who can tell you a great deal about me and my early life in Missouri. He was the greatest friend I ever had in my life. I shall never forget that April Sunday in 1860 when I, a boy not yet eighteen years of age, landed in the little village of Lebanon, Laclede County, Missouri, with a small box of law books, a much smaller bag of clothing, and only $20 in my pocket, when I made the acquaintance of your fellow-citizen, Dr. Joseph L. Moore. In answer to inquiries I told him I was a lawyer from the State of Illinois en route to Springfield, Missouri, to practise law. I never shall forget how he literally took me in his arms and forced me to stop right there and locate in Lebanon; how he took me into his office and did not ask for rent; how he put my books on his shelves; and how he encouraged and praised and helped me. How, when from burning the midnight oil and working myself to death to master my profession, I simply collapsed from overwork, he doctored me, nursed me day and night and brought me back to vigorous health. I shall never forget how he induced his friends to employ me as their attorney and how he put me on my feet and made a man of me before I was fit to shed my school books. I see him here in the audience today. (*Cheers.*)

I shall never forget the day we parted after the election of Mr. Lincoln, and he felt it his duty to come South and I felt it my duty to join the Union Army—we both shed tears, for neither of us ever expected to see the other again. But we met here today and we had a great reunion. He is the same dear friend he was in 1860 and he can call on me for my life's blood if it will serve him. (*Cheers.*)

I told the people that I had no doubt but they had all heard of me through the newspapers and the grand speeches delivered from that platform. I told them that if half of the lies the newspapers had told about me were true, I ought to be in the penitentiary for life, thereby depriving them of the services of the best Governor the State had ever had in its history. I told them that my great-grandfather was born in Virginia, and that my father was born in Tennessee, that I commanded a Missouri Regiment in the Civil War, and that every drop of my blood was Southern.

I apologized to them for my Democratic political friends and told them that they knew how hard it was for those gentlemen who were so hostile to me to be deprived of the flesh-pots of Egypt; that they had so long lived on the fatted calf that now to be deprived of the loaves and fishes was more than they could stand.

I begged them to remember that it was the Democratic Party that brought on the War, and that, although a majority of the people of Louisiana were against Secession, the Democratic

Governor forced the issue, seized all of the forts and arsenals in the State, paroled all of the United States soldiers, and set up a secessionist government before actual war was declared. They lost the War; they lost their sons and brothers; they lost their fathers, by the thousands; they lost their offices. I told the people that these politicians could stand losing the War; they could stand losing their sons and brothers; they could stand losing their fathers, and their slaves; but when it came to losing their offices, it was more than they could bear. So that if the boys resorted to vituperation and slander, and even downright lying against the officers of the State Government, they ought to take pity on them and help them to bear their sorrow. (Everybody laughed heartily.)

I told the people how our Legislature had extended the time for paying their back taxes. I told them what we had done to restore their public schools, and that I had not forced the race issue upon them. I told them what we had done to repair and rebuild their levees. I told them that I could promise them a railroad to New Orleans and to Houston, Texas, within three years. I told them that we proposed, by an Amendment to the Constitution which was to be voted on at the coming election, to strike the shackles from the limbs of every ex-Confederate in the State.

I told them that I had appointed Lieutenant-General James Longstreet (one of the great heroes of the Confederate Army) my Adjutant-General of Militia; that I had appointed Major Penn Mason, once an officer on General Robert E. Lee's staff, a Major-General of Militia; that I have appointed Major-General M. Jeff. Thompson, once a Major-General of the Confederate Army, my Chief State Engineer, and that I had organized twenty-five hundred young Rebels into the State Militia.

I told them that I spoke for General Grant, the President of the United States, as well as for myself when I said that we wanted every old "Rebel" and every young "Rebel" to come in and join the Republican Party. (Applause.)

After I had finished my speech, our circus band played some of the national airs, including *Dixie,* and then General McCleary introduced General Sheridan to the audience.

General Sheridan began his speech by a most beautiful, eloquent, and pathetic tribute to General Robert E. Lee, who had just died, as a man and as a soldier. He said that he spoke *as* a soldier *for* a soldier. In less than five minutes every man in that great audience was shedding tears like a child. Within fifteen minutes every chair on that big platform was filled, and men were hanging on to the sides wherever they could get a hold. Every sentence of General Sheridan was cheered to the echo, and when he finished his magnificent speech the great audience rushed to shake our hands, and they placed the brass band at the head of the procession and escorted us in a body to our hotel, where we had to speak again. I never witnessed such a demonstration before or since in my long life. The result was that we carried the Parish of Caddo by an overwhelming majority, and the State by over 22,000 majority. I never forgot those people.

It was admitted by everybody in the State that the election of 1870 was the quietest and fairest election ever held in the State of Louisiana up to that time. The Returning Board did not throw out or reverse a single poll in any Parish of the State, and Lieutenant-Governor Dunn, as a member of the Returning Board, signed all of the returns without protest.

We elected the Republican State ticket; we elected every Republican candidate for Congress; and we elected a good working majority in both houses of the State Legislature.

We elected as Mayor the Republican candidate, ex-Governor B. F. Flanders, and all of the administrators for the City Government of New Orleans.

We adopted, by large majorities, all four of the proposed constitutional amendments, including the one making me eligible for re-election, and it would seem that my triumph was complete.

After the election of November, 1870, I visited General Grant in Washington. He received me most cordially, and asked me to dine with him in the White House. It was a simple family dinner, there being present only Mrs. Grant, Miss Nellie, one or two of the boys, and old Mr. Dent, Mrs. Grant's father. We had a pleasant time talking of old times and old friends. After dinner, the President and I retired to his library and talked until eleven o'clock.

General Grant congratulated me heartily on our victory of November. He strongly approved of the liberal policy which I had pursued in our State. He himself had appointed General Longstreet to an important Federal office. He especially expressed his approval of the amendment to our Constitution striking out Article 99, which had disfranchised a large number of ex-Rebels. He approved of my policy in appointing friendly conservatives to office, and he was plain in his views against making Louisiana an African State. He agreed with me that we should protect the colored people in all of their political and civil rights, provide them with schools, give them appointments to offices whose duties they were capable of discharging, and encourage them in every way possible; but he did not purpose to make the white people of the South feel that they were not a part of this Republic.

When I left General Grant, I felt that I had reached a complete understanding with him; and that he would support me cordially in my policy of liberality to the people who had opposed us, but who now showed a disposition to accept fully the results of the War and Reconstruction, and to co-operate with us in building up the State and Union.

Everything went well with me until the new Legislature met on January 1, 1871, only two months later. Up to this time

Collector Casey and his friends were in entire accord with me. He was a member of our "Auxiliary State Committee," so bitterly condemned by Lieutenant-Governor Dunn, Chairman Packard, and their Radical followers. He was a large contributor to our campaign fund, and Senator Herwig, his chief deputy, was its treasurer.

The new Legislature was largely Republican in both houses. It was organized by the election of Mr. Mortimer Carr, a former speaker of the House of Representatives. Lieutenant-Governor Dunn, of course, presided over the Senate.

I extract the following from my message:

State of Louisiana, Executive Department,
New Orleans, January 11, 1871.
Gentlemen of the Senate and House of Representatives of the State
of Louisiana:
I congratulate you upon the favorable auspices under which you assemble. . . .

A growing spirit of harmony and good will between the different classes of our people has been strikingly evinced during the last year. It has been seen in a strongly pronounced disposition on the part of all good citizens in most parts of the State, without respect to partisan differences, to preserve order, enforce the laws, and render obedience to all constituted authority. The devices and machinations of evilly disposed demagogues and restless and irrepressible parties, who seek to profit by times of alarm and violence, have been set aside by the good people of the State, who are most deeply interested in its peace and prosperity. The result has been that this disposition, aided by salutary laws passed by the General Assembly and by Congress have secured, during the last fall, the most quiet, peaceable, and orderly election the State has witnessed for many years. In former elections, even within two years, New Orleans and the State have been the scenes of violence, riots, and bloodshed which have disgraced their names and greatly injured all their interests. This fall an important and exciting election was held without any conflict or disturbance and with scarcely an arrest. Such a thing was never known in New Orleans before. I feel especially grateful to be able to lay this before you as a matter of record; because the last General

Assembly, deeply impressed by the alarming and increasing violence and lawlessness displayed in our elections, and their lamentable effects upon every interest of the State, had, with a view to remedying these evils, enacted stringent penalties against such offences, and for their more certain enforcement had clothed the Executive with ample powers. I have endeavored to use these powers with moderation and impartiality, but with firmness, and with the simple aim to preserve the peace and to secure to all men, irrespective of party, race and color, the free exercise of all their rights as citizens. That I have been able to do so without arraigning against the law any class or party, may be accepted as a proof that the laws were wholesome and wise, and that the people, as a whole, have been satisfied that their Executive was faithful and impartial.

I cannot pass from this subject to other details, in justice, without calling your attention to the general and peaceable acquiescence of our people in the results of the Reconstruction policy of the general Government. Their acceptance of it as a finality has been much more satisfactory in Louisiana than in any other State in the South. This must be attributed to the patriotism and wisdom of our people and to those features of State policy which have led to this great and desirable result. It has always been my sincere conviction that it is safe to trust to the good sense, the honor, and the sober second thought of the people. This conviction has determined my course in matters of State policy, even in matters where I was forced, for a short time, to differ from many of my political friends. The peaceable character of the late election and the favorable condition of Louisiana as compared with many other Southern States, have, I think, convinced both friends and foes that I was right. I have refrained from any severe and arbitrary measures or recourse to mere force, appealing on all occasions and in all localities to the justice and discretion of the people themselves. Under all circumstances, however, I have held myself in readiness to employ all the resources at my command, both civil and military, to enforce the laws, and preserve order, and protect any citizen in his rights so far as authority of the executive could be lawfully used. The good results of this spirit of harmony on all sides, upon the prosperity of the State, cannot be estimated.

It has been my pleasant fortune, during the past season, to visit a good portion of the State, in answer to repeated and cordial invitations from many of my fellow-citizens, which were extended to me by gentlemen of all political parties. I had been led to believe, from the assurances of many prominent citizens, that I would find the leading, most influential and enterprising people of the different localities imbued with better and more advanced ideas than those petty partisan animosities and sectional hates and prejudices which, swaying the hearts of a small class of men more noisy than important, had hitherto caused much of this domestic trouble in our State and brought disgrace upon its name; and that the good people of the State had taken its peace and order into their own hands, as was proper, and that the power of these bad and restless spirits was gone. I am glad to say that these assurances have been realized. I have everywhere been received by that wonted cordiality and hospitality for which Louisiana is so deservedly famed. What is more important, everywhere I saw evidences that the people were determined that the laws should be obeyed, and the rights of all men, under the law, respected. I was met with assurances from all parties that in every effort to advance the welfare, credit and the great interests of the State, I should receive the hearty support of the people.

Amendments to the Constitution

The last General Assembly proposed four important amendments to our Constitution, which were duly ratified by the votes of the people at the last election. The first amendment repealed the 99th Article of the Constitution. This Article, by reason of its disfranchisement of an influential class of our citizens for political reasons, was obnoxious to them and their friends; and as the result has proved, was distasteful to almost all. Incorporated in our Constitution through an unwise spirit of retaliation, and by its peculiar phraseology serving mainly to irritate and humiliate, while debarring from suffrage and office only the most scrupulous and upright of the class it was aimed against, and admitting all others, it had all of the most odious features of disfranchisement and none of its good effects, if such there be. It is to the lasting credit of the first Republican Administration of Louisiana that the amendment to strike out this last vestige of the War in our Constitution was passed with the unanimous Republican vote of the General Assembly and indorsed unanimously by the people. It is no longer a part of the Constitution. Henceforth in Louisiana all disabilities resulting from the War are removed, and no citizen is disfranchised by its laws except for crime or mental disability.

The second amendment limits the total amount of State indebtedness that can be contracted up to the year 1890 to the sum of

$25,000,000. All indebtedness of whatever character contracted above this amount before that time is illegal, null and void. This voluntary limitation by the people of the amount of indebtedness which they will incur for a term of years will have the double effect of increasing the credit of the State securities, thus lessening the interest the State will have to pay on any future loans, and of compelling rigid economy on the part of the State Government.

The third amendment prohibits all officials who have held public moneys from voting or holding office until they have procured from the proper authorities receipts in full for all funds which they have thus held. The former history of the State, with regard to many of its public funds, is a sufficient proof of the wholesomeness of this measure.

The fourth amendment removes the ineligibility for a succeeding term that was imposed by the Constitution upon any incumbent of the gubernatorial office. Under this amendment, the reëlection of a Governor is left like that of any other officer, to that last and best arbitrant of all free governments—the good judgment of the people. While this might seem to most minds a sound principle, yet I did not feel at liberty, owing to my personal attitude toward the question at issue, to take any part in the discussion for or against it. The amendment was spontaneously and voluntarily presented to the public by the General Assembly, and has been ratified by a majority approximating 24,000 votes.

At the proper time, a United States Senator had to be chosen to fill the seat of Senator John S. Harris, whose term would expire on the fourth of March, 1871. There were a number of candidates, among them the Lieutenant-Governor and Senator P. B. S. Pinchback.

The colored members of the Legislature held a caucus and made a formal demand that a colored man of their choice should be chosen to fill the place; and they selected by a considerable majority State Senator Pinchback as their candidate over Lieutenant-Governor Dunn.

Early in the session I was visited by State Senator P. F. Herwig, who was also Chief Deputy Collector of Customs under

Collector James F. Casey, the President's brother-in-law. He told me that he came to ask me to support his Chief, Collector Casey, for the seat in the United States Senate to become vacant on the fourth of March following. He told me that Mrs. Casey was the favorite sister of Mrs. Grant; that she was not very well and that our climate was too hot for her; and that the President would like to have Collector Casey sent to the Senate so that his wife might be near Mrs. Grant.

I told Senator Herwig that I had recently been with the President and dined with him and Mrs. Grant, and that neither of them had said a word to me about Casey and the Senatorship; but that I would do almost anything I could to please the President, and that if he would intimate to me in some way his desire to have Casey sent to the Senate I would do what I could to bring it about, although I doubted very much that even with my support he would succeed.

I never heard from the President, and as I thought that Herwig, who expected to be Casey's successor to the collectorship, had made this the real object of his visit to me, I forgot all about it; and another gentleman, a distinguished Union General, was elected to the Senate. This was early in January, 1871, which seems to be about the date of the beginning of the estrangement between Collector Casey and myself.

The white Republican members of the Legislature refused to go into caucus, or be bound by the nomination of Senator Pinchback, the result being that the contest was a free fight for all candidates.

The white Republicans of the Legislature united on General Joseph R. West, who was a Union soldier during the War; and some of the Democrats, fearing that possibly Pinchback might slip in, threw their votes for General West, and he was elected. Lieutenant-Governor Dunn, Collector Casey, and Senator Pinchback held me responsible for their defeat. Lieutenant-Governor Dunn and Collector Casey never forgave me.

It seems that from this date my friend, Collector Casey, began to become dissatisfied with me, and to withdraw his support from me and my friends. There were no fewer than fifteen members of the Legislature who held positions in the New Orleans Custom House, Chief-Deputy P. F. Herwig being one of the State Senators. Other matters arose during this session of the Legislature to give Collector Casey additional cause for complaint against me and to increase our estrangement.

At this same session of the Legislature a bill was passed entitled "An Act to incorporate the New Orleans Levee Shed Company," which proposed to monopolize the entire levee front from Common to Poydras Streets (New Orleans), with authority to build sheds and to tax all merchandise landed under them, and all steamboats and steamships that landed their goods on the wharves. Collector Casey and Chief-Deputy Herwig were the promoters of this measure. I felt obliged to veto this bill, but both houses of the Legislature passed the bill over my veto. However, I refused to issue the $1,400,000 of bonds authorized by the Act, and they were never able to force me to do it.

A Congressional investigation later disclosed the fact that Collector Casey had locked up in his safe in the Custom House $18,000 of money contributed by the stockholders to control eighteen votes in the State Senate, and when the bottom dropped out of the scheme through my veto and my refusal to issue the bonds, the money was returned to the stockholders. Captain John C. Sinnott, one of the incorporators, who had paid his $5,000 to this fund, testified before the Congressional Committee that Collector Casey opened the Custom House safe in his presence and handed him his money.

From that time on Collector Casey and Senator Herwig joined actively with Lieutenant-Governor Dunn, United States Marshal Packard, Senator Kellogg, Collector of Internal Revenue

Joubert, and Postmaster Lowell, in their warfare upon me and my friends.

Soon after my inauguration as Governor of Louisiana, there came to New Orleans a man by the name of George W. Carter. He was a native of Virginia but more recently from the State of Texas. I had met him some years before, but only for a few hours at that time. He called on me at the Capitol to renew his acquaintance with me. He was an engaging and prepossessing man, of very fine education, had been a Methodist preacher, and had held some high position in that connection. He had been President of a women's college at Oxford, Mississippi, and afterwards occupied a similar position somewhere in the State of Texas. It was said that at the breaking out of the War he had organized a Confederate cavalry regiment and officered it with members of the Methodist Church, and was himself the colonel of the regiment. It was especially armed, as I have learned since, with revolvers and Bowie knives, and seems to have displayed a very sanguinary spirit. But it seemed strange to me, learning to know Colonel Carter as I did, that he could have been such a bold, bloodthirsty man, for he was one of the most gentle, simple, and attractive men that I have ever known.

He was, as I have said, a man of exceptional education and polish, and was gifted with a remarkable ability to state and illustrate a proposition. He was a fine speaker, and I was attracted to him at once, and showed him various social courtesies. And later I appointed him to a lucrative office under the State administration.

At the time the Republican Party began to organize for the General Election of 1870, Colonel Carter came to me and said that he thought he would like to be a member of the new State Legislature and asked me to use my influence to secure his nomination for a seat in the House of Representatives from his ward.

I told him that I should be much pleased to have him in the Legislature as he seemed especially gifted for such a position.

I suggested his name to the leaders of his ward and district, but they had already made arrangements to name some one else; and I confess to much disappointment and some chagrin that I had not been able to get him a place on the ticket, for I felt sure that he would make an able member of the House and be of great service to the administration in carrying through measures for the good of the State.

The Legislature during its late session had passed an act to create the Parish of Cameron, taking a part of the large Parish of Calcasieu. I had not as yet signed the bill and had the right, under the Constitution, to hold it up until the first day of the next session of the Legislature. My recollection is that I did not regard the territory composing this proposed Parish as having sufficient population to warrant its organization into a Parish. But I was so anxious to get my friend, Colonel Carter, into the Legislature to help me carry on the government, that I conceived the idea of signing this bill and so communicated my views to Colonel Carter, who entered into the spirit of the move at once.

So I signed the bill creating the Parish of Cameron on March 16, 1870, and sent Colonel Carter down there as Parish Judge with a salary of $2,000 *per annum*. I gave him blank commissions for the Sheriff, Justices of the Peace, Police Jurors, Registers of Voters, Constables, etc., with instructions to fill all of the offices with the best people he could find in the Parish.

The reader will not be surprised that with all of this power Colonel Carter was able to fulfill his ambition and my wishes by being elected a member of the Louisiana House of Representatives from Cameron Parish. He was unanimously elected, and when he returned to the city he boasted that "he had been elected to the Legislature as a Republican on his Confederate record."

The new Legislature met in January, 1871. Mortimer Carr, the former Speaker, was elected Speaker of the House, Colonel Carter supporting him. But it was not long before Carter and Speaker Carr fell out about something, and the disagreement culminated in the resignation of Carr as Speaker, through a combination of Republicans and Democrats, and the election of Colonel Carter in his place.

During the session it became known that Speaker Carter was at the head of a ring, composed of Democrats and negro and white Republicans, which proposed to control all legislation which could stand a liberal "blackmail." The fact became a public scandal and the result was a break between Speaker Carter and me, after a very plain interview in which the matters were fully and frankly discussed.

I discovered that this mild-mannered, able, and accomplished man was absolutely demoralized; that he was dishonest, faithless, and in a position where he could do great harm. He had surrounded himself with a number of the most desperate men in New Orleans, who were his constant associates. He developed a fondness for drink, and his bar-room tirades and threats against me and my friends were being constantly reported to me.

Speaker Carter of the House and Lieutenant-Governor Dunn, President of the Senate, combined for the purpose of controlling all legislation. When the Journal of the House was published in the official journal some time later, it was found that a number of the House Committees had been authorized to sit during vacation, with authority to travel over the State, their *per diem* and traveling expenses to be paid on the warrant of the Warrant Clerk, approved by the Speaker. It was well known that no such authority could be given these committees by the House alone, and it was also well known that no such resolutions were introduced or passed by the House of Representatives. They were put into the record by Carter without ever having been introduced or read in the House.

After the adjournment of the Legislature, I found Speaker Carter in close communion with the Custom House—the Dunn-Packard-Casey faction. He was made the editor of their newspaper, *The National Republican,* and became most prominent in his leadership against me and my friends. He was appointed an inspector of customs by Collector Casey. He did not work but drew his pay.

About this time I met with a severe accident, which required a surgical operation on my right foot. I was laid up for several months, and finally I was carried just over the State line to a summer watering-resort, at Pass Christian, Mississippi. There was great delight among my enemies, and they enjoyed the many reports circulated to the effect that I would not recover.

The combination against me was very considerable. It embraced the Lieutenant-Governor, with his following; United States Marshal Packard; the Chairman of the State Committee, Collector Casey, with all of his Custom House following; Postmaster Lowell and all of the employees of the New Orleans City Post Office, and Speaker Carter, with his many friends in the Legislature.

Taking advantage of my technical absence from the State, notwithstanding that my secretary brought me my mail every morning, and inspired by these gentlemen, Lieutenant-Governor Dunn intruded himself into the executive office without any suggestion from me, and proceeded to discharge the duties of Governor of the State. He made removals of officers; appointments to fill vacancies; granted pardons and reprieves to criminals in the penitentiary, and exercised all of the functions of a Governor. It tickled my enemies very much. The Democrats liked to point at what had come to the proud people of Louisiana in having a negro for Governor, and some of the Democratic press did not fail to say that they preferred a "nigger" Governor to a carpet-bagger.

STORMY DAYS IN LOUISIANA

The Lieutenant-Governor received crowds of his followers at the State House to congratulate him on his accession, and not a few, perhaps, offered up silent prayers that the threatened lockjaw might take me off. So the Custom House faction was confident that the party organization would drop like a ripe apple into their laps at the Convention to be held on the 9th of August.

Lieutenant-Governor Dunn being installed in the State House and being President of the Metropolitan Police Board, it was thought to be a good time to hold a State Convention. So Mr. Packard, the Chairman of the State Committee, called a State Convention to meet in the Hall of the House of Representatives on the 9th of August, 1871. There was no State, Congressional, or Parish election to be held that year. The only purpose of the call was to take advantage of my illness and absence, and to strengthen their hold on the party organization.

In the meantime, the fight for delegates to the Convention progressed throughout the State. The Lieutenant-Governor addressed the following letter to all of the leading colored Republicans of his acquaintance:

General Assembly of Louisiana, Senate Chamber,
New Orleans, July 26, 1871.

John Simms, Esq., Opelousas, St. Landry Parish, La.

My dear Sir: Being very much interested in the success, politically and otherwise, of our race, I write to you to ask of you your support and influence in behalf of the colored people. We have a great work before us, and in order to be successful we need the aid and coöperation of every colored man in the State. An effort is being made to sell us out to the Democrats, by the Governor, and we must nip it in the bud. Just look at his recent appointments of Democratic Judges, Constables, Justices of the Peace, Tax Collectors, Police Jurors and other Officers, in many of the Parishes. We have remonstrated with him, but it is still continued, and it is said that he declares that if he is elected in 1872, no colored man shall hold any office. Now, not satisfied with this base betrayal of the trust reposed in him, he seeks to force us to elect such delegates to the coming State Convention as will endorse

[113]

and support him in this outrageous treatment of our race. I ask you to use your influence to elect good, honest men, that will look out for the interests of the colored man, and not be duped by the money or the promises of Governor Warmoth, and above all do not elect as a delegate any of his office-holders, who being under obligations to him for position will be compelled to support his policy. Let me hear from you immediately.

Respectfully,
(Signed)   Oscar J. Dunn

The object of these leaders was made clear: it was to be a personal fight on me; it was to organize the party against me, and the Lieutenant-Governor drew the race issue as his strongest card.

My friends had a thorough organization in every Parish of the State, my patronage was very large, and I had as gallant a lot of friends, both white and colored, as ever followed a leader. It was the same organization that less than twelve months before had carried the State by over 22,000 majority, notwithstanding the machinations of the Dunn-Packard cabal, and had adopted an amendment to the State Constitution making the Governor eligible to reëlection for a succeeding term.

A few days before the date fixed for the meeting of the State Convention, it was published in the evening papers that I was *in extremis* at my temporary residence at Pass Christian, Mississippi. But on the day before the meeting of the Convention, to the consternation of Lieutenant-Governor Dunn, Speaker Carter, Collector Casey, United States Marshal Packard and Postmaster Lowell, I arrived in New Orleans on crutches, but ready for a fight to a finish. My enemies became demoralized, a hurried meeting of the clans was called in the United States Marshal's Office in the Custom House, and it was the unanimous opinion that it would not be safe to hold the Convention in the State House as usual: it was too close to the Governor's Office, and although he could not stand alone on his feet, he might be too much for them in their plans to pack the Convention with their bogus delegates. So Mr. Packard changed the place of meeting of the Convention to the United States Circuit Court Room in the Custom House building. He was in entire charge of the court buildings as United States Marshal.

He appointed forty or fifty deputy marshals—to preserve the peace, so he said. He claimed that he and his executive committee, composed of Lieutenant-Governor Dunn, himself, and Collector Casey, should make up the temporary roll of the State Convention and appoint the temporary chairman and secretary, and that no one should be admitted to the Convention Hall unless he first obtained a ticket through a window of the post office. But yet he was still afraid that he could not carry out his scheme to pack the Convention, and he wanted more help; so he telegraphed the following to General J. J. Reynolds, United States Army, San Antonio, Texas:

New Orleans, La.
August 8th, 1871

The Republican Convention meets here tomorrow, and much trouble is anticipated from thugs and bruisers. I desire to have a guard of soldiers from the Barracks to protect the Custom-House and other public property. Please give General Sully the necessary orders immediately.

(*Signed*)   S. B. PACKARD
U. S. Marshal

There is no doubt that General Reynolds was imposed upon. Mr. Packard did not telegraph as Chairman of the Republican State Committee; he telegraphed as United States Marshal. He did not tell the General that he was to hold a political convention in the Custom House Building, but he skilfully suppressed everything that would let General Reynolds know that he wanted the United States troops to help him pack a Republican Convention. With this official statement of the United States Marshal, General Reynolds directed General Sully, in command at New Orleans, to furnish the troops. So General

[115]

Sully sent Captain Smith with a company of United States troops and two Gatling guns, to the Custom House with instructions *"to report to the United States Marshal and to consult with him as to disposing of his troops so as to guard the Government property against any injury that evilly-disposed persons may attempt."*

Still not satisfied, United States Marshal Packard and Collector-of-Customs Casey had all of the doors of the Custom House building boarded up with heavy timbers and guarded by some forty or fifty armed Deputy United States Marshals, under Chief Deputy Marshal De Klyne.

When our delegates assembled in the street in front of the Custom House we were told that we could not enter the building unless we went to the United States Post Office and obtained tickets of admission, issued by Marshal Packard as Chairman of the State Committee. So off we went and got such tickets as Postmaster Lowell was pleased to issue to us. Not half of our delegates were allowed tickets. The seats of many of them were contested.

The Convention had already been packed, and it was plain to us that if we could not get our men into the building, the game was up. But, nevertheless, we determined to see it through and to make up the record. So, leading my friends despite the fact that I was on two crutches, we climbed the great wooden stairs of the Custom House to the second floor, to find drawn up in front of us, at the top, a company of United States Infantry and two Gatling guns. We passed the troops and proceeded to the United States Circuit Court room where the Convention was to be held. Armed United States Deputy Marshals at the door told us that we could not enter before twelve o'clock. It was then much after eleven. While we were demanding admission, a door in front of us leading into the United States District Court room, which adjoined the Circuit Court room, opened and we beheld all of the Dunn, Carter, Packard, Lowell, and Casey members in caucus and being addressed by the Hon. George W. Carter.

I was lame and ill, but not so stupid as to fail to see the game that was to be played upon us. The plan was that these delegates just before twelve o'clock were to pass from this room into the Circuit Court room and, before we could get admission, they would have precipitated their temporary organization. Our protests would have been met by armed Deputy Marshals, who, supported by United States soldiers, would have marched in and put us out.

They were determined to control the Convention, and it is readily seen that they had the power to do so. It was only necessary for me to mount a chair and to denounce the whole proceeding in my choicest vocabulary. Captain Smith of the United States troops approached me, took me by the arm, and demanded that I should desist. I retorted that we would submit to the United States Army. So we retired from the building to find standing at the door, in the street, nearly one-half of our delegates, who had been refused tickets of admission by the Postmaster on the ground that their names were not on the roll furnished by Mr. Packard. There was nothing left for us to do but to go to another hall (Turner's Hall) and hold a Convention of our own.

The Custom House Convention elected Lieutenant-Governor Dunn President and proceeded to read me and all my friends out of the Republican Party. It indorsed President Grant for reëlection, appointed a new State Committee, and adjourned *sine die*.

Our Convention met at Turner's Hall and organized, by electing Senator Pinchback as President, denounced the conduct of Dunn, Carter, Packard, Casey, Lowell, Herwig, and Kellogg, and appointed a committee of twenty to visit President Grant at his summer home at Long Branch, New Jersey, and to lay all the facts before him.

The Committee was received by General Grant coldly. He said that he did not see what harm the presence of United States soldiers could do to a Republican Convention. He resented some statements made as to the conduct of his brother-in-law (Collector Casey), and closed the interview by saying that he would take their report and investigate the facts. It is now fifty years since that time and no reply has ever been received.

On November 6, 1871, the Packard Custom House faction established a newspaper called *The National Republican* to lead the war upon me and my friends. It was edited by Speaker George W. Carter, and it certainly was a lively sheet. If anything of a bitter, personal, or outrageous character was left unsaid, it must have been by accident. It was filled with scurrilous and vindictive diatribes. My public and private affairs were laid bare and foully misrepresented. It said so many bad things about me and published them so often that I almost began to believe some of them myself.

Thousands of people came to my active support who probably would never have done so if they had not discovered that my traducers had only one object, and that was to overturn me, in order to get control of the State government for themselves.

The Democratic politicians of New Orleans, strange to say, gleefully united with the Custom House faction. But the conservative people—the thinking people and the property-holders, especially in the country Parishes—stood by me.

Amid this seething conflict, Lieutenant-Governor Dunn died on November 21, 1871. It was a very serious misfortune for me as it presented an issue that I could not avoid. It was necessary that he should have a successor immediately. Had anything happened to me, George W. Carter, Speaker of the House of Representatives, would, under our law, have become Governor of the State.

I was advised by a number of my conservative friends to assume the right to fill the vacancy by appointment. I submitted the question to the Chief Justice of the Supreme Court, United States District Attorney J. R. Beckwith, and Messrs. Christian Roselius, Thomas J. Semmes, and Harry T. Hayes, eminent leaders of the Bar, and it was their opinion that the Senate only could fill the vacancy by the election of a President of the Senate, who, in turn, would be Lieutenant-Governor. Following this advice, I issued a proclamation on the 24th of November, 1871, convening the State Senate in extra session.

The question then arose as to whom my friends in the Senate would select for the place. We were greatly embarrassed. We knew of the caucuses of the Custom House leaders—Casey, Packard, Antoine, Ingraham and Burch, with Eustis, Voorhies, Cotton and Hunt of the Democratic State Committee. We knew that the Custom House Democratic combination had agreed to support Senator T. V. Coupland, one of Collector Casey's deputy collectors, and that the seven Democratic members of the Senate had agreed to vote for him. With the seven white Custom House Senators and the two negro Senators, Antoine and Ingraham, they would have sixteen votes.

There were four negro senators on our side—Pinchback, Barbour, Kelso, and Butler, together with fourteen white Republicans, giving us eighteen votes.

So the reader will see that the four negro senators, Pinchback, Barbour, Kelso and Butler, held the balance of power. These colored Senators claimed with good reason that, as Lieutenant-Governor Dunn was a negro and as the Republican Party had a large majority of negroes in it, the colored element of the State was entitled to the right to select the Senator for the place of Lieutenant-Governor and that my white friends in the Senate ought to support its choice. I thought that these arguments were unanswerable, and so I urged my white friends in the Senate to support Senator Pinchback, who was the choice of the colored members of the Senate.

It was with considerable difficulty that my white friends in the Senate were induced to support Pinchback. He was a restless, ambitious man and had more than once arrayed himself against me and my policies. He was a free lance and dangerous, and had to be reckoned with at all times. He was very distasteful to my conservative friends, and many of them openly condemned me for his election until they became aware of the situation and realized the political necessity for the action we had taken.

The Senate met on December 6, 1871. Only two Senators were absent and it proceeded at once, without protest, to elect a presiding officer, who became *ex-officio* the Lieutenant-Governor of the State. There was no objection made to this call by any one. My friends proposed the name of Senator P. B. S. Pinchback, and the opposition proposed the name of Senator T. V. Coupland, a Deputy Collector of Customs under Collector Casey. Three negro Senators—Antoine, Ingraham, and Pinchback—voted with the Democrats, and the white Custom House Senators for Senator Coupland, giving him 16 votes.

Three negroes—Senators Kelso, Barbour, and Butler—and 14 white Republicans, including Senator Coupland, voted for Senator Pinchback, giving him 18 votes; and Senator Pinchback was formerly proclaimed the Lieutenant-Governor of the State. And after confirming some appointments made by the Governor during vacation, the Senate adjourned on the 7th *sine die*.

The Legislature was to meet on January 1, 1872, only twenty-five days later, in regular session. When it did meet, a large number of the members of the House of Representatives had their pockets filled with illegal warrants for *per diem* and traveling expenses during vacation, approved by Speaker Carter, all of which were dependent for payment on an appropriation by the Legislature approved by the Governor. It was well known that I would never sign a bill appropriating money to pay these illegal warrants.

The city seethed with excitement as the day for the meeting of the General Assembly approached. It was known that leading Democratic politicians of the State Committee were in daily consultation with Marshal Packard and Collector Casey at the Custom House. I was kept informed of the conspiracy as it progressed.

These conferences led to a combination between Marshal Packard, Collector Casey, Chief Deputy Collector and State Senator Herwig, Deputy Collector Coupland, and two negroes, Senators C. C. Antoine and J. H. Ingraham, on one side, and James B. Eustis, Frank B. Jonas, Frank Zachary, E. L. Jewell, J. B. Cotton, Carlton Hunt, and ex-Lieutenant Governor Albert Voorhies, members of the Democratic State Committee, on the other. The object of the combination was declared to be to secure what they called "Reform."

I will let the Hon. J. B. Eustis of the Democratic State Committee tell the story in his own language, as sworn to by him before the Congressional Committee.

New Orleans,
February 9, 1872.

J. B. Eustis sworn and examined by Mr. Spear:

I reside in New Orleans, and am a lawyer by profession; I am a native of this city.

Question. And a large owner of real estate?

Answer. My wife is an owner of real estate to a large extent.

Q. Will you please give the committee, in your own way, a statement of the condition of things in this State?

A. I am a member of the Parish Executive Committee of the Democratic Party, which is composed of seven members of the Democratic State Central Committee. When Governor Warmoth issued his proclamation calling a session of the Senate to elect a Lieutenant-Governor, propositions were made to that committee that we should give our influence in the Senate to secure the election of a Republican for

Lieutenant-Governor, on the condition that we were to have control of certain committees; and the Custom House wing of the Republican party, from whom this proposition came, pledged themselves, for their part, to vote for the repeal or modification of certain laws. We selected Mr. Coupland. We knew very little of him, and for that reason we selected him. He was reputed to be a proper person. We failed for the reasons that have been stated to the Committee, and Mr. Coupland was defeated afterward. I think about a week before the 1st of January, a proposition with regard to the modification of these laws was made to us, substantially to the same effect as before. We again agreed to use our influence with Democratic members and Senators to induce them to vote with this wing of the Republican party. I will state that the Central Committee in their address had advocated, as part of the policy of the party, not to make any practical alliance with either faction of the Republican party, and in the resolution which we passed to co-operate with the Custom House wing, we expressly stated that it was a temporary arrangement for these specific purposes. We used all the influences we could control to make this co-operation effective. It was not made public for the simple reason that it was supposed that the program involved merely a question of combination with regard to these particular laws, and nothing else. It was distinctly understood, of course, that the principles of neither party were compromised by this arrangement; on the contrary, the reason why we believed this program could be carried on was that the agreement had reference only to the laws affecting election and registration. We considered we had three elements to attack, which gave these enormous powers to Governor Warmoth—one was the patronage placed in his hands, and the others were the frauds which could be perpetrated under both the election and registration laws. We understood perfectly well from the situation of affairs that the anti-Warmoth wing of the Republican party was in precisely the same difficult situation that we were in; that they had the same reasons to apprehend the use or abuse of these laws against themselves that we had; and in fact in discussing these matters we considered that the motive of self-interest with these gentlemen was sufficient to secure the punctual fulfilment of their part of this arrangement. We, of course, had nothing to do with weighing or comparing the antecedents of either faction. We did not consider the personal merits of either leader involved in the controversy. We looked merely to political results.

Q. Was it part of your agreement that the Governor should be impeached?

A. As soon as these propositions were acted upon by the Parish Committee, I remember distinctly that after the gentlemen who had submitted them had left the room, the question of the impeachment of the Governor was discussed, and before we took any part in this matter we wanted to see where this was going to lead us. After considerable deliberation we unanimously decided that as a matter of party advantage we would oppose the impeachment of Governor Warmoth, because our idea was, of course, to keep the Republican party divided as long as we could. If Governor Warmoth had been impeached, the Republican party would have presented to us but one front, because, he failing, I have no idea that such a thing as a Warmoth party would have survived fifteen minutes after the fall of the Governor. Affairs afterward took a very peculiar and unexpected turn. Nobody ever supposed that the Legislature would be disrupted or that anything like a quasi-revolution would be the result of this very simple arrangement. When the troubles commenced and the attempt was made to eject Speaker Carter from the chair, we made one advance step which was not in the original program, and it was this: it was to protect the House of Representatives from executive control and executive interference. It was only then we threw ourselves forward and came before our people, and assumed the responsibility of what we had done up to that time, and the further responsibility of maintaining the fact that Carter was the legal Speaker of the House of Representatives. Of course, our view of the matter was that the Governor, as an act of self-defense, had resorted to this extraordinary proceeding of calling an extra session during a regular session of the Legislature, and as far as the Democratic party is concerned the leadership of Speaker Carter during this juncture was purely accidental. While we considered it a disadvantage to be called upon to appear under the wing of either faction of the Republican party, we assumed that responsibility absolutely at this time, and did the best we could. I do not know that the subject was ever discussed by the Democratic committee, but it was certainly my opinion, and I believe the opinion of individual members of the committee, that the Governor should be impeached; that was my opinion, and I did everything I could to carry it out.

Q. Why were you in favor of impeaching the Governor?

A. Because we discovered that he had resolved to resort to the most extraordinary measures to maintain his power, and that our only chance of success was his removal. We had never heard before of a Governoɪ holding armed possession of a Legislature. We supposed that he resorted to this revolutionary mode of proceeding for the purpose of maintaining what we were determined to overthrow, that is, what is popularly known in this State as the one-man power. After having considered that attitude, we considered this coalition would be without results as long as Warmoth remained Governor of this State. We considered it a gauntlet thrown down to the people and the Democratic party; a declaration that he intended to maintain and preserve those laws which we were seeking to repeal or modify.

Their program was as follows.

FIRST: They were to get control of the State Senate. To do this they bought one of our Senators—Senator Lewis of Sabine Parish—giving him a place in the Custom House. They were still short one Senator, in order to obtain whom they proposed, at the meeting of the Legislature, to declare my call for the meeting of the Senate in extra session on December 6th, to be illegal, and the election of Senator Pinchback to be President of the Senate to be void.

SECOND: They then proposed to elect Senator Coupland, a deputy to Collector Casey, President of the Senate and Lieutenant-Governor, and to overthrow all that had been done at the special meeting of the Senate on December 6th and 7th. Having accomplished the control of the Senate, they would address themselves to keeping Speaker Carter and his faction in control of the House of Representatives. Having secured the control of both Houses, they proposed to have the House of Representatives impeach the Governor for "high crimes and misdemeanors." That could be done by a simple vote of a majority of the House of Representatives.

By our Constitution the presentation of articles of impeachment against the Governor works his suspension from office, and Mr. Coupland, the Custom House Senator and Lieutenant-Governor-elect, would automatically become the acting Governor of the State. They did not expect to try me by the Senate. It requires a two-thirds majority of the Senate to convict an officer. They knew that they could not get that, but a simple majority of the Senate could hang up the trial, and they could hold on to the Governor's office indefinitely. This was all to be done in the interest of "Reform." It was a great scheme, and word was passed around by Collector Casey that President Grant was in sympathy with it.

Undoubtedly, General Grant was disappointed that I did not support his brother-in-law Casey for the United States Senate at the late election. He was also informed that our Convention did not endorse him. Mrs. Grant made no concealment of her antipathy to me. Mrs. Casey was her favorite sister and it would have been fine to have her near herself in Washington— the wife of a Senator who could have the "back door" entrance to the White House at all times.

The Democratic politicians were in high glee. Having secured the negro following of the late Lieutenant-Governor Dunn, together with the Federal office-holders and their immense patronage, and with the assurance of the sympathy of President Grant, they thought they saw within their grasp the power which they had sought so long without success.

The "Knights of the White Camelia" were reorganized—the "Grand Cyclops" was again in the saddle. Mysterious notices with cabalistic signs began to appear in the city newspapers. I was in daily receipt of threats against my life. The "Innocents," a Sicilian gang, paraded through the streets, and preliminary arangements were made to take possession of the State Government by force, if necessary.

Finally the day, January 1, 1872, arrived. There was a quorum in the House of Representatives but not in the Senate. Only fifteen Senators answered to their names; all of the Democratic Senators, except Senator Futch of Union Parish, Senator

Thomas of Bossier Parish, and Senator Anderson of St. Landry Parish, were hidden away in the top of the Custom House with the two negro and six white Custom House Republican Senators, in order to avoid being arrested by the Sergeants-at-Arms to make a quorum in the Senate.

These Senators remained for several days and nights in the top of the Custom House, but, finding it very unsanitary, they took refuge on the United States Revenue Cutter "Wilderness," under the control of the Collector of the Port, Casey, and enjoyed sweet converse with each other for several days and nights—eating, drinking, and sleeping together, riding up and down the Mississippi River under the protection of the United States flag, and out of the reach of the Senate Sergeant-at-Arms.

I telegraphed the facts to the President, and on January 6th the following telegram from Washington was read in the Senate:

Washington, Jan. 6th, 1872

To P. B. S. Pinchback
   President of the Senate
      New Orleans, La.
   Collector has been directed to order "Wilderness" to New Orleans at once.

(Signed)   T. F. HARTLEY
Acting Secretary

After this, these bolting Democrats, negro, and white Custom House Senators took refuge over in the State of Mississippi at the town of Bay St. Louis, where they went into camp and remained for some twenty days in sweet concord. In the meantime, the Senate was without a quorum.

The House of Representatives met on January 1st with 89 members present, but adjourned until the following day, out of respect for the late Lieutenant-Governor Dunn. On the following day, Mr. Lott (colored) of Rapides offered the following resolution:

STORMY DAYS IN LOUISIANA

RESOLVED: That we, the members of the House of Representatives, have unabated confidence in the efficiency and integrity of Hon. G. W. Carter, Speaker of this House, and do hereby pledge to him our hearty support during the continuance of the present General Assembly.

After some manoeuvering and at least one member refusing to vote, the resolution was adopted 49 to 45. The membership of the House was 106—12 members absent.

Having won the first step the House adjourned until 12 M. the next day. In the meantime, other members arrived, and when the Speaker ordered the reading of the Journal of the day before, the House by a vote of 49 to 46 postponed the reading and approval.

Speaker Carter arose from his seat and apologized to a member whom he had grossly insulted on the day before. He then called the Honorable J. C. Moncure (a Democrat) to the Chair and took the floor on a question of privileges. It was to answer charges of gross scoundrelism of the Speaker which had been published in *The New Orleans Republican* of that morning.

The charges were that Speaker Carter had taken advantage of the great confusion of the last night of the late session of the House of Representatives to put into the Journal, as having been adopted by the House, resolutions authorizing various Committees to sit after adjournment, and during vacation, and to travel over the State on various investigations—their traveling expenses to be paid by warrants issued by the Warrant Clerk on the State Treasury, approved by the Speaker; that the members of these Committees had obtained from the Speaker many thousands of dollars of warrants for their *per diem* and mileage and traveling expenses. The Speaker practically admitted the truth of every charge. He claimed, however, that he was not to blame because the House itself had passed these Resolutions. He said that he had asked the gentleman whether he really did introduce these resolutions, and he said that he had, and he said

that he had also asked the Clerk of the House whether the resolutions had really passed the House, and both had confirmed
the fact. He admitted that he had ordered the proceedings of
the House to be printed in a number of country newspapers,
which had cost sixty-eight thousand dollars. The Committees,
he said, had cost $46,000, and their traveling expenses had been
$40,000; that the House had given the employees of the House
$12,000 extra compensation. He said to them: "I was out of
the House at the time the resolutions were passed."

Great confusion followed this speech and Mr. Carter resumed
the Chair. He had attempted to make the members of the
whole House responsible for his gross frauds and the enormous
expenses of the last Session.

There was indignation and revolt. Finally a motion was
made to declare the Speaker's Chair vacant. Carter refused to
put the motion. Still greater excitement and confusion. He
ordered the lobby cleared of spectators. Finally, when order
was restored, Ex-Speaker Carr moved to declare the Speaker's
Chair vacant. Again the Speaker refused to put the motion,
whereupon Mr. Carr put the motion himself to the House and
declared it carried. A rush was made for the Chair. The
Speaker was immediately surrounded by a number of armed
men hitherto concealed in his private office just off the platform,
and the members of the House were driven back.

The Speaker said: "Take your seats, gentlemen. I will not
allow any such resolution to be brought before the House. Take
your seats, gentlemen, this is revolutionary and degrading in the
highest acceptance of the term. I should like to see the man
who will dare to displace me from this Chair. You can put
Speaker Carter out of the Chair, but you must use different measures to do so."

Order was finally restored when Messrs. York and Matthews,
representing the Speaker, and after a conference with him,
approached the leaders of the opposition and assured them that

Carter would resign the Speakership the following day if they would consent to adjourn at once. Accepting and relying upon this pledge, the House consented to the adjournment until 12 M. the next day.

That afternoon a conference was held in the office of United States Marshal Packard, in the Custom House, there being present (besides Mr. Packard) Collector Casey, Deputy Collector Herwig, Postmaster Lowell and Speaker Carter of the Republican faction, together with Messrs. James B. Eustis, Frank B. Jonas, Ex-Governor Albert Voorhies, Frank Zachary, J. B. Cotton, and E. L. Jewell of the Democratic faction.

It was agreed that Speaker Carter had lost control of the House and that something had to be done to regain control of it. Various plans were discussed, but none seemed to assure success but one, and that was finally adopted after Marshal Packard returned from an interview with General Emery, commanding the United States troops at Jackson Barracks, who agreed to bring his troops into the City to "preserve order."

The plan adopted was for an affidavit to be made before a United States Commissioner, "charging the Governor, Lieutenant-Governor, four members of the Senate, and thirteen members of the House of Representatives with a conspiracy to obstruct the laws of the State, and also the laws of the United States, in depriving the Representatives of the General Assembly of the State of Louisiana of equal rights under the Constitution and Laws; that by means of said conspiracy the said parties had attempted by violence to eject the Speaker of said House, and had been engaged in bribery and corruption of divers members of said House of Representatives and had used means of intimidation to deter others from discharging their duties, and to incite riot—all against the peace and dignity of the United States." The affidavit was sworn to by Representatives Shoemaker, Stevens, Kearson and Wilson—four Democratic Members of the House of Representatives—on January 4, 1872.

This remarkable affidavit was prepared by ex-Governor Albert Voorhies and James B. Eustis, members of the Democratic State Committee, in the office of United States Marshal Packard. Writs were issued by United States Commissioner Woolfley for the arrest of Governor H. C. Warmoth, Lieutenant-Governor P. B. S. Pinchback, Senators Hugh J. Campbell, A. B. Harris, A. E. Barber, members of the State Senate, together with thirteen members of the House of Representatives; also General A. S. Badger, the Superintendent of Police of the City of New Orleans; Captains Edgeworth and Flanagan of the Police Department, together with several other gentlemen who were in no manner connected with the Legislature. General Emery brought to the city two companies of infantry to assist the United States Marshal in executing the writs should resistance be made.

The House was to meet at 12 M. At 11:30 A.M. a number of United States Deputy Marshals, under Chief-Deputy De Klyne, accompanied by a gang of city Democratic politicians, appeared at the State House, and arrested the Governor, Lieutenant-Governor, four members of the Senate, thirteen members of the House, and others whose names were in the warrant. There was no resistance made to the arrest and all were marched through the mob to the Custom House and arraigned before the United States Commissioner, who pretended great difficulty in finding any blank bonds. We were detained for nearly two hours in the Custom House on the pretense that blank bonds could not be found, before we were admitted to bail.

Promptly at 12 M., Speaker Carter called the House to order, but he did not have a quorum. He sent out a Sergeant-at-Arms and arrested a number of members and brought them into the House. Yet he could muster only 51 members, counting himself. The House was composed of 106 members. Finding he could catch no more members he declared a quorum present and proceeded to business. The first act was as follows:

STORMY DAYS IN LOUISIANA

House of Representatives
New Orleans, La.
January 1st, 1872.

To the Honorable Speaker and Members of the House of Representatives.

Gentlemen: During the vacation, since the adjournment of the last session, your Committee on Elections and Qualifications have examined into the cases of alleged disqualifications of several persons returned as members of the House, and now sitting as such, and after considering the facts and the law, they find that L. C. La Saliniere of St. Martin, D. L. McFarland of St. Martin, W. R. Wheyland of Sabine, and L. J. Souer of Avoyelles, had no residence in these Parishes they claim to represent on the day of election, as is required by the Constitution to render them eligible, and recommend that they be disqualified by virtue of such ineligibility for membership of this House, and that their seats be declared vacant.

(*Signed*)   C. C. ANTOINE (Colored)
JAMES M. THOMPSON (Democrat)
HARRY H. STEVENS (Democrat)
J. B. WANDS (White Republican)
R. M. J. KENNER (Colored)

There had been one full session of the Legislature since the election of 1870. There had never been any contest filed against any one of these members. The whole movement was "cooked up" within the last few hours in order to diminish the opposition to Speaker Carter and his faction in the House of Representatives.

A remarkable fact was that Carter, who represented Cameron Parish, was never in that Parish sixty days. The fact was that I signed the Bill creating the Parish of Cameron and sent Carter down there to organize it and to get himself returned to the House. If, admitting the charge, these six men were ineligible for want of residence in their respective parishes, how was it as to the Speaker himself?

These members were unseated by a vote of 42 to 8, *no quorum voting,* but the Speaker declared the report adopted.

The House then adjourned until 12 o'clock the next day.

When I was finally released on bond and returned to the State House, Speaker Carter and his followers had done their work and adjourned. There was great glee at the Custom House, in Democratic Headquarters, and in the drinking saloons of the city that afternoon. The dram shops did a fine business. Speaker Carter was the center of a great crowd at the Gem Saloon, and he freely declared, between drinks, their program of "Reform" agreed upon: it was to impeach Warmoth and to declare the extra session of the Senate of December 6th illegal, and the election of Pinchback as Lieutenant-Governor void; and, as the Senate had not yet been able to get a quorum (sixteen Senators being away on the Revenue Cutter "Wilderness") he (Speaker Carter) would be the Governor of the State within a week.

All this time the troops of General Emery were within striking distance, and the mob was ready to make a rush for the State House at the signal agreed upon.

I telegraphed all the facts to Senator West at Washington, who laid them before President Grant, and he communicated the following to Senator West:

Governor Warmoth's dispatch of this date to you, received. His report of the proceedings of the United States Marshal is of such extraordinary character that I will have the matter investigated at once. Please show this dispatch to the Attorney-General.

(*Signed*) U. S. GRANT

There was but one of two things for me, as Governor, to do. One was to lie down and accept the situation, the other was to declare an emergency and recall the Legislature and to protect it from violence. There being an extraordinary condition of affairs, I issued a proclamation as follows:

State of Louisiana, Executive Department,
New Orleans.
January 4th, 1872, 1:30 P.M.
Whereas, A conspiracy has developed to overthrow the State Government by illegal and revolutionary means, which was shown by the

arrest of the Governor, Lieutenant-Governor, and members of the Senate and House of Representatives at the moment of assembling, by the United States Marshal, on a writ of a United States Commissioner, upon a false and frivolous charge; and

Whereas, While these said officers and members of the General Assembly were detained in arrest, an illegal and revolutionary attempt was made to eject certain members of the House of Representatives and seat other persons in their stead, there being at no time during these proceedings a quorum present, and deeming that the present condition of public affairs presents an extraordinary occasion, I do hereby, in virtue of the power in me vested by the Constitution and Laws enacted thereunto, convene the General Assembly of the State of Louisiana in extra Session at half-past four o'clock this evening, this fourth day of January, 1872, to take such steps as may be necessary to preserve the peace and protect the interest of the Commonwealth.

Given under my hand and the seal of the State this fourth day of January, A.D. 1872, and of the Independence of the United States the ninety-sixth.

(*Signed*)   H. C. WARMOTH

By the Governor
J. W. Fairfax,
   Assistant Secretary of State.

This proclamation was distributed throughout the city by editions of the evening papers. Extra Sergeants-at-Arms and messengers were sent out to notify members of the House and Senate.

At the time appointed the Lieutenant-Governor called the Senate to order. There not being a quorum it adjourned at once.

The House of Representatives was called to order by the Clerk. Fifty-five members out of 106 answered to their names. The Hon. T. G. Davidson, the oldest member and a prominent Democrat from Livingston Parish, was called to the Chair temporarily.

The House proceeded at once to adopt the following resolution:

Whereas, George W. Carter has sought in the most arbitrary manner, and by the use of means unworthy of a Representative and Member of this House, to deprive a clearly expressed majority of the exercise of its will, and did outrage this House by the introduction of armed personal supporters during the session of yesterday; therefore, be it resolved by the House of Representatives of the General Assembly of Louisiana that the seat of George W. Carter of Cameron Parish be and the same is hereby declared vacant, two-thirds of the members thereof concurring.

This resolution was adopted 49 to 5.

A resolution was adopted declaring the Speaker's Chair vacant, and the House proceeded by unanimous vote to fill it.

The Honorable O. H. Brewster of Ouachita Parish was elected Speaker.

On motion of Mr. Marvin of Catahoula Parish, the following resolution was adopted:

Resolved, that the Speaker appoint a Committee of three to wait upon the Governor of the State and request him to take all measures necessary to protect the General Assembly and the Capitol from violence and the members from intimidation.

The Speaker appointed Messrs. Marvin, Davidson, and Fontellieu to wait upon the Governor. Later the Committee reported that it had called upon the Governor and had the honor to report that he would comply with the resolution and have sufficient force to protect the Capitol from violence and the members of the House from intimidation.

The House then adjourned until 10 A.M. the next day.

General James Longstreet, who was then the Adjutant-General of the State, on my order called out one regiment of State Militia made up of ex-Confederate soldiers, and one regiment of colored militia, who were stationed about the Capitol, together with a battery of Artillery. The following telegram was received by the Hon. J. R. Beckwith, United States District Attorney, at New Orleans:

STORMY DAYS IN LOUISIANA

Washington, D. C.
January 5th, 1873.

Keep the legal processes of the United States from being abused for political purposes. Collision with the State Government must be avoided if possible.

(*Signed*) A. T. ACKERMAN
Attorney General

A second set of warrants were issued by United States Commissioner Weller on the 5th of January. I wrote the facts to General Emery, in which I stated to him that I refused to be arrested a second time, or to allow the Legislature to be interfered with.

Mr. Beckwith at once ordered the United States Commissioners to discontinue their proceedings, and so informed Marshal Packard by letter, and General Emery withdrew his troops from the City. Ex-Speaker Carter and his "rump" Legislature went into session in a room over the Gem Saloon on Royal Street, and sent out Sergeants-at-Arms to arrest such members as they could find. They killed one member, Mr. Wheyland, of Sabine Parish, on Canal Street, who refused to be arrested. In several instances they invaded the residences of city members at midnight, took them out of their beds, frightened their wives, mothers, and children, and kept them at the Gem Saloon for days and nights under guard. But they never were able to obtain a quorum. A number of Carter's followers abandoned him after a day or so and returned to their seats in the Capitol. So Carter and his advisors became the laughing stock of the city, while the country press, both Democratic and Republican, together with the whole press of the nation, denounced their proceedings from beginning to end as an outrage, especially condemning the Federal officials for their infamous conduct.

On several occasions, public meetings were held in the city at which the most violent threats were made against me and the

State Government. The streets thronged with a mob ready for anything. On one occasion, a mob of several hundred men called upon General Emery and demanded that he "clean out Governor Warmoth and his State Government." General Emery told them "that they deserved to be cleaned out themselves with grape and canister, that if they wanted to interview him they could send him a Committee and he would give them a hearing." Frank Zachery and two others constituted themselves a Committee. They asked General Emery to use his force to turn Governor Warmoth out. General Emery told them that he could not favor either faction; that he could not interfere with the Executive of the State; that the Executive of the State had the right to call upon him for forces to protect his authority. That was the end of the mob. It reluctantly dispersed.

But this did not end the Gem-Saloon-Custom-House combination.

On the fifth of January, J. C. Moncure, a member from Caddo Parish and a Democrat; a colored member, J. Henri Burch, from Baton Rouge, and J. B. Wands, a member from Tangipahoe, addressed the following communication to General Emery:

Hall, House of Representatives,
Royal Street, New Orleans,
January 5, 1872.

General: We have been appointed a committee by the Speaker of this House to present to you the inclosed resolution this instant adopted, and to ask from you the protection which the resolution contemplates. We think the action of the Governor is revolutionary and subversive of law and liberty, and ought to call forth the power of the United States authority to protect the Legislative branch of the State Government of Louisiana against the Executive, sustained as he is by his police and militia.

The Speaker is unwilling to permit the members of the committee to present the resolution in person at this time, because information has been received that they will incur the hazard of arrest. The committee will however wait upon you at the earliest period practicable.

We are, with greatest respect, your obedient servants,

(*Signed*) J. C. MONCURE (White Democrat)

J. HENRI BURCH (Negro Republican)

JAMES B. WANDS (White Republican)

Major General Emery *Committee*

Commanding Department Gulf.

Whereas H. C. Warmoth, Governor of the state of Louisiana, aided and assisted by the metropolitan police and other evilly disposed persons, has taken illegal possession of the Hall of the House of Representatives and placed armed policemen around the State House, preventing and hindering the House of Representatives of the State of Louisiana from meeting; and is endeavoring, by force and violence, to intimidate, coerce, and obstruct the Legislative department of this State in its exercise of its legitimate function: Therefore, be it

Resolved, that the commanding General of the Army of the United States for this department be requested to furnish without delay a sufficient number of troops to protect the members of this House in the exercise of their official duties, to prevent riot and bloodshed, to preserve peace and order, and to replace this body in full possession of the Hall of the building used as the State House.

(*Signed*) G. W. CARTER

Speaker House of Representatives

J. H. McVEAN

Assistant Clerk of Representatives

W. T. GENTRY

Captain Nineteenth Infantry, Assistant Adjutant General

Official copy.

A true copy.

On January fifteenth, General Emery addressed the following letter to G. W. Carter:

Headquarters Department of the Gulf.

New Orleans, Louisiana

January 15, 1872

Sir: I have the honor to acknowledge the receipt of your letter, dated 10 o'clock, but not received by me until midnight, and to say that I promptly disavow any intention of insinuating, directly or indirectly, your complicity in instigating a riot; but I do mean to say that the effect of publishing my letter to you, accompanied by the preliminary editorial, remarks and headings, was calculated to do so, and, unless disavowed, would have had the effect of making both you and me parties to any riot that might have ensued.

It must be recollected that the first call by which the troops were moved from their barracks to this city was made by United States officials under the "enforcement act," who, it appears, are your personal friends. I have made an honest attempt to disengage the troops from all participation in this imbroglio, but the untoward events of last evening have prevented or at least retarded it.

I am now awaiting and momentarily expecting full instructions from the President as to my future course in this matter; meantime, however, as the peace of the community is threatened, and as my action under similar circumstances during the past week met with the entire approval of the President, I shall hold my command in readiness to quell any riotous disturbance and prevent bloodshed, without reference to the parties originating the riot.

I have the honor to be your obedient servant.

(*Signed*)   W. H. EMERY
Brevet Major General, Commanding
W. T. GENTRY
Captain Nineteenth Infantry, Acting
Assistant Adjutant General

Hon. George W. Carter

He censured Carter for an editorial in his paper, using a letter from him leading to riot, and saying that the first call for troops was made by his friend, Marshal Packard.

Two days later, Mayor Flanders asked the President to declare martial law and received the following reply:

Washington,
January 12th, 1872.

Benjamin F. Flanders, Mayor, New Orleans:

Martial law will not be proclaimed in New Orleans under existing circumstances, and no assistance will be given by Federal authorities to persons or parties unlawfully resisting the constituted authorities of the State.

(*Signed*)   U. S. GRANT

[138]

On the twentieth of January, Carter issued a proclamation announcing that on Monday at 11 A.M. he proposed to take possession of the State House, and called upon the people to arm themselves and to report to him for service; concluding his call as follows:

The premises considered, we earnestly invite the citizens irrespective of race or party to organize and arm themselves as well as they may be able and to report in force in the neighborhood of 207 Canal Street, where they will be provided with necessary commissions and sworn in as Assistant Sergeants-at-Arms and thus within the law be prepared to protect their rights. I want a force so potent in numbers and so representative of the community as will preclude bloodshed and insure us from further interference with the General Assembly on the part of the Executive.

General Emery promptly telegraphed the proclamation to the War Department and received the following reply:

Washington, D. C.
Jan. 22nd, 1872

General W. H. Emery, Commanding Department of the Gulf:

The President directs that you hold your troops in readiness to suppress a conflict of armed bodies of men should such occur, and to guard public property from pillage and destruction. Keep the Department informed of your action.

By order of the Secretary of War.

(*Signed*) E. D. TOWNSEND
Adjutant General

Several hundred armed men appeared at the Clay Statue at Canal and Royal Streets. The merchants put up their shutters and closed their doors. There was intense excitement in the city. There could be nothing but bloodshed if Carter attempted to carry out his threat. One thousand old Confederate soldiers under Colonel Squiers, and one thousand negro militia under General Barber, together with seven hundred Metropolitan Policemen under Superintendent Badger, with a battery of artillery, all under the command of General James Longstreet, were quite able to protect the State House from the rabble of Carter, Packard, Casey, Eustis, Jonas, Voorhies, Zachary and Jewell.

While Colonel Carter was addressing his mob and telling them how to attack the State House, he was served with the President's telegram to General Emery. After reading it twice he threw up his hands and declared that "he surrendered to superior forces."

In the meantime the Custom House and Democratic Senators were in hiding at Bay St. Louis, Mississippi. Senator Futch of Union Parish, a Democrat, was seriously ill at his home. Senators Thomas and Anderson were also absent.

One day I received a telegram from a friend stating that Senator Thomas had passed through his town on his way to join the Bay St. Louis encampment in Mississippi, and that he would reach a certain station on the railroad that night to take the train. I sent my friend, Colonel Jack Wharton, to intercept him and to ask him to come to New Orleans and confer with his friends with my assurance that he could do so without danger of being arrested by the Senate. Colonel Wharton did meet him, and Senator Thomas came with him to the city. He was soon called upon at his lodgings by General Richard Taylor, who assured him that the best people in the city of New Orleans were on my side in this controversy. An hour later Dr. Newton Mercer called on him and confirmed what General Taylor had told him, and then invited him to dinner that evening at his palatial residence on Canal Street.

Here Senator Thomas met thirty of the leading citizens, all of whom confirmed General Taylor's and Dr. Mercer's statements.

The next morning Senator Thomas came to my office and told me that he was ready to take his seat in the Senate. Senator Anderson had already arrived, and so we had a quorum in the Senate. Hearing of the fact, the six white Custom House

Senators, with their two negro colleagues and the five Democratic Senators, who had been in hiding for twenty days over in the State of Mississippi, came sneaking back to their duties, looking like whipped curs and encountering the gibes of their fellow-citizens in the State and city.

Thus ended the war organized by the Federal office-holders of the Custom House, guided and supported by the leaders of the Democratic State Committee, but opposed by the masses of the white and colored people of the State.

After the conflict in the Legislature of January, 1872, I felt it was my duty to present all of the facts to General Grant; to ask him to support our Government, and to remove his brother-in-law, Colonel Casey, Collector of Customs at the Port of New Orleans, United States Marshal Packard of the Eastern District of Louisiana, Postmaster Lowell of the city of New Orleans, and the other Federal officials who had so wantonly conspired with leading Democrats to overthrow me and our State Government.

So I prepared a full statement of all of the facts, together with a plain demand for their removal. This I signed, together with Lieutenant-Governor Pinchback. This letter of protest and demand was silently ignored by President Grant, who preferred to accept the statements of his brother-in-law, Collector Casey, and to recognize him and the other Federal officials. They charged that I was at heart opposed to his renomination at the coming Presidential Convention.

In his letter to the President, Mr. Packard told the President that "the Republican Party of Louisiana is composed of 90,000 voters, 84,000 of whom are colored people," and that should Governor Warmoth receive a nomination for Governor in any manner, "the State will be lost to the Republican Party."

On January 15, 1872, a committee was appointed by the National House of Representatives on motion of Mr. Dawes of

Massachusetts, "whose duty it shall be to proceed to New Orleans and to inquire into the origin and character of the difficulties which have arisen between the Governor and the officials of the State of Louisiana, and the United States officials of said State, and their conduct growing out of the same, and to report to the House with such recommendations as they deem expedient."

Hon. G. W. Schofield of Pennsylvania, Hon. G. W. McCreary of Iowa, and H. Boardman Smith of New York (Republicans), Stevenson Archer of Maryland and R. Milton Spear of Pennsylvania (Democrats) constituted the Committee.

On January 29, 1872, the Committee met in the city of New Orleans.

The Committee was composed of three Republicans, all intimate friends and supporters of General Grant, and two Democrats with most bitter prejudices against both the Republican State officials and the Republican Federal officials, but strong friends of the Democratic Party and intensely interested in shielding the acts of its leaders in the late contest.

It is needless to state that all three Republican members were determined to find an excuse, if possible, to free General Grant's brother-in-law and his officials from any blame, and that the Democratic members were determined to aid their Democratic friends in Louisiana in besmirching me and ruining all of the Republican leaders, but especially the leaders who were so antagonistic to their party interests and welfare. Such being the case it was the full purpose of all members of the Committee to destroy me and my friends, if possible.

It can be said truly that the Committee was packed against me—that everything in my favor would be ignored and everything that could reflect upon me would be exaggerated to the fullest extent. The reader can well understand my embarrassment and that of my friends in this situation. Five hundred and fifty-three pages of testimony were taken by this Committee.

Every personal and political enemy of mine was given a chance at me, and they all availed themselves of their wonderful opportunity.

They were allowed to state not only any facts they claimed to possess, but also their suspicions, their inferences, their fears and their beliefs; and not only this, but they were allowed to state what had been told to them or what they had read in the newspapers, and were not even required to tell from whom they had heard their lies and slanders.

One witness was allowed to state that he "had heard" that I was turned out of a boarding-house before I was elected Governor because I could not pay my board, and that he "had heard and believed" that I was worth a half-million dollars at that time.

The United States Marshal, Packard, was given ninety-five pages in the book. He presented fourteen specific charges against me, and asked the Committee to summon ninety-six witnesses.

The charges were political, official and personal. They related to about every act of my administration, from the removal of officials who had criminally abused their offices to controlling the Legislature in its legislation. Nothing was left out; if one per cent of the charges had been true, I should still, after sixty years, be in the State Penitentiary.

After Mr. Packard had fired all of his ammunition, Chairman Schofield of the Committee asked:

Q. Are you now testifying to facts?
A. I am reciting facts which are generally believed and which I believe for reasons which I can state to the Committee. It is a subject of notoriety, and I state these charges to the Committee as one of the reasons why I differ from the Governor of the State, and oppose his administration. These charges I believe can be substantiated by the persons named, and I believe them to be true. Of course, I cannot have any personal knowledge of many of the charges set forth, but I can

furnish such evidence as I think will satisfy the Committee of the truth of them if they will summon the witnesses I have named.

Q. What is the Governor's reputed wealth?

A. I have seen some newspaper articles estimating it at from half a milion to two or three millions. I have no information upon which I could give any well-grounded opinion on the subject.

Marshal Packard put in evidence a long letter from the late Lieutenant-Governor Dunn to Horace Greeley, giving their side of the use of the Custom House for the Republican State Convention, and defending the use of Deputy United States Marshals and United States troops to control its organization. This letter was allowed to go in with the evidence. It ended:

In conclusion, permit me to speak frankly and advisedly of the feelings and purposes of the Republicans of Louisiana.

There are 90,000 voters in this State, 84,000 of whom are colored. In my judgment, a fair and untrammeled vote being cast, nineteen-twentieths of the Republican Party in the State, including a majority of the elective State officers and all of the Federal officers with a few exceptions, are opposed to the administration of the present State Executive.

The party is not divided, nor does it propose to be, but it is resolved that its servant, the present Executive, shall not assume mastership over the people who made him, and shall not use the prerogative and power that were given him by the people to oppress and crush them.

We want for ourselves and for the people of all parties better laws on the statute-books and better men to administer the same, and we are persuaded that neither of these wants will ever be met so long as the present Executive exercises any material control over the politics of Louisiana. We are engaged in no strife of factions, but the people gravely and earnestly are fighting for their personal and political rights against the encroachments of impudent and unfaithful public servants.

In your lecture, delivered to the citizens of New York, after your return from Texas, you refer to a class of men found in all the Southern States, as elements of the Republican party hurtful to its integrity and dangerous to its safety; and you are pleased to characterize their conduct as "carpet-bag scoundrelism." You stated that the good name and safety of the party demanded that when these men should press to the front and assume leadership of our hosts, we should say to them, "Go back, thieves."

Would you be greatly surprised, Mr. Greeley, to be informed that, in the judgement of the good people of this State, irrespective of party, the young man who now occupies the executive chair of Louisiana, whose crimes against his party and his people you charitably ignore, and whose championship you so boldly assume, is pre-eminently the prototype and prince of the tribe of carpet-baggers who seem to be your pet aversion.

Well-attested facts from the official history of his Excellency will show that the people are not mistaken in assigning to him the leadership of the class you denounce.

In all candor, we believe that his Excellency Governor H. C. Warmoth is officially derelict and politically untrustworthy. He has shown an itching desire, as manifested by repeated negotiations with certain leaders thereof, to secure the personal support of the Democracy at the expense of his own party, and an equally manifest craving to obtain a cheap and ignoble white respectability by the sacrifice of the confidence and support of colored Republicans, and he is much more concerned to have the entree into good southern society than he is to do the arduous but honorable work of elevating the masses of that race who elected him, and to perfect harmony between the races by an impartial and honest enforcement of the law. He has so frequently violated the Constitution he has sworn to obey, and maladministered the laws he has sworn faithfully to execute, that he has succeeded in destroying public confidence not only in himself but in officials generally. He has so deceived the public faith and disappointed the public hope by the facility with which he makes, and the recklessness with which he breaks, his pledges, that we, in self-defense, have been compelled to withdraw our confidence from him.

We cannot and will not support him, even though *The New York Tribune* should remain his champion, for such support would inevitably involve the disastrous defeat of the Republican party in the State of Louisiana.

Mr. Packard in a letter to the President, justifying himself for his conduct on the 9th of August, 1871, said:

On the 9th of August, Mr. President, I had no personal interest to subserve; no nominations of State or Federal officers were to be made at the Convention. I saw the delegates hunted from their primaries, and denied a place of assemblage. I heard upon one side their pleas for protection, and upon the other the threats against their lives. I felt that the United States Government would not begrudge citizens an asylum from bloodshed under a United States roof, and I prefer the responsibility of having thrown open to them the door of a vacant United States courtroom, rather than today to be charged by my brethren with standing upon its threshold in pitiless indifference to their peril.

In conclusion, Mr. President, permit me to say that the Republican problem in Louisiana is to be mastered chiefly by 85,000 colored men. In their political inexperience, they mistook certain of their pretended friends in 1868. They have seen a demagogue reëstablish the old ethics of slavery so far as to enforce a partisan servitude to himself, and, if need be, invoke violence to promote his selfish ends. They now propose to clearly disavow all mischievous men and measures, and husband their confidence from further abuse as a sanction for crime. To this end they have declared in convention that H. C. Warmoth, having shown clearly that he would sacrifice the Republican party to advance himself, can no longer be safely followed as a Republican leader; having pronounced for a thorough reform in matters of local administration, and addressed themselves to a better solution of the national question in 1872 than their official incumbrances permitted them in 1868.

I respectfully submit this statement, with accompanying proofs, as my answer.

(*Signed*) S. B. PACKARD
United States Marshal, District of Louisiana

Mr. B. F. Joubert, Collector of Internal Revenue, belonging to the Custom House faction, was one of the witnesses who testified against me. He swore that "four-fifths of the colored people of the State were opposed to Governor Warmoth's renomination for Governor."

The following is a reply to his testimony:

New Orleans,
February 10, 1872.

Dear Sir:
The attention of the undersigned, colored members of the Senate and House of Representatives, having been called to the statement made

STORMY DAYS IN LOUISIANA

by B. F. Joubert, United States assessor of internal revenue, before the Congressional Committee, that "four-fifths of the colored people of this State are opposed to Governor Warmoth," would respectfully beg leave to enter their protest against the injustice and untruthfulness of this statement. They would also state from their personal knowledge derived from an intimate acquaintance with the views and feelings of their own race throughout the whole State that the political principles and course of Governor Warmoth are generally approved.

P. B. S. Pinchback, Orleans
A. E. Barber, Orleans
George Y. Kelso, Rapides
E. Butler, Plaquemines
David Young, Concordia
Henry Demas, St. John Baptist
R. R. J. Kenner, 4th representative district
E. C. Morphy, 70th representative district of Orleans
C. A. Verretof, Terrebonne
George Washington, Assumption
Henderson Williams, Madison Parish
P. Darensbourg, Point Coupee
Henry Raby, Natchitoches
Raford Blunt, Natchitoches
Milton Morris, Ascension
Cain Sartain, Carroll

George Washington, Concordia
H. C. Tounoir, Point Coupee
William Crawford, Union
W. B. Barrett, Orleans
R. G. Gardner, Jefferson
John J. Moore, Caddo
H. Mahoney, Plaquemines
P. G. Deslonde, Iberville
A. Overton, Rapides
Thomas Murry, Orleans
J. W. Quinn, 3rd representative district of Orleans
V. E. McCarthy, representative of 6th ward
A. Belot, Orleans
C. W. Ringgold, Orleans
Henry Riley, St. Mary
T. B. Stamps, Jefferson

Hon. G. W. Schofield, Chairman Congressional Committee

I was summoned before the Committee on February 5, 1872, and kept on the rack until the 7th. One hundred and thirty-five pages of the book were consumed by my examination.

I was allowed to file my protest against the range of the testimony, and also a statement of my side of the controversy, and at the end I used the following language:

That, gentlemen, is the substance of the statement of this case as far as I am able to give it to you. I am now ready to be interrogated, and I desire to say to the Committee that so far as I am personally concerned, or officially concerned, I shall be glad to answer any questions however personal they may be which the Committee shall see proper to ask.

Right here I desire to state that the Chairman of the Committee, Mr. Schofield, and also Mr. McCreary, were fair, just, and decent in their examination of me, and sought to confine the inquiry to the resolution adopted by the House of Representatives. Their report in the main was a fair statement of the whole case. But H. Boardman Smith, the other Republican member, showed at once, by his examination of the witnesses, and especially his cross-examination of me, that he was a bitter and relentless partisan and determined to protect President Grant's brother-in-law and the other Federal officials at any cost. He approved or excused their every act. And Messrs. Archer and Spear, the Democratic members, were no less bitter, and showed that they were determined to excuse the Democratic conspirators in their alliance with the Federal officials against me, and to destroy me politically and personally if it were possible to do so. Their report was a stump speech leaving nothing unsaid that would help the Democratic party and throw blame and shame on its opponents.

This statement will be fully proven by reading the questions they propounded to me, the language they contained, and the aggressive manner in which they conducted my examination. Many of their questions were irrelevant, and their manner most offensive. They were such as one might expect in a Recorder's Court where the petty lawyers were defending a thief for stealing chickens.

I am glad to say, after these long years, that I maintained my temper and overwhelmed them with my complete answers, so much so that Mr. Spear said to me after it was over, "We cannot determine whether you are an angel from Heaven, or a devil from Hell." Reading his report it would seem that he adopted the latter conclusion.

Every witness who did not support the Custom House and Democratic side was treated as if he were a criminal, and from the harrying cross-questions it looked as though he must be guilty of some kind of criminal offense. Even United States District Attorney Beckwith and General Emery, commanding the Army, were grilled by these fierce partisans as if they were criminals. So with every friend of mine.

General James Longstreet resigned his office as Surveyor of the Port in protest against the proceedings of Casey, Packard and company.

Custom House,
Surveyor's Office,
New Orleans, March 5, 1872.

Hon. Geo. S. Boutwell,
    Secretary of the Treasury.
Sir:
I have the honor most respectfully to submit my resignation of the office of Surveyor of Customs at New Orleans.

I find it inconsistent with my views of sound Republican philosophy to approve the efforts of prominent Federal officers in this city to displace by violence the civil authority of the State. As I cannot identify myself with such adventures, it seems fitting that I withdraw from this office as soon as you may be pleased to appoint a successor. . . .

I am profoundly thankful for the noble act of the President and his marked personal kindness in selecting me for a practical illustration of his readiness to encourage and receive those who recognize and support the law; and I beg leave to assure you, sir, of my appreciation of your uniform official and personal kindness.

I am, sir, with great respect,
Your most obedient servant,
(Signed)   JAMES LONGSTREET
Surveyor

The prompt acceptance of the resignation of General Long-

[149]

street as Surveyor of the Port of New Orleans, and more especially the appointment in his place of the negro State Senator,
James H. Ingraham, who had been most conspicuous in all the
recent revolutionary proceedings against me and my friends,
showed clearly that the President had taken sides against me and
had given Casey and Packard a free hand thereafter in the war
on me.

I was at war with the Legislature from the beginning of my
term until the end. I was obliged to veto over thirty-nine bills
passed by the Legislature, some of which were passed over my
veto; and to defeat several in which I invoked the aid of the
courts. The Legislature from the beginning was besieged by
people and interests which would have involved the State in
immense liabilities, and I was obliged to antagonize not only
these promoters but many members of the Legislature, thus
piling up against me an increased number of enemies. As an
example, I print the following agreement entered into by the
banks of the city of New Orleans:

This agreement made and entered into this 22nd day of April, 1869,
Emile H. Reynes and Avegno & Willoz, of this City of New Orleans,
of the first part, and the several banks hereinafter named, represented
by their respective presidents, duly authorized by their boards of direc-
tors, of the second part, witnesseth:

Whereas the said banks are holders and owners of certain bonds
issued by the State of Louisiana under and by virtue of an act of the
Legislature thereof approved the 23rd day of January, 1862, entitled
"An act to raise money for the State treasury," &c. And whereas the
said Emile H. Reynes and Avegno & Willoz, parties of the first part, are
desirous and willing to undertake to have the validity of said bonds
admitted by the State, or to obtain compensation for the same:

Now, therefore, it is hereby stipulated, covenanted, and agreed, by
and between said parties of the first part and second part, as follows,
to-wit: The said E. H. Reynes and Avegno & Willoz hereby agree and
bind themselves to use all their influence and exertions, and to make
every effort either to obtain some compensation for the said bonds, or
to procure some relief to the parties of the second part, holders and

owners of said bonds. They further bind themselves to make all necessary advances of money, and to bear personally and alone all the cost, expenses and outlays of money that may be necessary to reach the proposed end.

In case the said Emile H. Reynes and Avegno & Willoz should succeed in their endeavors, either to have the validity of said bonds admitted or to obtain some compensation for the same, by the issue of new bonds by the State in lieu of the old ones; then, and in that case, the said parties of the second part hereby agree and bind themselves to transfer and turn over in full ownership to the parties of the first part twenty-five per cent, or one-fourth, of the whole number of the said bonds which they now hold or own in full compensation for their services in the premises.

In case any of the bank parties to this agreement should not have their bonds in their possession by reason of having surrendered the same by error to the United States authorities during the War, but hold the receipts of said authorities for the same, the said banks agree and bind themselves to contribute in the same manner their *pro rata* out of any new bonds or compensation they may receive from the State of Louisiana, in lieu of the old bonds or of the receipts of the United States authorities for the bonds surrendered by them.

It is hereby acknowledged and agreed that the amount of bonds held by the said banks and individuals respectively is as follows, to-wit:

The Louisiana State Bank	$537,248
The Canal Bank	700,000
The Bank of Louisiana	700,000
The Citizens' Bank	743,000
The Mechanics' and Traders' Bank	342,500
The Union Bank	200,000
The Bank of New Orleans	145,000
The Merchants' Bank	100,000
The Crescent City Bank	26,000
Making a total of	$3,493,748

It is expressly understood between all parties that this agreement and contract shall not extend beyond the last day of the next regular session of the Legislature of the State, at which time if Messrs. Reynes and Avegno & Willoz have not succeeded in and by virtue of acts of the Legislature, then, and in that case, the agreement shall *ipso facto* be null and void.

Thus done in duplicate, in the city of New Orleans, this 22nd day of April, 1869.

JULES A. BLANC
President Louisiana State Bank
GEORGE JONAS
President Canal and Bank Company
E. E. WILLOZ
P. H. MORGAN
J. F. IRVIN
Commissioners
SAM BELL
President Union Bank
E. H. SUMMERS
President Crescent City Bank
E. H. REYNES
AVEGNO & WILLOZ

Witness:
Robert Kerr
A. Cassard

The promoters of this legislation spent large sums of money among the members of the Legislature and actually invaded my office and offered my private secretary $50,000 of the proposed issue of bonds for his influence. I was obliged to go before the Senate in person and expose the people who were engaged in the attempt to bribe the Legislature and the Governor. In this way I killed the scheme.

The Legislature was most extravagant in its expenditures, as I exposed in my message to the Legislature of January 1, 1872, and from which I quote as follows:

I respectfully call your attention to the fact that the extravagance of the Legislature at its last session has produced a most noticeable sensation throughout the State, and has given the opponents of the Government the means of sowing distrust and producing the greatest dissatisfaction among the people. The last session is known to have cost the State, for the Senate $191,763.85, and for the House of Representatives $767,192.65—an average cost of $5,300 for each Senator and $7,300 for each member of the House, or an average of over $6,800 for each member of the entire body, or of $113.50 per day for each member during the session. It is necessary that I should comment upon this subject with a view of bringing the evils to your attention, in order that you may guard against them in the future. A careful calculation of the expenses of the General Assembly for mileage and *per diem,* even at the enormous rate of twenty cents per mile, each way, shows that the total expenses ought not to exceed $100,000 for the sixty days of the annual session, and the legitimate contingent expenses of both houses ought not to exceed $25,000. Then what has become of the excess, $833,956.50? It has been squandered by the officers of the Assembly in paying extra mileage and *per diem* of members for days' service never rendered; for an enormous corps of useless clerks, pages, etc., for publishing the Journals of each house in fifteen obscure newspapers, some of which have never existed, while some of those that did exist never did the work they were employed to do, although every one has received the compensation for it; in paying committees authorized by the House to sit during vacation and to travel throughout the State and into Texas, and in a hundred other different ways. The enrollment committee of the House had over eighty clerks, most of whom were under pay during the whole session at eight dollars per day, during which time only one hundred and twenty bills were passed, which did not require more than eight or ten clerks to perform the whole labor of enrollment.

Permit me to suggest that neither House has any right to spend the public money for purposes for which the law has already provided. The publication of the Journals of the General Assembly being provided for by the printing law, it was not competent for either house separately to direct and pay for such services. It is not legitimately a part of the contingent expenses of either house.

The people of Louisiana plunged into bad luck from the beginning. There was an element so extreme and vicious in action as to give excuse for the most extreme measures against them. The murderous violence practised by the leaders of the Democratic Party at the Presidential election of 1868 forced the Republican Legislature to enact stringent registration and election laws to protect their voters at future elections. The executive powers were supreme, and if abused might lead to frauds and injustice. But it seemed that the only way to meet violence and fraud was to lodge in some tribunal the power to meet them; and whether this power was abused depended upon the man or men selected to administer the laws. These laws, of course, met with the most violent and fierce opposition of the Democratic Party.

The election of 1870, at which two State officers, five Congressmen, a new Legislature and the Parish officers of the State were chosen, was conducted by me. It was the most peaceable and fair election ever known in the State up to that time. The Returning Board had no complaints of violence, unfairness or frauds before it, and the official returns of the election were simply tabulated and the result promulgated.

Recognizing the power of the Executive, the extreme element in the Republican Party composed of Federal officials and aspirants for future political promotion, disappointed and embittered against me for aspiring to reëlection and by the endorsement by the people of the amendment to the State Constitution which made me eligible for a succeeding term, found the patronage of the Governor and his power under these laws a menace to their ambitions. They made it the issue and sought for allies to help. They found the Democratic Party politicians only too glad to join them. They did join them, and in the prosecution of their campaign resorted to the most violent and revolutionary proceedings. It was this combination of Federal Republican officials and Democratic politicians that first invoked the power of the United States Courts. It was this combination that prepared affidavits signed by four Democratic members of the Legislature on which they obtained writs to arrest the Governor, the Lieutenant-Governor, four members of the Senate and thirteen members of the House of Representatives, with which the United States Marshal arrested them at the moment of the meeting of the Legislature, holding them in the United States court room, located in the United States Custom House, until they had revolutionized the House of Representatives by removing six members of the House and seating six others in their places and confirming their man as Speaker of the House of Representatives. The Democratic State Committee could not object to the intervention of United States Courts in our political controversies after that. This precedent was shot into our faces when we contested the right of Judge Durell to take jurisdiction of a purely State controversy in 1872. What could the eminent lawyers, J. B. Eustis, H. D. Ogden, J. B. Cotton, Frank Zachary, Carlton Hunt, and others, have to say after having advised the proceedings and invoked in 1871 the intervention of the processes of the United States Courts as described above.

If it was legal for a United States Court to arrest the Governor, Lieutenant-Governor and members of the State's Senate and House of Representatives in a political controversy in 1871, why was it not legal for Judge Durell, a United States Judge, to seize the State Capitol, install a Legislature, and set up a Governor and State Government to suit President Grant in 1872?

Mr. Eustis alleges the Election and Registration Laws adopted by the Legislature in 1870 as the object upon which the Custom House faction, led by Marshal Packard, Chairman of the Republican State Committee, begged and obtained the coöperation of the Democratic leaders, led by Eustis and his friends.

Now let us analyze the case. The Registration and Election laws existing before 1869 were such that the Democratic Party was able by violence to carry the State by 88,000 majority for Seymour and Blair against Grant and Colfax. It was to protect the voters from violence and fraud that Marshal Packard, Lieutenant-Governor Dunn, and their followers devised the Registration and Election laws of 1869. They prepared the bills and put them through the Legislature. They conferred great power on the Governor and the Returning Board. The election of 1870 was conducted under these new laws. It was the most peaceable and orderly election ever held in the State up to that time.

There were 106,762 votes polled, and the Republican Party elected its State ticket by over 20,000 majority. It elected five Republican Congressmen, a good working majority in both houses of the Legislature, the Mayor and officers of the city of New Orleans—all without protest. Lieutenant-Governor Dunn, as one of the Returning Board, signed all of the returns. What right had these Republican leaders to find fault with me for the administration of the Registration and Election Laws at the late election?

The Democrats might have found fault with me, since they failed in everything. All of their candidates for Congress were defeated. Their candidates for Auditor and Treasurer lost; they failed to win the control of either House of the Legislature; their candidates for Mayor and the five Administrators of the city of New Orleans all were defeated—they had a right to feel disappointed and chagrined. But as for the batch of Republican leaders holding Federal offices and controlling the Republican State Committee, they did not have any honest cause of complaint. We must look somewhere else for an excuse for their bitter opposition to me.

Mr. Eustis, the Democratic leader, in his testimony before the Congressional Committee, tells the story. He said:

We considered we had three elements to attack, which gave these enormous powers to Governor Warmoth—one was the patronage placed in his hands, and the others were the frauds which could be perpetrated under both the Election and Registration laws. We understood perfectly well from the situation of affairs that the anti-Warmoth wing of the Republican Party was in precisely the same difficult situation that we were; that they had the same reasons to apprehend the use or abuse of these laws against themselves that we had, and in fact in discussing these matters we considered that the motive of self-interest with these gentlemen was supposed to secure the punctual fulfillment of their part of this arrangement. . . . After having considered that attitude, we considered that this coalition would be without results as long as Warmoth remained Governor of the State. We looked merely to political results.

The people of the late election had just adopted an amendment striking out Article 50 of the State Constitution by which I had been made ineligible to reëlection as Governor. The Custom House wing of the Republican party was afraid that I might receive the Republican nomination for reëlection; the Democrats were also afraid that I might be the Republican nominee—so here the Custom House leaders and the Democratic leaders found an issue of self-interest on which they could unite and did unite. If the people had rejected the amendment to the State Constitution making me eligible to election for a succeeding term as Governor, there would have been no call for help from the Democratic leaders. It was to keep me out. It was on me that the war was inaugurated. The Custom House Republicans knew that they could not defeat my nomination by a free Republican Convention, and both the Democrats and the Custom House Republicans knew that I would carry the State at the election, in spite of both of these forces. So I was the man who was the cause of all this trouble.

THE GREAT STEAMBOAT RACE—
"Robert E. Lee" *vs.* the "Natchez"

There was a great rivalry between the officers of the "Lee" and the "Natchez."

There was a Yankee by the name of Asa S. Mansfield in New Orleans, during the war, representing Oakes Ames of Massachusetts. Mansfield controlled large sums of money belonging to Ames. He used it to buy cotton inside the Confederate lines, got it out and shipped it North. He had the good will of the

Federal authorities and made a great deal of money. I was his attorney.

At the end of the War he invested some of it in the building of a splendid Mississippi steamboat, and, having an eye to its popularity, he named it after the most beloved man in the South—Robert E. Lee. It did a wonderful business and was patronized by all of the Southerners in the Valley of the Mississippi.

Captain Leathers, an old steamboat man, built another splendid steamboat, which he called the "Natchez." These two were rivals for the river trade; a fierce contest was carried on between Captain Leathers of the "Natchez" and Captain Cannon of the "Lee," both Southerners. But only a few knew that the "Lee" was owned by Mansfield and Ames. Each boat had its patrons and friends.

A little man well known as Johnny Hawkins, who kept the finest bar-room in New Orleans, and was a friend of the "Natchez" and Captain Leathers, decided that he was prepared to bet $10,000 that the "Natchez" could beat the "Lee" in a race from New Orleans to the city of St. Louis. He soon found takers of his bet, and the race was arranged for the 30th of June, 1870.

I had been to Baton Rouge to attend the commencement exercises of the State University and to deliver the diplomas of the graduates. The exercises were ended by a grand ball. Dr. A. W. Smyth, Chief Surgeon of the Charity Hospital of New Orleans, accompanied me. At 2 A.M. we went on board the steamer "W. S. Pikes" for New Orleans. There were no railroads from New Orleans to Baton Rouge then. The packet was the only means of transportation. We stopped at every landing, and were from 2 A.M. until 4:30 P.M. getting to the city.

When we landed at the wharf we saw the largest crowd, I think, that I had ever seen together in the city of New Orleans. They were there to see the steamboats start on the great race.

Dr. Smyth, who was an old friend of Captain Cannon, suggested that we go aboard the "Lee" and see the Captain. We found the boat stripped for the race. The boilers were carrying every pound of steam allowed by law. Everything was eagerness and excitement. The "Natchez," lying just above, was in the same condition for the race. Captain Cannon pressed us to go with him and, as we were carried away by the excitement and enthusiasm, we accepted the invitation. Within a few minutes the bells rang and both boats pulled out into the stream, amid the cheers of the multitude on the shore.

The "Natchez" got out first. But before she had straightened out into the river and got going, the "Lee" was beside her, and within a very few seconds the "Lee" took the lead, which she never lost until the end.

The river banks all the way up were crowded with excited and enthusiastic people, day and night.

We had been under way but a short time when the fearful news came up from the engineer that the "Lee's" boilers were leaking. The Captain, who stood with Dr. Smyth and myself on the upper deck, went below at once; he was greatly concerned. The Captain was gone for some time; then he returned to us, all smiles. The engineer had pumped some sort of material into the boilers that settled into the openings and stopped the leak.

The boat's carpenter came up to the Captain and told him that he thought the boat was too rigid, and that the hog chains should be loosened, so that it could lie down as a dog lays his ears back on his head in a race. He said that he wanted the boat to lie as flat and have as little resistance as possible. I don't know whether the carpenter loosened up the hog chains or not, but we ran all night up the river, the banks on both sides being lined with people who made bonfires, fired guns, and cheered the race with all their might. The race continued as we passed Baton Rouge, Natchez, and Vicksburg, all of which were decorated; cannons were fired and the wildest enthusiasm and excitement displayed.

My friend Dr. Smyth and I occupied the same stateroom on the "Lee" that night. The Doctor was an Irishman with some brogue and, besides, he stammered a little in his speech. As we undressed for bed I thought to make a little fun, so I said: "Doctor, if you had not come to this country but had remained in Ireland, it would have been a long time before you could have slept with a Governor."

And with true Irish wit and with plenty of brogue and lots of stammering, he replied at once: "Oh, yes! If we both had lived in Ireland it would have been a d—d sight longer time before you would have been a Governor!"

We got right into bed and slept until daylight.

During the second night, the steamer "Frank Pargaud" came alongside the "Lee," and without slowing down, loaded a hundred cords of pine knots on to the "Lee." During this time Dr. Smyth and I transferred ourselves to the "Pargaud" and returned to New Orleans.

The "Natchez" never caught up with the "Lee," and long before it reached Cairo abandoned the race. The "Lee" was by all odds the stronger and faster boat. This was one of the greatest steamboat races in the history of the Mississippi River.

Apropos of my dear friend, Dr. Andrew Smyth, it was he who saved my life after an accident to my right foot, and nursed me back to perfect health. He would receive no pay for his services, so I sent to Tiffany's in New York and bought the best watch that they made and presented it to him.

The Doctor was surprised when I presented it to him in the presence of a number of friends. He was given to droll remarks and always stammered in his speech. After looking the watch over with care, he remarked that "if he had cut my head off instead of my toe the Democrats would have given him a d—d sight better watch than that!"

CHAPTER V

The conduct of the Federal officials in Louisiana was so revolting and the President's nepotism and military despotism was such as to arouse a tremendous opposition to his renomination for a second term. Senator Sumner of Massachusetts, Senator Lyman Trumbull of Illinois, Senator Carl Schurz of Missouri, Horace Greeley of New York, and hundreds of other staunch old Republican leaders, together with many leading Republican newspapers, declared against Grant's renomination.

The movement finally took form in the calling of a National Convention at Cincinnati, Ohio, on May 1, 1872.

I was forced to sympathize with this movement. General Grant had violated his understanding with me; he had taken sides with his brother-in-law, Collector Casey, Marshal Packard, Postmaster Lowell, and the other Federal officials who had so grossly abused their positions in their efforts to outrage and humiliate me, Lieutenant-Governor Pinchback and the people who supported me in my efforts to build up a Republican Party in which the conservative and honest white people of the State should have a share. We believed that the attempts of the Federal officials to Africanize Louisiana were bound to lead to civil war and to the ultimate destruction of the rights of all our colored citizens. I tried to harmonize the two races and to secure justice for both, and their consent to live together on the basis of equal civil and political rights. I took to the Convention at Cincinnati 125 delegates, one-third of whom were colored Republicans. It was the largest delegation that any State sent. We had a splendid reception by the delegates from the other States.

I, with a part of our delegates, supported Lyman Trumbull of Illinois for President, but the Convention finally nominated Horace Greeley of New York, with Governor B. Gratz Brown of Missouri for Vice-President. I was appointed a member of the National Committee for Louisiana.

Later, in June, the Campbell-Pinchback faction of the Republican Party met in convention at New Orleans, and nominated me as its candidate for Governor. I promptly declined the nomination in the following letter, after which the Convention adjourned without further action:

STATE OF LOUISIANA

Executive Department

New Orleans, June 13, 1872.

Dear Sir:

In returning thanks to the Convention over which you preside for the distinguished compliment extended to me in the unanimous presentation of my name for reëlection to the office of Governor, justice to you, no less than to myself, requires that I should frankly state the reasons which force me to decline the honor thus tendered. Whilst I value highly the confidence of any portion of the public, I cannot conceal from myself that the Convention is about to assume an attitude entirely inconsistent with the views of State and national policy which I have already expressed; and with the course which I have determined to pursue, I could not become its candidate without doing violence to my dearest convictions, and sacrificing a principle for which, in common with yourself, I have so earnestly contended during the last year.

It now appears to be the intention of the majority of the members of the Convention on its reassembling at Baton Rouge, to attempt an alliance with the Custom House party, which is to meet at that place on the same day, for the purpose of reuniting with those whom I consider the most dangerous enemies of the country and the State, with the arrogant, dictatorial and corrupt administration of General Grant, and with the party which, under the leadership of his followers and agents, would subject the State to a continuance of a rule of ignorance, venality and corruption unparalleled in the history of any other community. The success of General Grant at the ensuing Presidential election would be a calamity such as cannot be contemplated without alarm. It would be the perpetuation, perhaps the permanent establishment, of personal government in its worst form. It would be the commencement of imperialism in politics, and the utter and hopeless degradation of political morality. It would be the continuance of an odious executive and legislative tyranny which tramples with equal indifference upon the rights of persons and of communities; which overturns all the muniments of public liberty, and drags thousands of peaceable citizens to the common jail on a false pretense of secret conspiracy; which uses the bayonets of its soldiery to overawe a convention of the people, and prostitutes the courts of the country and the officers of the law to the service of an audacious attempt to overthrow the government of a State.

It was in order to avert these evils and to join in the general protest against these infamous acts, as well as to save this State from the further depredations of the ring of Federal officials who have persistently used their personal and political power to suborn and corrupt the Legislature, that I went to Cincinnati and participated in the nomination of Greeley and Brown. It is with the view of assisting to prevent the triumph in this State of a party whose success would fill the Legislature with the representatives of organized ignorance and unblushing venality, would cause irreparable injury to our commerce, would irretrievably ruin our credit, and bring contempt and scorn upon even the beneficial results of Republican reconstruction, that I have resolved to devote all my energies to the service of the Liberal Republican party and the allies who may act with it in this contest.

I believe that the country can be saved from Grantism with its attendant tyranny and corruption, and I believe that the State can be rescued from the nameless evils which the triumph of the Grant-Custom-House party would inflict upon it. I believe that a thorough union of the parties and portions of parties which have this object in view will suffice to accomplish that end, and I think you know me too well to suppose that any personal advantage or allurements of ambition could swerve me from my purpose to oppose with all the vigor of my nature the party with which, unfortunately, you are about to ally yourself, and to support with equal zeal and determination the party which alone, in my judgment, can save the State from desolation and ruin.

I again thank the Convention for the honor conferred upon me, and trust you will communicate to them the regrets which I feel in finding myself compelled to separate from the friends who have so long and so faithfully supported me.

Very respectfully your obedient servant,

H. C. WARMOTH.

To Hon. H. J. Campbell, President Republican State Convention.

Later, in July, the National Democratic Convention met at Baltimore and indorsed the Greeley and Brown ticket, and a little later the Republican National Convention met at Philadelphia and renominated Gen. Grant for President and Henry Wilson of Massachusetts for Vice-President.

On my return from the Cincinnati Convention it appeared to me to be my duty, as one of the leaders of the Liberal Republican National Committee for Louisiana, to exert myself to bring about a union of all of our people favorable to our national ticket. I devoted myself to this work.

We proceeded to organize a provisional State Committee of the Liberal Republican Party pledged to the support of the Greeley and Brown ticket. We issued an address to the people which was printed and distributed in every Parish of the State, and many thousands of our people—white and black—signed their names, approving of our movement, and sent them in to our committee.

The State Committee selected Colonel Davidson B. Penn, a distinguished ex-Confederate soldier, as its chairman, and Major Andrew Hero as its secretary.

Later, the committee with the approval of more than 25,000 citizens issued a call for a Liberal Republican State Convention to meet at the Academy of Music at twelve o'clock on the fifth day of August, 1872, to consolidate all elements opposed to Grant and Wilson and the Custom House State ticket headed by W. P. Kellogg and C. C. Antoine.

The greatest enthusiasm prevailed throughout the State. The movement spread among Democrats, Reformers, Liberals, and Republicans, both white and black, like wildfire.

I had, in the course of my administration, made many personal friends among the conservative white people of the State. I had appointed quite a number of them to important offices. I had appointed Gen. James Longstreet, one of the greatest Confederate leaders, as my Adjutant-General. President Grant had already appointed him Surveyor of the Port of New Orleans. I had appointed Col. William Penn Mason, lately a member of Gen. Robert E. Lee's Staff, a Major-General of Militia; I had appointed Miller Owen, an ex-Confederate soldier, a Colonel of Militia; I had appointed Gen. M. Jeff Thompson, an ex-Confederate soldier, Chief State Engineer in charge of all the levees and other public works of the State. I had organized twenty-five hundred young Rebels into the State Militia; I had made many appointments of conservative citizens as judges of district courts and district attorneys, as well as other officials in the various districts and Parishes. I had induced the Legislature to propose an amendment to the State Constitution to strike out Article 99, which disfranchised thousands of ex-Confederate soldiers; I had vetoed a civil rights bill which was intended to force social equality by means of a criminal procedure. So the reader can see that I had made many friends for the Republican Party, which gladly followed me into the Liberal Republican movement.

But, of course, my administration was exceedingly obnoxious to the colored Lieutenant-Governor, Oscar J. Dunn, to *The New Orleans Tribune,* to United States Marshal Packard, to Senator Kellogg and the "Pure Radical" Federal officials, who looked only to negro voters to support the Republican Party. They claimed that in my appointment of conservative white men to office, I was guilty of treason to the negro people. It was, in fact, the paramount issue of the Custom-House-Federal-Officials faction, who claimed that "of the 90,000 Republican voters 84,000 were negroes," and their support was "the problem of the Republican party."

But strange as it may appear, there were a number of the leading Democrats who bitterly opposed me in my efforts to harmonize the people. They were mostly politicians living in the city of New Orleans, but they were all-powerful with their State Committee. They were the same men who but a few months before were in a combination with Lieutenant-Governor Dunn, C. C. Antoine, James H. Ingraham, and J. Henri Burch, all negroes, together with James F. Casey (President Grant's brother-in-law), United States Marshal Packard, United States Senator W. P. Kellogg, and George W. Carter, ex-Speaker of the House of Representatives, all of the Custom-House-Grant faction, to overthrow me and to revolutionize the State Government and put one of Collector Casey's deputies in the office of Governor.

These Democratic leaders hated me with a holy hatred. I stood in the way of their political ambitions. I had built up a strong following among their own people. In every country Parish I had numerous and strong friends. *The New Orleans Picayune* complained that "the gravest crime of which he [Governor Warmoth] had been guilty is this: he has deliberately gone to work to debauch our citizens by means of largess distributed among them under various pretexts. He might have taken from the State millions of dollars without inflicting such an injury as this."

The people had but recently adopted an amendment to the State Constitution, striking out Article 50 which made the Governor ineligible to reëlection for a succeeding term. These Democratic politicians hated me and found common cause with the Custom House Republican politicians who hated me for the same reasons.

The Legislature adjourned on the 23rd of February, 1872, and the city was still in a violent ferment resulting from the revolutionary attempt of the Custom House and Democratic State Committee to overthrow me and the State Government. It was thought by these politicians a good time to hold a Democratic State Convention, so the Democratic State Committee called one to meet on April 18, 1872. It met, of course, in the city of New Orleans. The apportionment gave the city of New Orleans a very large proportion of the delegates. When it met it was found that distinct differences between the city and the country delegates existed; the galleries were filled with a howling mob, supporting every move of the city leaders.

It was only on the second day that the Convention could agree on the selection of President and other officers. Several delegates had to fight for their seats against the charges that they had been too friendly with Governor Warmoth. One city delegate moved to expel the venerable Thomas Green Davidson of Livingston Parish, because he was a friend of Governor Warmoth. After great excitement and confusion and howls of "put him out," "give him a hearing," etc., he was allowed to speak. In the midst of profound silence, Mr. Davidson arose from his seat and spoke as follows:

Mr. President and Gentlemen of the Convention, it seems very hard that a man like myself, who has been a Democrat since 1826, and who always defended the Democratic party, should be questioned on this matter today. The people of the Parish of Livingston have known me since the year 1831, and have approved of my course in everything that I did. If the gentlemen who are so strong in their accusations would look at the resolutions adopted at the mass meeting in Livingston— one of the largest ever held there—they would see that my course was doubly approved, and they sent me here as a delegate to represent their feeling at this Democratic Convention.

Mr. President, this whole affair is entirely uncalled for, for the reason that the people of Livingston approve of my course. I represent them, and they are my constituents, and to them alone am I responsible. The meetings held in New Orleans have nothing to do with me. They may hold their mass meetings and censure me, but, sir, did you ever hear of a citizen being condemned without a hearing? They never heard me. They never gave me the chance to be heard. They condemned me before I had the opportunity to explain my position, although I have been a Democrat since 1826. And, sir, I did not know before that the Democratic State Central Committee was so composed that it could destroy a man—a true Democrat—without his being heard.

How did we stand in the House? We Democrats stood 26 to 104; in the Senate 7. Now, what show had we? My people desired to have certain acts passed for their benefit in reference to taxed lands. Now, if I had not taken the position I did, I never could have accomplished anything for my people. As I said before, what show could I have possibly stood? We, with sometimes but 5 in the House, stood against 55, a majority, I believe, of 104. Now, what good could I have rendered the Democratic cause by fighting this large majority?

The point has been raised that "I am no Democrat." I will leave that to any sensible person who has watched my career since 1826. I have worked, labored and defended the Democratic cause. My people will not say I am no Democrat, and who are better judges of my actions than the people I represent—my constituents? I am judged by them and they indorse my conduct.

That there was corruption in the Legislature no one doubts; but it was not confined to the Republicans alone. But I have never been accused of being influenced by corrupt motives, and say here that my actions were fully sustained by my constituents in Livingston.

I have stood by the Democratic party faithfully, but the convention wants to expel me because I am a friend of Governor Warmoth. I *am* a friend of Governor Warmoth. I do not understand that any opposition can be offered to my making friends with anyone. When the whigs and the Democratic party were at loggerheads, I had several warm friends in the Whig party. Because I am Democratic it does not stand to reason that I cannot have friends on the other side. It does not make me unfaithful to them. Am I by this to be judged because of some personal animosity? There is no doubt but that you can expel me. I can go back to my constituents, and they will send me back. It will not injure my reputation among them. They have too much faith in me. They know, and I respect them for it, that I will do my duty under all circumstances.

Gentlemen, I have said all I deem necessary under the circumstances. You should not judge me by what a meeting in New Orleans says or does. I am not responsible to them—I am responsible to my constituency alone. They have deemed it wise and prudent to send me here. I intend to represent them to the best of my ability. Do not let personal motives or prejudices gainsay your better judgment, but give to the accused a fair and impartial hearing.

Mr. Davidson was not unseated.

After the organization was finally settled, the Hon. Carlton Hunt of New Orleans introduced the following resolution:

RESOLVED: That this Convention is of the opinion that Governor Warmoth is unworthy of the respect and confidence of the people, and that any political connection with him would be dishonorable and injurious to the best interests of Louisiana.

It is to be noted that the whole Hunt family later supported Grant; and Wm. H. Hunt, one of the family, was one of Kellogg's attorneys before Judge Durell.

Mr. Brigham of Morehouse Parish, on the motion to refer Mr. Hunt's resolution of condemnation of Governor Warmoth to the Committee on Resolutions, said:

I am sorry, Mr. Chairman, that this resolution has been offered before this Convention, as there can no possible good come of it, and there may be great harm. We have assembled as Democrats from all over the State to consider questions of vital importance to the whole people, and in every caucus and private discussion, and constantly before this Convention, the name of Governor Warmoth was thrust into prominence and made the leading and all-important matter of consideration. I do not attach so much importance to the individual in question as other gentlemen in this House do, to the extent that it must engage the entire time of the Convention, nor am I afraid of the great bugbear held up to constant gaze.

He said he thought the party had assembled in Convention to inaugurate measures of reform and invite recruits from all parties to help bear the Democratic banner on to victory, and correct extravagance, corruption and misrule; that to accomplish this we were trying to recruit our forces from all parties now opposed to us, and it made no difference to him from whence they came. He was sorry to see so many of the young Democracy, and particularly of this city, so full of bitter vituperation and denunciation. No good could possibly come of all this. Living in the atmosphere of the recent political excitements in New Orleans, they were red-hot in their extreme views, and had come into this Convention in a blaze of excitement, when the people and the times demanded cool and deliberate council. He had been called in his section an extremist, and it was true that after the "straitest sect of his religion" he had been a Democrat. But to gain strength to carry out the objects for which we cherish so holy a zeal, we must do nothing to expel men from us; must not ostracize this party or that party, this faction or the other, because they differ with us. The object of every true patriot was first to redeem the State, and then to draw nice party distinctions. He called on them to rescue their land and its oppressed people from the burdens which weighed us down as a mighty incubus, and then to make choice of their special political associates.

The resolution before the Convention should be referred to the Committee on Resolutions, for the reason that it was opening a grave question, and men could not in the heat of debate fully comprehend its compass and true import. In his mind it was ambiguous and loosely worded, and should be properly laid before a committee and pruned of its more objectionable features and reported for action, if the Convention must have an expression on what he thought was a matter injudiciously sprung upon the Convention.

He said that we had met not to condemn Warmoth or Grant, but to save the State of Louisiana, and if there were men in any of the factions who would aid us in that, he, for one, was ready to welcome them to our ranks—not to march in the lead with banner in hand, but to fall into the rear and push up the column to vote for the men we placed in the field as our standard-bearers. The resolution was well calculated to drive men off, not to conciliate them; to insure our defeat, not to help us to rout the enemy. The eyes of the entire people of the State were upon us, and the greatest anxiety was felt that we be not too harsh, too dictatorial or too unreasonable in our demands. If so, where was our strength to come from to redeem the State? The meeting of the Convention was a farce, and the efforts to be made in the approaching contest worse than negative, if we pursued this course.

Gentlemen who professed to be posted in the political affairs of this State seemed to overlook the fact that we had to rely to a very great extent upon a certain portion of our population in the country, now manipulated by the factions in power, for the support necessary to achieve a success. Was this the course to pursue in order to do this? He thought not. He hoped the resolution would go before a committee of able and discreet gentlemen, and be by them weighed and well considered. "Let us be calm and reasonable men, and act with common prudence and sagacity. We cannot afford to lose any who will and can come to us; let us not be guilty of that folly, no matter from what quarter they come; let us lead, and not be led. We can do it, if we will!"

This speaker was frequently applauded, and his remarks, happily delivered, were well received.

The Convention declared itself in favor of referring the resolution to the Committee on Resolutions, and this was done.

Mr. J. A. Fuqua offered the following resolution:

That it is inexpedient to nominate a State ticket at this time; that the Convention adjourn, to meet at a future day, and invite all men who are opposed to corruption, Federal and State, to meet and nominate a State and presidential ticket.

In support of this measure, Mr. Fuqua declared there should be another body in any event. Shame upon those who, expressing the fear that the members of the Convention would be corrupted *ad interim,* had lost all faith in Democratic virtue. Proper action in the present emergency could be taken only when the lights shed by the Philadelphia and the Cincinnati Conventions were before them. The prophecy of an overwhelming majority in the city for the young Democracy was like the snowball in the sun. Hasty action was pregnant with discord. Mr. Eustis opposed the postponement of nominations. The people had sent them hither to make nominations and put a ticket in the field.

Delays are dangerous. My friend who has just spoken cannot deny that a great many of the Democratic members of the Legislature were influenced by the promises of "that young man" who occupies the executive chair, and, as they know, were deceived. It is useless to deny he holds great power. Let us be guided by the National Convention. What does the State of New York propose to do? What does the State of Wisconsin propose to do? What does the State of Ohio propose to do? They propose, sir, to nominate a straight Democratic ticket and thus go out in the field. I have never voted any other ticket than the Democratic one, and never intend to. I have always been a Democrat, and shall always be while a Democratic party exists. (Cheers.)

J. B. Cotton followed in a long speech favoring the Hunt resolution and bitterly denouncing Governor Warmoth. He said he was in favor of making nominations for State officers at once, that he feared delay. He criticised the Boston Club, saying: "All these coalitions and combinations are being fixed up." He was asked: "How about Grant? Are you for Grant?" The Judge said he did not know what right they had to ask him that question, but, the inquiries being persisted in, he answered that he had always been a Democrat and never voted any other ticket. He continued to speak strongly against postponement of State nominations.

The Hon. Michael Ryan of Rapides Parish arose. He said:

"It was my understanding that the Convention in assembling from all parts of the State had agreed to unite and combine with all elements; throwing away no votes but taking all they could get. What in the name of God have we to do with Governor Warmoth or with his supporters? Let us bid good morrow to the devil himself in case we meet up with him."

Mr. E. H. McCaleb of Orleans, favored the resolution. He said:

"Charges have rung through the State that the Democratic party is going over to Warmoth, and I wish to vote on the question now. Denounce all men who have betrayed the State and the people. If the old banner is to go down, let it sink like the flag of the Alabama,

untarnished and leading the hosts in a fight we believe right. The
party has not fed at the public crib for years. Better that it should
never attain power again through such means." (A voice: *"How about
Grant?"*)

Mr. McCaleb said: "I want no coalition with either Grant
or Warmoth. Let us maintain Democratic principles."

Ex-Governor Hyams said that he strongly favored the resolution. "Avoid all coalitions; stand or fall upon principles."

Mr. McGloin of Orleans strongly favored the resolution.

Mr. Kernan opposed the Hunt resolution. His speech follows:

"I am not a humorous man but I will begin by telling a story. Hearing
that the parson was coming to the home, the boy went out in search of
game, and while he was setting a trap for a woodchuck the parson
came that way. 'You ought not to catch that woodchuck on a Sunday.' 'Ah,' said the boy, 'I'm obliged to catch him, 'cause the
parson's coming to our house and we are out o' meat!' Gentlemen,
the Democratic party is in that condition; we're out o' meat and Parson
Greeley is coming in November. But too many prejudices still stand
in the way of a Democratic success. Ah, gentlemen, are we not giving
way to our prejudices?

"The Democratic party has been fighting its forlorn battles since
General Lee surrendered his sword, and no matter how such a man may
love his party, he must have recognized the fact. I do not come here
to 'chaffer about men,' for it is nothing but the lack of men that has
produced defeat of the Democratic party for the past five years. The
Republican party being divided, victory is easy with the accessions from
other parties sure to come to it. We are fighting for the existence of
ourselves and our families. We must have allies. The party alone
cannot be successful. There is much opposition to Governor Warmoth
here. It has been said that there are portions of the party that will
bolt if he is taken up. Why he should be denounced I cannot say.
What has this convention to do with Warmoth? We have heard much
said against him, but he is also to be recommended for his good acts.
(A voice from the gallery: *'Name them!'*)

"Well, I will name them. When the Baton Rouge prisoners were
brought down here, from whom did they receive protection but from
Governor Warmoth? Besides, I well remember he would not send
militia up there, and in my Parish he has turned out bad officers and
put in good ones. I do not stand here favoring Governor Warmoth—

no man opposed him more bitterly than I did in this State; but I want to do him a simple act of justice, for I would not knowingly do any man an act of injustice.

"I am glad to see the Convention in such a good humor. It plainly shows that you intend to see justice done. I do not know anything criminal that Governor Warmoth has done, and I am too good a lawyer, if not too old a one, to make a charge which I cannot prove."

A Hibernian voice from the gallery rang out: "I want to save Louisiana—I am willing to cohabit with the Devil—I am willing to cohabit with the Republican party—I am willing to cohabit with the naygur, but I am d—d if I will cohabit with Governor Warmoth!" (Laughter and cheers.)

A long wrangle followed.

The adoption of the resolution condemning Governor Warmoth and for immediate nominations of a State ticket was supported vigorously by Messrs. Carlton Hunt, T. G. Hunt, James B. Eustis, J. B. Cotton, H. D. Ogden, Albert Voorhies, E. H. McCaleb, B. F. Jonas, ex-Governor Hyams, and all city delegates; while Messrs. Brigham of Morehouse Parish, Ryan, Judge Manning, Texada of Rapides, ex-Attorney-General Herron, J. O. Fuqua of East Baton Rouge, Reese of Tensas, Kernan of East Feliciana, J. M. Sandidge, Judge Young of Claiborne, E. J. Ellis of Tangipahoe, Lott of Carroll, Levy of Natchitoches, all spoke strongly for a coalition with all elements opposed to Grant and Kellogg and against immediate nomination of a State ticket.

In the last hour of the last session of the last day the hot, weary and disgusted delegates adopted a resolution denouncing Governor Warmoth and General Grant. On the motion to adopt a substitute the Hon. E. John Ellis took the floor and condemned Grant for his nepotism and tyranny. He said that "all of the evils coming from Governor Warmoth were due to the agency of General Grant. Unless the stream is purified at the source, it is useless to purify it at the bottom. All the evils that have afflicted Louisiana had flowed from Washington sources of Reconstruction."

The Convention then adjourned to the third day of June, inviting all persons and all elements opposed to State and National corruption to join in an effort to save the State.

The Democratic Convention met again on the 3rd of June and was in session for over six days and nights. It was as obdurate and stubborn as it had been in April. It refused all propositions for union or coalition that did not give the Democratic organization the control of the State. It was still hopeful that the Democratic National Convention would repudiate the Greeley and Brown ticket. The Liberal Republican Committee and the Liberal German Committee made an appeal to the Democratic Convention to unite in a general movement for a State and electoral ticket, as the following will show:

> Headquarters of the Liberal Republican
> State Central Committee of Louisiana,
> New Orleans, June 6, 1872.

To the Conference Committees of the Democratic and Reform Conventions.

Gentlemen:

We have the honor to submit a proposition agreed upon by the conference committee of the Liberal Republican Executive Committee. We submit it as the deliberate opinion of the committee that it is the only solution of the difficulty in the way of an honorable coalition. Hoping that it may commend itself to your approval, we have the honor to be very respectfully, your fellow-citizens and obedient servants.

> (*Signed*)   E. NORTH CULLOM
> Chairman of joint committee of conference,
> Liberal Republican party of Louisiana

> (*Inclosure*)
> Committee Room, New Orleans,
> June 8, 1872.

In order to effect a thorough and efficient combination of all parties in this State having National and State reform for their object, the following arrangement is proposed by the representatives of the Liberal Republican party:

1. The Democratic and Reform conventions to approve and accept the platform of principles adopted at Cincinnati on May 4, 1872, by the Liberal Republican Convention.

2. The delegates chosen by the Democratic State Convention, now in session, to represent Louisiana in the National Democratic Convention to be held at Baltimore on the ninth of July next, to be instructed to vote to accept the plaform of the Cincinnati convention, and to indorse and ratify the nomination of Greeley and Brown.

3. Inasmuch as it is necessary to adopt a State ticket on which Democrats, Reformers and Liberal Republicans can unite, it is agreed that each of the three organizations shall name ten persons to constitute an executive committee, which shall be authorized to call a Liberal Reform convention, to meet at some future day, to nominate a State, Congressional and Electoral ticket.

4. It being absolutely necessary that harmony of action be assured in order to accomplish the purposes of this arrangement, that national reform may be forwarded and State reform guaranteed, it is further agreed that the conventions shall respectively adopt the following resolution:

RESOLVED: That we accept and pledge ourselves to support, in good faith, the State and Congressional tickets to be nominated by the Convention to assemble in accordance with the above resolution.

Respectfully submitted by

E. NORTH CULLOM
J. M. DIRRHAMMER
JOHN B. ROBERTSON
JAMES LONGSTREET

Liberal Republican State Committee.

DANIEL W. ADAMS
P. O. HEBERT
THOMAS A. HARRIS
D. B. PENN
JACK WHARTON
E. D. RARESHIDE

Executive Committee of Greeley and Brown ratification meeting held at St. Charles Theatre.

J. HASSINGER
WILLIAM P. GERRARD
GEORGE FOERSTER
LOUIS SCHWATZ
GEORGE STROMEYER

Of the Liberal German Republican Committee.

STORMY DAYS IN LOUISIANA

Parlor O, St. Charles Hotel, New Orleans,
June 6, 1872.

E. North Cullom, Chairman of the Joint Committee of Conference
Liberal Republican Party of Louisiana.

Sir:

We have the honor to inclose the accompanying resolution of the conference committee of the Democratic and Reform Conventions, together with the grounds of their action. We note with regret that it is "the deliberate opinion of your committee that your proposition is the only solution of the difficulty in the way of an honorable coalition," as the door is thus closed by your own action to further consideration of the subject. Respectfully, your obedient servants,

(*Signed*)   J. D. HILL
Chairman Reform Conference Committee.

(*Signed*)   E. JONES MCCALL
Chairman Democratic Conference Committee.

Room of the Joint Committees of Conference
of the Reform and Democratic Parties.

RESOLVED, That the proposition made by the committee of the Liberal Republican party be rejected,

1. Because the Reform party, being organized and existing for State purposes only, cannot entertain questions affecting National policies.

2. Because the committee of conference of the Democratic Party has not been intrusted with powers to pronounce on any subject affecting National politics.

3. Because the adoption of the proposition would involve the virtual abandonment of the Democratic and Reform parties; and the Conventions of both these parties in adopting the report, and the resolutions of the joint committees of conference under which these joint committees were created, expressly declared that neither party would relinquish its separate organization.

(*Signed*)   B. R. FORMAN
Secretary.

We had at this time in Louisiana four distinct political party organizations. There was first the extreme, aggressive, violent, and relentless Last-Ditch Democratic party led by James B. Eustis, B. F. Jonas, Albert Voorhies, George W. McCranie of *The Ouachita Telegraph,* J. H. Cosgrove of *The Natchitoches*

Vindicator, H. J. Hearsey of *The Shreveport Times,* and Daniel Dennett of *The St. Mary Banner,* all of which newspapers had advocated violence; had palliated or excused, if not justified, murder and assassination, and the extermination of the colored population, and most especially all of the white men who had in any manner affiliated politically with the negro population.

Then there was the Reform party, composed mainly of Democrats who had broken away from the leadership of the extremists; it was led by G. T. Beauregard, James I. Day, I. N. Marks, August Bohn, Charles H. Thompson, George Williamson, W. M. Randolph, and others who eschewed national politics.

Then there was the Radical Custom House or Grant Republican party, led by U. S. Marshal Packard, Collector Casey, U. S. Senator Kellogg, Postmaster P. W. Lowell, C. C. Antoine, J. H. Ingraham, all of whom held Federal offices.

Finally there was the vigorous Republican party organization, of which Senator Hugh J. Campbell was the leader, and with which Lieutenant-Governor Pinchback and the masses of the colored people affiliated. I had up to the beginning of the Liberal Republican movement been associated with this organization and had its cordial support.

Mr. Pinchback, the Lieutenant-Governor and admittedly the leader of the colored race in Louisiana at this time, was most bitter and outspoken against the Grant-Custom House faction. He had been subjected to every outrage and humiliation by these Federal officials, and he had joined with me in a letter to President Grant demanding, for the reasons stated, that the President should remove his brother-in-law (Collector Casey), U. S. Marshal Packard, and certain other Federal officials who had joined them, and the Democratic politicians of the city of New Orleans in their violent and revolutionary proceedings to annul his (Pinchback's) election by the Senate to fill the vacancy of Lieutenant-Governor made by the death of Oscar J. Dunn.

In one of his speeches he said that he had always loved General Grant and had always supported him, "but if he found that

General Grant sustained these Federal officials in their outrageous treatment of him and his fellow-citizens, he would leave that stand as his deadliest enemy."

Governor Pinchback at the time of the inauguration of the Liberal Republican movement was in close touch with and followed the leadership and advice of Senator Sumner of Massachusetts, and he was in entire accord with me in taking a delegation of our friends to the Cincinnati Convention. Only a decent regard for the situation would have brought this powerful leader and his element to our support. But the Last-Ditch Democrats denounced the Conservatives and colored people who joined in the Liberal movement as "Warmoth's hirelings." They said that Horace Greeley had favored everything against the South, and that B. Gratz Brown was the son of old John Brown of Ossowatamie, and that the Cincinnati Convention closed its session by singing "John Brown's Body."

The New Orleans Bee declared editorially that overtures had been made by Collector Casey to the Last-Ditch Democrats to give them the control of the State if they would let Grant have the electoral vote. It is certain that Eustis, Jonas, Voorhies, the Hunts, Cotton, and others looked upon the scheme most favorably.

But the New Orleans city delegates, with some other extreme Last-Ditch Democrats from the country parishes, constituted a majority of the Convention, and after wrangling for six hot days and nights in June, they were finally able to force the nomination of the following State ticket, but they neglected to indorse Greeley and Brown. A considerable number of the country delegates withdrew from the Convention before the balloting began.

For Governor	John McEnery of Ouachita
For Lieutenant-Governor . .	B. F. Jonas of Orleans
For Auditor	Daniel Dennett of St. Mary
For Att'y General	H. N. Ogden of Orleans
For Supt. of Education . . .	R. M. Lusher of Orleans
For Congressman-at-Large . .	James B. Eustis of Orleans

It will be observed that out of the six candidates on the State ticket four of them came from the city of New Orleans.

But the assembling of the Liberal Convention on August 5 amazed these Last-Ditch Democratic leaders. Five hundred of the best and most distinguished men in the State came as delegates to the Liberal Convention, among them being many of the gentlemen who had participated in the April and the June Conventions.*

Every parish in the State (except Calcasieu, Cameron, Caldwell, Jackson, Lafayette, Union and Washington, seven in all) and every ward in the city was represented by a large delegation.

The Convention met at twelve o'clock at the Academy of Music; the galleries were crowded with spectators who cheered the delegations from each parish as they entered and took their seats.

The decorations were most artistic and effective and indicated both taste and judgment on the part of the committee.

In the rear of the stage was placed a representation of the Arms of Louisiana, the pelican upon a pedestal of Italian marble. The latter bears the inscription: "Union of the People for the People's Good. Confidence in the Constitution and the Laws. Justice to all Races, Creeds, and Political Opinions."

Facing the delegates from the farther corner of the right and left proscenium boxes respectively were the life-sized profile pictures of Horace Greeley and B. Gratz Brown.

The flies were enveloped in American flags, a large ensign in the center and smaller ones at the sides. The second circle was further ornamented by groups of American flags. To the right was placed a quotation:

Liberal Republican Party

Its hold upon the popular heart is the miracle of the day. It would seem as though the tranquil masses from whom safety ever comes were

* See Appendix J for list of delegates.

aroused by some impending peril to the nation, and were intent upon effecting a deliverance regardless of any forms or of customs following.

(*Signed*)   B. GRATZ BROWN.

In the center was placed the following:

For thirty years I have battled for the liberation of the slaves, but never did it occur to me that I should be called upon to assist in the liberation of the masters.

(*Signed*)   HORACE GREELEY.

Colonel D. B. Penn called the Convention to order in the following remarks:

"It is my pleasant duty to welcome and address the delegates to this Convention called by the Joint Committees of the Liberal Republican Party.

"It is a matter of congratulation to see that the people of Louisiana have at length aroused themselves from the political lethargy that has been existing, and have responded to that call of the great Liberal Republican Party which will be the salvation of the State and the whole nation, by their enthusiastic support of Greeley and Brown. I see around me many familiar faces, gentlemen who were never in any political organizations in the State before, and I also see gentlemen who were representing many other political organizations in the State, blended together in this great movement, and to raise their voices against the corruption and despotism of the past few years, rejecting all party affiliations and combining into one great party which will give back this great State to its people.

"If the Cincinnati platform has taught me anything it is this: the importance of uniting all of the conservative elements of the State against Grant."

Colonel Penn concluded his remarks by nominating General Andrew S. Herron of East Baton Rouge as temporary President, and invited General Allen Thomas and General B. B. Sims to escort the gentleman to the chair.

General Herron said:

"Gentlemen of the Convention, I thank you heartily for the honor conferred upon me in calling me to preside even only temporarily over

[181]

your preliminary proceedings, and I feel that the duty will be an easy one, for I feel that for the brief period that I shall preside over your deliberations, from the character of the men I see here as delegates, representatives of the best elements of the people all over the country, there will be found a co-operative agency to preserve order and decorum that will relieve the Chair of most of its trouble and responsibility.

"The common sense of the people all through the country forced them to the conclusion that this condition of affairs should not exist any longer. If we have to live together it must be as brothers and sisters, as it has been. We must bury the past with all its animosities and bitterness; bury all the hostile feelings that one section of the country entertained against the other. We must put all of these things behind us; we must forget the prejudices and passions of the past; in the words of Horace Greeley, 'We must shake hands across the bloody chasm, and become once more co-equal members of this great Union.' That is the only policy that can ever restore the country to peace and true prosperity; the only means of blotting out forever those hostile feelings which have been so long cherished, and which, if kept up, will bring about the dissolution of that Union, for the perpetuity of which men who have fought and shed their blood were willing to make such great sacrifices. A great movement has been started in Cincinnati, and it is to consummate the work begun there, to carry it out and complete it, that we have met here today. In that same spirit of harmony and conciliation which has actuated the invitation of this return to fraternal relations all over the country, we meet here today men who have belonged, as the President of the Central Committee has just stated, to political parties of all shades and political opinions. We should, therefore, in the very beginning of our deliberations, ascend to an elevated standpoint, lifted far above the clouds of petty prejudices and passions, a standpoint from which we shall survey clearly the whole field around us, whence we can behold all those elements that can be united in one common mass for the purpose of resisting the aggressions of our common enemy. We must recognize, as thinking men, that the only hope we have in this conflict is to carry out the program which has been initiated, to unite on a common platform and for a common purpose all the elements of opposition to extreme Radicalism. Without it we fail; with it we have the assurance of a most glorious victory—not merely a petty partisan victory, not merely one of those victories which parties crow and halloo over, not merely to put one man out of place and to put another man in, but a victory that will result in the salvation of the State, in the benefit and good of the people all through the country, and the return of that era of fraternal feeling for which we have so long prayed." (*Great applause.*)

Major Andrew Hero, Jr. was nominated temporary secretary. The usual committee on credentials was appointed and the Convention adjourned until 2 P.M.

On reassembling, the Committee on Credentials asked for further time. During this delay eloquent speeches were made by Judge Cullom, General Thomas A. Harris and others, at the conclusion of which the Committee on Credentials made its report.*

The report was unanimously adopted.

Major E. A. Burke of Orleans then nominated the Hon. W. W. Pugh, of Assumption, as Permanent President of the Convention.

The Hon. T. C. Manning, of Rapides Parish (afterwards Chief Justice of the Supreme Court of the State), was nominated but declined.

On motion of Judge Manning, the Hon. W. W. Pugh was unanimously elected as Permanent President of the Convention with great applause. On taking the Chair, Mr. Pugh said:

"Gentlemen of the Convention: When I look around upon the well-known faces in this house, I feel that there is life in the old land yet. It is encouraging in these times of oppression to see so many of my old friends assembled, who have come here with the honest intention of taking this State from the slough of despond in which it has been plunged. (*Applause.*) The same object urges us all to come forward to carry on the good work. It is nothing but right that I should say one word personal to myself. As I have been a member of the other Convention, some of my opponents have objected to my being here at this time. I will state that although a party man for the last thirty or forty years, and in the habit of following strictly the lines laid down, on this occasion I found it necessary to depart from that course, and to come here and assist my friends in doing what we could for what we all have at heart—the good of the State. (*Applause.*)

"A great revolution is at hand. The scientist who prophesied the coming of a great tidal wave which was to engulf us and destroy our

* See Appendix K.

planet was mistaken as to the element which was to work such great changes among us. This element is the revolution in the opinions and politics of the masses of our countrymen, a tidal wave which affects the minds of men, and not the material objects of earth; a wave which leaves destruction in its onward career, but, like the electric fluid which oft pervades the atmosphere of our sunny clime, has served to purify and liberalize the minds of our people. This awakening, this arousing of the public mind to that which is pure and noble, was reduced to a tangible shape in Cincinnati, and culminated in a bright and glorious reality in Baltimore.

"The grand old Democratic party, whose foundation was based on the principles bequeathed to us by Jefferson, one of Virginia's great statesmen, could show no greater reverence to its antecedents, pay no greater compliment to its past triumphs, than by the furling of its proud banner on such an occasion to secure the peace, happiness and prosperity of our common country.

"In the time to come it will be a source of heartfelt pride that we acted with a party which had not only the moral courage and magnanimity to ignore the bitterness and prejudices of the past, but to extend the hand of good fellowship to those who have reviled and oppressed us, make their cause our cause, and unite in a common effort to elect Greeley and Brown, in order to arrest the corruption which is gradually but surely undermining the great and substantial fabric bequeathed us by our forefathers.

"The example of our friends in Baltimore must not be ignored; it is too pregnant with great results at this time. For years to come no more fitting time than the present could present itself for the baptism of the Liberal Republican party, which is destined hereafter to be a power in the land, and if properly and tenderly nursed, to exercise an influence for good and pure government which is essential for the preservation of our institutions and the avoidance of the doctrine of centralization, whose spread already begins to exercise a baneful effect.

"We are happy in having such sponsors for the new party as Horace Greeley and B. Gratz Brown. With their nomination an era of prosperity begins to dawn upon us, and the rainbow of promise makes our hearts glad, and pushes away those dark clouds which have so long hung like a pall on our beloved State. The future prosperity of Louisiana rests with us; by the selection of honest and intelligent men as our standard-bearers in the coming canvass, we shall most assuredly triumph, and make a new departure towards securing that prosperity and happiness to which our people have been so long strangers.

"Gentlemen, we have come here for the same purpose, and I hope that this Convention will be influenced by a spirit of harmony and good feeling, in order that we may unite all the parties opposed to the Custom House ticket and Grant, and secure the triumph of our own ticket. (*Applause.*)

"Everything rests with us. If we select a good ticket, our triumph is secure. We will see the whole country swept as it was in 1840 in the Harrison campaign. If we pursue the proper course there is no doubt of our success.

"In conclusion, allow me to thank you for the honor you have conferred upon me. I have presided at several Conventions, but I recollect none in which I have experienced more pleasure; and I hope, with your assistance, to carry on our proceedings with order, facility and pleasure."

Major Andrew Hero, Jr., of New Orleans, was then elected Permanent Secretary by acclamation.

Mr. Leonard, of Caddo, offered the following:

Resolved, that a Committee of Conference composed of fifteen—three to be elected by the delegates from each Congressional District—be chosen with instructions and authority:

1. To call upon and confer with the Democratic Central Executive Committee; and meet the Executive or any other committee of the Republican organization presided over by H. J. Campbell, with a view to bringing about a fusion of all elements opposed to Grant and Kellogg.

2. To exhaust all reasonable means to effect a union of all these organizations and the formation of a ticket—State, Electoral and Congressional—acceptable to all the united parties.

3. Resolved further, that the committee so appointed report in writing as early as practicable, in order that their action may be ratified or rejected by the Convention.

Mr. Burke offered an amendment: "that the committee have no authority to close or make terms touching a coalition or fusion, without further vested power from the Convention." The amendment was adopted.

Later, the President was authorized to appoint the Committee, which he agreed to do on the recommendation of names by the delegates from each Congressional District. Adjourned to 10 A.M. next day.

The Committee of Conferences

First District
Effingham Lawrence, Plaquemines
Thomas G. Davidson, Livingston
Patrick Swan, 7th Ward, Orleans

Second District
E. A. Burke, 2d Ward, Orleans
Louis Bush, Lafourche
R. L. Preston, 12th Ward, Orleans

Third District
Joseph A. Breaux, Iberia
Thomas J. Foster, St. Mary
E. W. Robinson, East Baton Rouge

Fourth District
Louis Texada, Rapides
A. H. Leonard, Caddo
J. P. Harris, Point Coupee

Fifth District
J. C. Eagan, Claiborne Parish
W. W. Farmer, Ouachita
J. M. Gillespie, Tensas

At the Session of August 7, J. Sella Martin, a colored man, addressed the Convention pledging the co-operation of the colored people in the movement, and denouncing Kellogg, Packard and Antoine. He said he spoke for Lieutenant-Governor Pinchback and pledged his co-operation.

Louis Bush was selected Chairman of the Liberal Committee on Conference.

I addressed the following letter to my friend, the Hon. Effingham Lawrence:

August 6, 1872.

Hon. Effingham Lawrence.
My dear friend:
I ask you to say to Mr. Bush, the Chairman, and to your Conference Committee of Fifteen, that I would esteem it to be the greatest honor

of my life to receive the nomination of your splendid Convention for the office of Governor of this State, which you and others assure me that it is the disposition of a large majority of the delegates to give me. But I am convinced that your Committee can never get the Democratic party organization to agree with you on my nomination, and we shall need every vote to carry this State.

Ex-Governor Voorhies, James B. Eustis, Benjamin F. Jonas, and Frank Zachary, who absolutely control the Democratic party organization, all of whom were but six months ago in a close combination with the Custom House crowd, led by Collector Jas. F. Casey, President Grant's brother-in-law, United States Marshal Packard, Postmaster Lowell, United States Senator W. P. Kellogg, and the negro State Senators, C. C. Antoine, J. H. Ingraham, and Representative J. Henri Burch, in their violent and revolting attempt to overthrow me, and who have worked so hard to make me odious with their following, will never consent to accept my nomination by your Convention, or support me if nominated.

So I request your Conference Committee to withdraw my name from consideration as a candidate for Governor or for any other office.

If you can induce the Democratic Conference Committee to accept Colonel D. B. Penn as the fusion candidate for Governor and can put Lieutenant-Governor P. B. S. Pinchback on the ticket as our candidate for Congressman-at-Large, we will carry the State by 30,000 majority. Governor Pinchback tells me that he will accept this nomination on our ticket.

Yours very truly,

H. C. WARMOTH.

After several days and nights were consumed in conferences of the Liberal Republican Committee, the Democratic, the Reform, and the Campbell Republican Committees, Chairman Bush of the Liberal Committee was finally obliged to make the following report to the Convention:

New Orleans,
August 9, 1872.

Honorable W. W. Pugh,
President Liberal Republican Convention.
Sir:

The Conference Committee have the honor to report that, obeying the letter and spirit of your instructions immediately after the organi-

[187]

zation of the committee, the respective parties designated in your resolution were respectfully invited to meet us in conference as early as
practicable.

The different organizations responded by accepting our invitations,
and conferences were begun at 2 P.M. August 6th and were almost
continuous up to 2 A.M. of this instant.

The result of our labors briefly told is this: We endeavored earnestly
and honestly to conciliate and harmonize with the Democratic and
Reform parties and the Regular Republican party presided over by the
Hon. H. J. Campbell, and failed.

We presented a basis upon which in our judgment all parties could
reasonably and honorably combine, but we regret to state that our
propositions were declined by all parties.

We felt we were not authorized to vary materially this basis, and
therefore declined the Committee's propositions submitted to us at a
late hour last night.

We received from the Committee of the Regular Republican party
a communication enunciating, as we understood it, merely the opinion
of the Committee, and not distinct propositions. We, therefore, refer
their communication to the Convention.

In that communication the following suggestions are made:

That in the opinion of the Committee of the Regular Republican
Party, the following propositions could be adopted by the Ninth August
Convention of the Republican party, and said Committee agreed to
advocate the same.

That the Governor shall be some known Republican who has been
identified with the Republican party. That the Secretary of State shall
be a colored Republican. That the Congressman-at-Large shall be a
colored Republican. The Superintendent of Education shall be a Republican. That for the Second and Third Congressional Districts, Republicans shall be nominated. And finally that for the places conceded on
the ticket to the Republican party the names shall be dictated by them,
and that the whole ticket shall be nominated by both Conventions.

We announced distinctly at the outset to the Committees of the
Democratic and Reform parties that we were authorized to state that
the name of H. C. Warmoth would not be placed in nomination for
Governor in the event of these parties combining with the Liberal party.

The propositions last made by those Committees (the Democratic
and Reform Committees) to us are substantially as follows:

The names of John McEnery for Governor, B. F. Jonas for Lieutenant-Governor, and H. N. Ogden for Attorney-General, shall be retained as the nominees of the combined parties.

That the electoral ticket presented by said parties be withdrawn and that the Liberal Convention make all nominations except those above indicated.

At 2 this morning, we notified the Committees of the Democratic and Reform parties that any further communication they desire to make would be presented by us to the Convention.

It is simply impossible to prepare in the limited time allowed us an elaborate report. We therefore call your attention to the fact that the minutes of our proceedings contained full and explicit details.

In conclusion we desire to state that while we recognize, with regret, the fact that the people are seemingly widely separated in political opinion, we are nevertheless profoundly and unhesitatingly impressed with the conviction that through the Liberal Republican party alone can Louisiana be politically regenerated and redeemed.

(*Signed*)   LOUIS BUSH, Chairman
E. LAWRENCE
THOMAS J. FOSTER
ROBERT L. PRESTON
JOSEPH A. BREAUX
JAMES M. GILLESPIE
THOMAS GREEN DAVIDSON
J. PICKNEY HARRIS
A. H. LEONARD
LOUIS TEXADA
E. A. BURKE
E. W. ROBERTSON

A minority report was made in which it was recommended to accept the Democratic and Reform Parties' proposition, signed by W. W. Famer, J. C. Eagan, and Pat Swan.

Mr. Louis Texada said: "I stand here to show you that the idea of liberality as conveyed in the minority report is simply a myth." (*Loud cheering* from the body of the Convention and from the gallery.)

Pending the consideration of the Majority and the Minority Reports, the Convention took a recess until 2 P.M. On reassembling, great cries were made for Governor Warmoth to address the Convention, whereupon he was brought to the front of the stage, and delivered the following address:

"Mr. President, Gentlemen of the Liberal Republican Convention, and Fellow-Citizens:

"I thank you most sincerely from the very bottom of my heart for this grand reception at your hands. (*Great cheering and applause.*)

"Good people reading the speeches of eminent partisans supporting General Grant and what is known here as the Custom House Republican Party, together with those of their late co-adjutors and allies in the 'Last-Ditch Democracy,' and the editorials in the extreme opposition press, notably *The New Orleans Picayune, The Bee,* and the Custom House organ, *The National Republican,* will be amazed that this grand Convention should accord me such a splendid reception as you have given me today. (*Great applause.*)

"When I look into the faces of the five hundred members of this Convention, and see such men as Thomas C. Manning, Louis Texada, Andrew S. Herron, Thomas Bynum, W. W. Pugh, Taylor Beattie, Lewis Bush, Effingham Lawrence, D. B. Penn, Allen Thomas, Henry McCall, Bernard Lehman, S. M. Thomas, Samuel Armistead, A. H. Leonard, Joseph H. Breaux, A. W. Crandall, T. J. Shaffer, J. M. Gillespie, C. C. Cordill, J. C. Kernan, Chas. Provosty, J. C. Wise, E. A. Burke, and John Fitzpatrick—when I see a Convention composed of one hundred and twenty-five allotted delegates, but with every Parish sending from ten to thirty gentlemen of the highest standing to represent them, I find that my work has not been in vain. It is the proudest day of my life. (*Great applause.*)

"Fellow-citizens, I doubt if any man in this State has ever had more newspaper attention than I have had in the past four years. I have been accused of about every crime known to our code, and why I am not in the State Penitentiary instead of being welcomed by over five hundred of the grandest men of the State, our enemies will have to explain.

"Fellow-citizens, this is a land with a very warm climate, and we are given to the use of very warm language when we discuss any question. We are fond of adjectives, and when we talk of officials and politicians who stand in our way, we are inclined to seek out the very strongest words in the dictionary.

STORMY DAYS IN LOUISIANA

"I have been called a *Carpetbagger*, a *Czar*, a *Cæsar*, a *Dives*, a *Political Leper*, the *Pest in the Executive Chair*, a *Traitor to my Political Party*, a *Robber of the State*, and an *Oppressor of the People.*

"I have been accused of having made a fortune out of the office of Governor. They charge that I came to Louisiana a penniless Carpetbagger and that 'it is now said and believed that I am the possessor of a fortune of from half a million to three millions,' and some of them even charge me with having five million dollars, although when placed on the witness stand and under oath, Mr. Packard had to say that he had no facts to sustain his charges, but that *it is stated in the newspapers,* and that *he believed it.*

"There has been no limit to their language, their adjectives, or their lies.

"Because I have been most liberal in aiding the building of railroads and canals; because I have tried to restore our hundreds of miles of broken levees; because I have favored laws that protect all of our people in their citizenship; because I have sought to make the best people of the State my friends; because I have appointed General James Longstreet my Adjutant-General, and Penn Mason, late member of General Lee's staff, and Miller Owen, and Frank Paragaud, Major-Generals, and organized twenty-five hundred young Rebels into the State Militia; because I have appointed General Jeff Thompson my State Engineer, and such competent and friendly old citizens as Egan, and Watkins, and Lewis, and Beattie, and King, Judges of our District Courts; and because I associate with white men of conspicuous social standing like Dr. W. Newton Mercer, General Richard Taylor, Duncan F. Kenner, Thomas J. Semmes, Alexander Walker, and Christian Roselious—the leaders of the Dunn, Kellogg, Antoine, Packard, Burch, Casey, and Custom House Republican faction denounce me as a traitor to the negro race, who they say comprise 84,000 of the 90,000 voters in the Republican party.

"Because I would not let this Custom House faction, acting with James B. Eustis, Frank B. Jonas, H. D. Ogden, and Lieutenant-Governor Voorhies of the Democratic State Committee, put a Deputy Collector of the Custom House, an appointee of Collector Casey, in the place of the lamented Lieutenant-Governor Oscar J. Dunn, with a signed and sealed agreement that George W. Carter, J. Henri Burch, C. C. Antoine, and their House of Representatives should impeach me before the State Senate, and put this Custom House Deputy Collector into the office of the Governor of the State, and to hold me up by the eyelids till my term of office should expire, I have been accused of being a trickster, a briber, and a despot. (*Great applause.*)

"Gentlemen of the Convention, I have been the Governor of your State for nearly four years. I went into office against the wishes of a faction of so-called Republicans led by three San Domingo negroes who published a daily newspaper called *The New Orleans Tribune,* who sought to put a negro at the head of the State Government in 1868. I was able to beat their negro candidate for the nomination for Governor by a majority of two votes only; and though they with their friends bolted my ticket, and ran in opposition, I was able to beat them by a 22,000 majority at the election.

"I have had the strenuous, aggressive, and violent opposition of the Last-Ditch Democratic Organization, which declared that this is a 'White Man's Government,' and that 'no negro should ever vote or hold any office in this State.'

"With these aggressive and bitter factions fighting me without let-up or compromise from the beginning of my administration, resorting to the most violent and vindictive and unscrupulous methods, I have had all of the details of the administration of the laws of this great State of Louisiana to administer. My every official act was suspected, criticized and often condemned. It was enough to know that it was my act to have it meet with fierce opposition. It was charged that I controlled the Legislature, that no law I favored failed to pass, and that every law I opposed was defeated. I was held responsible for every act of the Legislative, the Executive, and the Judicial Departments of the Government. (*Applause.*) I was in a most trying position. I had an appalling responsibility. (*Cheers.*)

"I was working to get two peoples of different races, two peoples, one possessing the education, and property of the Commonwealth, to consent to live on equal political terms with a race equal in numbers but having been the slaves of the other, and freed by a gigantic Civil War; the one shocked, humbled, and outraged beyond description, the other supported by a victorious army, and not without arrogance and aggression; to get these to acquiesce in, agree to, and consent to accept, the awful, stupendous changes in political and social conditions.

"Is it a pretty picture? Would any of the great men of this Convention have liked to go through that ordeal? Could you have stood having Louisiana, the land of your birth, made a San Domingo—

made a Haiti, made a Liberia, made an Africa? (*Tremendous applause.*)

"That is what *The New Orleans Tribune* with its San Domingo editors and its Grant supporters wanted to do.

"That is what S. B. Packard, Oscar J. Dunn, W. P. Kellogg, Cæsar C. Antoine, J. Henri Burch, and George W. Carter would have brought about but for my standing up for a fair, free, equal, and just regard for the rights of all races and all classes of our people. (*Great applause and cheers.*)

"While I had the support of President Grant—and I did have it at one time—I was able to stand all criticisms and fault-findings, but when the exigencies of politics and the demand for votes for a Presidential renomination became such that he surrendered to these extreme radical elements in this State, and when the extreme 'Last-Ditch Democrats' like Eustis, Ogden, Jonas, Voorhies, and Zachary united with Packard, Kellogg, Casey, Antoine, Ingraham, and Carter, I was forced to stand up and fight for the people; and I am proud to stand here before this splendid Convention and this vast audience and to find that you are ready to stand up and fight with me for all of the people without regard to race, color, or condition. (*Great applause.*)

"I regard the coming together of this great Convention and this grand reception you have given me today as a complete vindication of my course, and as proof that you do not believe the lies of my enemies, that you approve of the work I have done to reconcile the very serious racial and political divisions that have beset our people. (*Great applause.*)

"Fellow-citizens, I want you to know that I am heart and soul with you in this great movement. I took a hundred and twenty-five delegates, one-third of them colored men, to the Liberal Republican Convention at Cincinnati last May, when we nominated dear old Horace Greeley as our candidate for President, and Governor B. Gratz Brown, of Missouri, for Vice-President. I have been working for months to bring about this great movement, and it is the proudest day of my life to look into your eyes and to hear your plaudits at what I am saying to you today. (*Great applause.*)

"Gentlemen of the Cenvention, I know that you have been criticized and denounced by the party leaders and the press of the two old political Parties as being the tools of Governor Warmoth, and that you are here to do my bidding. *The New Orleans Picayune* only two days ago, speaking of this Convention and me, said:

" 'He offers us his protection! Hee-hee! Yes, such protection as vultures give to lambs, covering and devouring them. The worst of all this man's crimes is, he has demoralized and corrupted too many of our people. He holds greater personal power in Louisiana than any monarch in Europe does in his dominions, and exercises it solely to promote his own personal ambitions.

" 'He is as false as he is deceitful; he is devoid of honor and principle. The Czar of Russia would not dare to exercise the same despotic sway over his people that this detested young man does over the people of Louisiana.'

"This is pretty strong language for a great newspaper having the slightest regard for decency or for truth. I am here to tell you, what the editor of the *Picayune* has known for days, that this Convention can do nothing for me. I am not a candidate for any office, and would not accept a nomination for any office at your hands. I can help the cause better by being free to speak, and to write, work for the ticket you shall name, and I pledge you my honest support. (*Great applause and cheers.*) I want you to win. (*Great applause.*)

"I ask this Convention to nominate a ticket that will command the respect and support of all of the white people in this State, and one that at the same time will command the confidence and support of all of the colored people, one that will be a covenant between them and you, that the colored people shall never be deprived of their civil and political rights. (*Great applause.*) That you will show to them that you will not look at the color of a man, but that in future you will only look to his character, his honesty and ability, making all men free and equal, in fact, guaranteeing every citizen every chance in life.

"If I can get the white people of our State and the black people of our State to lay aside their fears, their suspicions, and their prejudices, and come together and act together for the good of all the people, I believe I will have accomplished the greatest good and the grandest achievement of my life.

"I wish you, Fellow-citizens, every success, and I promise to be with you always and to the end."

A tremendous demonstration followed, the Convention rising and cheering.

The following is an editorial appearing in *The New Orleans Times* on Saturday, August 10th, 1872:

So the Convention, which *The Picayune* has been telling us all the time was controlled by Warmoth, and was convened for the express purpose of nominating him, has not nominated him, but, on the contrary, has nominated Colonel Penn. . . .

Seldom has there been witnessed in this State a spectacle so remarkable as the enthusiastic reception accorded to Governor Warmoth yesterday by the Liberal Convention and the multitude of auditors who crowded the galleries of the Academy. It would have been strange, indeed, if, after his entire withdrawal as a candidate, his frank declaration that all his influence and his abilities were at the service of the Liberal Party, whilst he asked no honors and no rewards at its hands, he had not deeply impressed his audience; but the tumultuous applause bestowed upon him showed deeper feeling than mere gratitude for promised services. It indicated that the public mind is at least prepared to be just as well as magnanimous, and that it is fatigued with the perpetual iteration of charges which are unproven, and denunciations which may be unmerited. It showed that the public are anxious to have the assistance of Governor Warmoth in the great contest which they have inaugurated, and will prove grateful for such services. A Convention of the five hundred delegates, embracing a large number of the most eminent men in the State—men of high intelligence and known integrity—would not have welcomed him with enthusiastic applause, if they did not feel that he was sincere; if they did not place implicit reliance on his pledges, and welcome him as an able ally in the grand scheme of National and State Redemption.

After Governor Warmoth's speech, the report of the majority of the Conference Committee was unanimously adopted, and the Convention proceeded to nominate Colonel D. B. Penn as its candidate for Governor by a unanimous vote, amid great enthusiasm, after which the Convention adjourned to the next day, when it completed the State ticket with the following nominations:

For Lieutenant-Governor . . .	John S. Young of Claiborne
For Secretary of State	F. E. Dumas of Orleans
For Auditor	Jas. Graham of Orleans
For Attorney-General	W. F. Kernan of East Feliciana
For Superintendent of Education .	J. W. McDonald of Webster
For Congressman at Large . . .	Geo. A. Sheridan

The Hon. Thomas C. Manning proposed the following resolution, which was adopted unanimously:

RESOLVED: That the Executive Committee to be appointed by the President be empowered and is hereby authorized to accept the resignation of any of the nominees on the ticket except that of D. B. Penn, and supply the places so vacated, if by such action a combination can be effected with the Democratic Reform and Regular Republican parties, and their votes be consolidated with those of the Liberal party; Provided that this combination be effected within thirty days after the close of this Convention.

This was intended to keep the doors open for conferences with the different factions, with a view to a fusion of all elements, a successful fight in the State for Greeley and Brown, and the defeat of the Kellogg and Grant ticket.

Having adopted a platform of principles, of which one is as follows:

RESOLVED: That we recognize the political and civil rights of all men, and pledge ourselves to maintain them, and we invite all men without regard to past political differences to unite with us in our honest efforts to accomplish such salutary reforms as are now, or may be, demanded by the people—

the Convention adjourned *sine die.*

CHAPTER VI

WHEN the Liberal Republican Convention adjourned in August Louisiana had five State tickets in the field. The first one was the "Last Ditch" Democratic ticket, headed by John McEnery for Governor and B. F. Jonas for Lieutenant-Governor. The second was the Custom-House-Grant Republican ticket, headed by W. P. Kellogg and C. C. Antoine. The third was the Pinchback Republican ticket, headed by P. B. S. Pinchback and A. B. Harris. The fourth was the Liberal Republican—Greeley and Brown—ticket, headed by D. B. Penn and John S. Young. The Reform Party had a ticket headed by George Williams, of Shreveport, for Governor.

The political situation was certainly mixed and it was left to the respective State Committees to untangle it.

The rejection by the "Last Ditch" Democrats and the Reform Democrats of the Liberal Republican proposition to consider a coalition with the Pinchback Republicans made it easy for the national Republican Grant leaders to conciliate the Pinchback element, and bring about a compromise ticket on which the Kellogg-Antoine ticket was merged with the Pinchback-Harris State ticket, and electors favorable to Grant and Wilson.

Many were the conferences between the Liberal Republican State Committee and the "Last Ditch" Democratic Committee and the Reform Democrats, which ended in an ultimatum from the "Last Ditchers": they demanded that unless their candidate for Governor (John McEnery) was accepted by the Liberal Republicans, they would keep their ticket in the field and refuse to support Greeley and Brown. This, of course, would have resulted inevitably in the election of the Kellogg State ticket and the giving of the State to Grant and Wilson. So the Liberal Republicans were forced to submit, and a fusion ticket was finally formed as follows:

For Governor . . . . John McEnery of Ouachita
For Lieutenant-Governor . . . . D. B. Penn of Orleans
For Auditor . . . . James Graham of Orleans
For Secretary of State . . . . . Samuel Armistead of Caddo
For Superintendent of Education . . R. M. Lusher of Orleans
For Treasurer . . . . Allen Jumel of Iberville
For Attorney-General . . . . . H. N. Ogden
For Congressman-at-Large . . . . Geo. A. Sheridan

The "Last Ditchers" gave up all of their candidates in order to keep the head of the ticket.

In this fusion of candidates on the Greeley and Brown State ticket, the "Last Ditchers" surrendered all of their candidates to save Colonel John McEnery, their candidate for Governor. B. F. Jonas, their candidate for Lieutenant-Governor, gave way to Colonel D. B. Penn, the Liberal Republican. James B. Eustis, their candidate for Congressman-at-Large, gave way to General Geo. A. Sheridan, the Liberal Republican. Daniel Dennett, their candidate for Auditor of Public Accounts, gave way to James Graham, the Liberal Republican. They accepted Allen Jumel, Liberal Republican, for State Treasurer, and Samuel Armistead, a black man and a Liberal Republican, for Secretary of State; R. M. Lusher for Superintendent of Education, and H. N. Ogden for Attorney General, the last two of whom were members of the Reform Party. So the extreme leaders were at last forced by public opinion to unite with the Liberal Republicans and to give up all of their candidates with the exception of the head of their ticket.

These disappointed candidates showed their chagrin at the final fusion by ever afterwards sulking in their tents. They not only sulked but they contributed to the overthrow of the fusion ticket after the election, by patting Kellogg and Casey and Packard on the back and with smiles and lifted eyebrows and covert criticisms encouraging them in their fight against what they termed "Warmoth's hirelings."

The Hunt family, two of whom were so conspicuous in the two Democratic Conventions for their hostility to Governor Warmoth and any fusion with the colored Republicans, are believed to have voted for Grant and Kellogg. The most eminent member of this distinguished family, Wm. H. Hunt, joined United States Attorney Beckwith and E. C. Billings in their disreputable proceedings for Kellogg and Antoine before Judge Durell; and his intimate friend, P. Hickey Morgan, was placed on the Supreme Bench to fill the vacancy caused by the resignation of Judge W. W. Howe. Hickey Morgan was appointed by Pinchback and confirmed by Kellogg's Senate during these proceedings as a "sop" to the Hunt family.

Another Democrat, Geo. W. Williamson, named by the Reform Democrats as their candidate for Governor, came out openly for Kellogg and Grant, and was rewarded by President Grant with a foreign mission; and after Pinchback was finally rejected by the Senate of the United States, we find Mr. James B. Eustis sitting in the seat, selected by Kellogg's Legislature and on the certificate of William Pitt Kellogg, Governor of the State of Louisiana.

The Kellogg-Pinchback State ticket was composed of five negroes, including the Superintendent of Education, with only three white men. This was in itself a strong appeal to the colored voters and produced to a large extent what I had striven so hard to prevent, a consolidation of the negro vote of the State against the white people.

The acceptance of Mr. McEnery as the head of our fusion State ticket was extremely unfortunate. Though an amiable and agreeable gentleman, he came from the Parish of Ouachita, which was considered by the colored people and the white Republicans as one of the most extreme and relentless of all localities in the State. Many negroes and several white Republicans had been murdered in that section of the State. And the acceptance of McEnery, who was recognized as an extreme "Last Ditch" Democrat, as the head of our fusion ticket produced a stampede among the colored voters and not a few white Liberal Republicans. By it we lost the support of *The New Orleans Republican* newspaper and a number of conspicuous Republicans. We lost the support of Chief Justice Ludeling, whose residence was in the same city as Colonel McEnery's. Judge Ludeling was a very influential man in his section of the State and he and his family and friends had suffered indignities and insults, politically and personally, from the McEnery following, and even from the McEnerys themselves. By it we lost the support of General James Longstreet who, up to that time, was an earnest supporter of the Liberal Republican movement. By it we lost the support of Senator John Lynch of East Carroll Parish, who was an influential Republican and a member, besides, of the Returning Board; and of General Herron, the acting Secretary of State, also a member of the Returning Board. The loss of the support of these men showed in the final round-up the grave mistake which the Liberal Republican Committee had made in surrendering to the "Last Ditch" Democrats the head of the State ticket.

Had the "Last Ditch" Democratic faction and the Reform faction consented to accept Colonel Penn as the fusion candidate for Governor, and Lieutenant-Governor Pinchback as our candidate for Congressman-at-Large, as they were urged to do, we would have carried the State by 30,000 majority. There could have been no split in the Returning Board, and no contest over the election, and the people would have been spared the four years of the dreadful Kellogg régime, and the lives of many of our people would have been saved.

In due time a fusion campaign committee was agreed upon, and I joined actively in the canvass of the State for Greeley and

Brown and the fusion State ticket. I was received by the people everywhere with enthusiasm. As an example: at a breakfast provided by the reception committee at the St. Martinsville Hotel, the following toast was given by Judge Fournet: "Here's to Governor Warmoth—the youngest but not the least illustrious of the Governors of Louisiana—once a formidable foe, now an all-powerful auxiliary!"

I appointed the election officers in the different Parishes of the State, as recommended by the fusion campaign committee, and did everything I could for the success of the ticket. There never was a more peaceable, free or fair campaign and election held in the State of Louisiana. There were no riots nor disturbances of any kind anywhere in the State. There were 121,552 votes polled, of which the McEnery ticket received 65,579 votes as against 55,973 votes for the Kellogg ticket. Col. Penn ran 2,672 votes ahead of Col. McEnery.

An episode occurred during the Grant and Greeley campaign that may amuse the reader. The Legislature of January 1872 passed two bills: an election bill and a registration bill; the latter was thought to modify the powers of the Executive of the State in the conduct of elections. These bills did not reach me until the last day of the session, so that I had, under the Constitution, until the meeting of the Legislature on January 1st, 1873, to consider them and to either sign or veto them.

As events arose, the Democratic Party, which had fused its candidates with our Liberal-Republican candidates, were not nearly so boisterous in their denunciations of the existing registration and election laws as they had been before the fusion, for they felt that I, being the Governor and supporting the fusion ticket, would see that our ticket had a fair chance.

The fusion of the Republican factions finally found Lieutenant-Governor Pinchback aligned with the Grant-Kellogg ticket, he being their candidate for Congressman-at-Large. So the Warmoth-Pinchback faction which had been fought so long and bitterly by the Custom House Grant faction was broken up—Pinchback taking up with the Grant-Kellogg side and leaving me with the Greeley-McEnery-Penn side.

The Grant-Kellogg party were anxious that the new election and registration bills should become laws, for they feared that I would give their opponents any advantage that the old laws might allow them.

The Grant and Wilson National Committee used Lieutenant-Governor Pinchback as a speaker to colored Republicans up in the New England States. In October I was called to New York on some important business. While there I met the Lieutenant-Governor on the street with his chum, State Senator A. B. Harris, a brother of U. S. Senator Harris from Louisiana.

Our meeting was cordial and ended in my inviting the Lieutenant-Governor to visit me that night (Saturday) at my hotel (the Fifth Avenue) at 10 o'clock. He accepted my invitation and promised to be there. I waited for him till nearly 11 o'clock but he did not appear. I concluded that he and his chum, Senator Harris, both gay young men, had fallen to the allurements of New York and had forgotten their engagement with me. So I went to bed and slept soundly till morning. After breakfast I descended to the office floor and the first man I met was Senator Harris. I asked him, "Where is your friend, Governor Pinchback?" He replied, "I don't know, I have not seen him since we met on the street yesterday afternoon."

As quick as lightning it flashed through my mind that Pinchback had slipped off to New Orleans, to get there ahead of me and to sign those bills which his friends thought would be helpful to them.

Major E. A. Burk was the Chairman of our campaign committee and he was also the Manager of the Illinois Central Railroad Company at New Orleans. I at once telegraphed to him the facts and told him I did not want Pinchback to get to New Orleans before me, and asked him to have a special car and engine for me at the end of his railroad, so as to get me into New Orleans first.

Major Burk appreciated the situation and went to work at once. He first found out by telegraph that Pinchback was on the New York and New Orleans train, and he put a car and engine at the proper place for me. But the fun of the thing is yet to be told.

When the regular train with Pinchback arrived at Canton, Miss., at 2 A.M. a messenger went into the car where Pinchback was sitting and called out loudly "Governor Pinchback" three times. Pinchback said "I am Governor Pinchback." The messenger said, "There is an important telegram in the office for you which will be delivered to no one but you in person." Pinchback rubbed his eyes and rushed out into the telegraph office, got his telegram, and without reading it rushed for the door, but found it locked. He then threw up the window and jumped out on the platform, but by the time he had picked himself up he found his train gone and he was left to read his telegram at his leisure. A little later I received a telegram saying, "Pinchback left at Canton."

The next morning about ten o'clock my car rolled up to the platform at Canton, where I found Governor Pinchback standing, tired, disgusted and sleepy.

He greeted me with "I told Bill Chandler [Secretary of the National Republican Committee] that I couldn't beat you to New Orleans—I want to go home!" I replied, "Governor Pinchback, step right into my car and I will take you home"— and I did. He told me that it had been fixed up that he should get to New Orleans before me and sign those bills, and that they had hoped for great advantage from them.

It is proper to remark here that I signed the bills later myself.

But Grant and Wilson carried the country by an overwhelming majority, receiving 286 electoral votes to Greeley and Brown's 80 votes. Grant and Wilson received 3,597,070 votes, while Greeley and Brown received but 2,834,079 votes. Grant and Wilson's electoral majority was 206 and their popular majority was 762,991.

The elation of the Grant and Wilson people may well be understood. The despondency of the Greeley and Brown people can hardly be described. Mr. Greeley died from a broken heart. The Kellogg forces in Louisiana at once sought for some scheme by which they could overthrow the election in this State.

There was a wild rush by politicians to get on the Grant band-wagon. Some Republicans in Louisiana who had supported Greeley and McEnery were after a time found in the camp of the enemy. The Kellogg-Custom-House faction at once determined to try to capture the Returning Board. The Returning Board was composed of Governor Warmoth, Lieutenant-Governor Pinchback, Acting Secretary of State Herron, and two Senators—Lynch and Anderson. It was known that Lieutenant-Governor Pinchback and Senator Anderson were ineligible, both having been candidates at the late election; so that the filling of their vacancies on the Returning Board was an important matter. If the Kellogg-Grant party could have captured the Returning Board they hoped to be able to throw out enough fusion votes, on one excuse or another, to change the result and give them the victory; so they addressed themselves at once to this matter. Old Republican friends of mine made a dead set at me to go into the conspiracy to reverse the result of the State election. They called my attention to the bitterness and vindictiveness and hatred always displayed by the Democratic-Reform factions toward me personally, which had prevented my nomination for Governor on the fusion ticket and which had been finally able to foist a "Last Ditch" Democrat upon the head of our State ticket—John McEnery. They were pathetic in their appeals; they urged that if McEnery should become installed in office as Governor, no single Republican in the State would ever have any consideration whatever and that, McEnery being Governor, he would be absolutely master of the situation. They called my attention to the awful charges and denunciations of me by the Democratic leaders for the past four years, and warned me that the "Last Ditch" Democrats would control everything hereafter.

Not satisfied that their appeals and arguments would move me to enter into the conspiracy, emissaries of Senator Kellogg dangled before my eyes the seat in the United States Senate which would be made vacant by the election of Senator Kellogg to the Governorship. In their interviews they did not hesitate to make it clear that we were expected to use unscrupulously, if necessary, the power of the Returning Board to vitiate the election and to wipe out the Greeley-McEnery majority.

In these interviews, I became aware of the plan that had been concocted to overthrow the election, and I learned that Senator Lynch and General Herron—I had appointed the latter Secretary of State temporarily, on the susupension of Bovee for criminal practice—had agreed to go into the conspiracy. All that I was asked to do in order to reap this wonderful reward that was dangled before my eyes and to punish the Democratic-Reform leaders who had so bitterly persecuted me was just to sit still and let matters take their ordinary course, the result of which would have been that the two vacancies on the Returning Board would have been filled by Herron and Lynch.

So the reader may imagine the surprise and consternation of Senator Kellogg and his followers when I removed Acting Secretary of State Herron, at the moment of the meeting of the Returning Board, and appointed Col. Jack Wharton in his place. Senator Lynch and General Herron both were greatly surprised and stunned by this proceeding, and while Senator Lynch was engaged in the act of reading my order of removal of General Herron and the appointment of Col. Wharton, Col. Wharton and I selected Col. Frank H. Hatch and Mr. Durant da Ponte to fill the two vacancies on the board, and they were immediately sworn into office.

Senator Lynch did not vote and he made no protest, nor did General Herron, both of whom a little later retired from the meeting. Later, after consultation with Kellogg and Packard, without notice to me, Lynch and Herron pretended to hold a meeting and selected two other gentlemen for their Board. They took the ground that I had no right to remove General Herron, notwithstanding the fact that his appointment by me was only temporary. If I had the right to suspend Bovee, who was elected Secretary of State, and to appoint General Herron in the first place, I certainly had the right to remove him in the second place at my discretion and to appoint his successor.

Having all of the official returns of the election in my possession, the Warmoth-Hatch-da Ponte Returning Board at once appointed secretaries and clerks and proceeded to tabulate the returns honestly, just as they came from the hands of the commissioners of election at the different polls, as required by law. But the so-called Lynch-Herron Board, without having a single return from any poll in the State, proceeded to fabricate and declare what they claimed to be the result of the State election. They declared that Grant and Wilson, Kellogg and Antoine and all of the Republican candidates were elected. At once Senator Kellogg, United States Marshal Packard, and Col. Casey, the President's brother-in-law, made a visit to the city of Washington and conferred with the President and Attorney General. On their return, the plan to overthrow the State Government and to reverse the result of the election developed itself; they had a bold scheme. There was never one like it before or since in the history of the nation.

Their first steps were to corrupt Judge E. H. Durell of the United States Circuit Court, to induce him to assume jurisdiction of their controversy, and to set up the Kellogg Government. This was not an easy job, for everybody knew that this court had no jurisdiction. Besides, Judge Durell was quite an elderly man and had passed the time of life when the spirit of adventure and revolution is supposed to exist, and finally, he was quite feeble in health and knew that he would very soon have to give up the discharge of his important duties.

But Judge Durell had two very close personal friends in New Orleans. They were his constant daily and nightly companions. One was a man by the name of E. E. Norton, who had come to New Orleans during the Civil War as a Captain in the Commissary of the Subsistence Department of the United States Army. He was from the State of New York and was a very shrewd man.

Captain Norton and his wife made it their business never to allow Judge Durell to want for anything in the way of creature comforts. They kept him under close surveillance and kept his closet well stocked with the choicest of wines and liquors. Judge Durell, in turn, appointed Captain Norton General Assignee in Bankruptcy. All bankrupt estates were assigned by Judge Durell to what was popularly called "this universal assignee," except in cases where it was possible under the law for the parties in interest to name their own assignee. There were many such cases after the War, and the assignee's fees and "pickings" were immense.

There was another gentleman in New Orleans at that time by the name of E. C. Billings, a member of the firm of Sullivan, Billings & Hughes, Attorneys-at-Law. They were also from New York, and were the attorneys of General Assignee Norton. Mr. Billings was the nightly companion of Judge Durell; they were inseparable, and were often together until late hours of the night.

It is to be noted that Mr. Billings had been a candidate for Governor before the Convention at Baton Rouge that nominated Mr. Kellogg, and had been defeated. He and his friends claimed that Kellogg, Packard, and Casey had packed the Convention with Custom House employees and defeated him by unfair means. So Billings and his friends bolted the nomination of Kellogg. A large public meeting was held in the city of New Orleans, in which the Billings' supporters exposed the trickery, denounced Kellogg and his methods in most bitter terms, and refused to support his ticket.

Col. Carter, late Speaker of the House of Representatives and editor of the Custom House newspaper, *The National Republican,* and a supporter of Mr. Billings, resigned his position as editor in a bitter protest at the manner of Kellogg's nomination. Mr. Billings telegraphed the President, denouncing and demanding the removal of Collector Casey, the President's brother-in-law, Marshal Packard and the other Federal officials who had packed the Baton Rouge Convention against him.

Senator Kellogg knew the ground he had to cover and the enormous difficulties he had to encounter, and nobody had greater skill than he in the management of such a situation. He knew that if he could in some way interest Captain Norton and Mr. Billings in his fight, he might be able to capture Judge Durell. So he sought an interview with these gentlemen, at which the program agreed upon in Washington was made known for the "safety of Louisiana to the Republican Party," and for the overthrow of the fusion party in Louisiana. Senator Kellogg assured these gentlemen that the President and the Attorney-General would support Judge Durell in his taking jurisdiction of the case, and would enforce any decree he might make. United States District Attorney Beckwith was reluctantly forced to take a hand in the contest.

The scheme was a bold one; it was thrilling, and appealed to both Billings and Norton. They saw at once that it would put them in close *rapport* with the new Grant Administration at Washington and make them worthy of special recognition and favors by President Grant.

To make it still more attractive, Mr. Kellogg called Mr.

Billings' attention to the fact that Judge Durell was old and feeble, and would soon have to retire from the bench; and Kellogg promised Mr. Billings that he should be Durell's successor, which promise in a little time later was fulfilled by General Grant, and Billings became Judge, Durell resigning. And Captain Norton was fixed with the promise that he should be elected United States Senator by the Kellogg Legislature, which was to be counted in by the proposed diabolical outrage.

The plans and terms were submitted to Judge Durell, and, after some delay, were accepted by him, and proceedings were begun to carry them out.

First, a suit was instituted in the Circuit Court of the United States, Judge Durell presiding, by candidates Kellogg and Antoine against McEnery and Penn. Mr. Billings prepared the papers and instituted the proceedings to overthrow the State election as returned by the legal Returning Board and the result as proclaimed officially by me as Governor of the State.

It is not necessary to recount in detail the various proceedings of this long and bitter litigation, but only to tell the result, together with the denunciations and condemnation of all the proceedings by every one and all of the tribunals which later came to pass upon them, all of which tribunals show the dastardly enormity and disgraceful conduct of this Judge, which finally led to his forced resignation of his office in fear of impeachment.

Judge Durell enjoined the State Returning Board, recognized by the Governor of the State, from declaring any election returns. He also declared that the bogus Lynch-Herron Returning Board was the legal Returning Board of the State, and he finally issued a decree naming the members of the Legislature who should be entitled to seats in the Legislature.

The Governor of the State called the new Legislature to meet in extra session at the State House on the 9th day of December, 1872. Judge Durell at his private residence late at night on December 5th was induced by Billings to issue an order, which the United States Senate Committee afterward unanimously declared to be "without parallel, and it is hoped it will remain so in judicial proceedings."

After reciting the proclamation of the Governor of the State, announcing the result of the election and convening the Legislature in accordance with law, he ordered:

Now, therefore, in order to prevent the further obstruction of the proceedings in this cause, and, further, to prevent a violation of the orders of this court, to the imminent danger of disturbing the public peace, it is hereby ordered that the Marshal of the United States for the District of Louisiana shall forthwith take possession of the building known as the Mechanics' Institute and occupied as the State House for the assembling of the Legislature therein, in the city of New Orleans, and hold the same subject to the further order of this court, and meanwhile to prevent all unlawful assemblage therein under the guise or pretext of authority claimed by virtue of pretended canvass and returns made by said pretended returning officers in contempt and violation of said restraining order; but the Marshal is directed to allow the ingress to and egress from the public offices in said building of persons entitled to the same.

(*Signed*)   E. H. DURELL

Evidently in anticipation of this order, and two days before it was issued by Judge Durell, United States Marshal Packard received the following dispatch from Attorney General Williams, which was undoubtedly shown to the Judge in order that he might know certainly that the President would support him in any act which he might take to set up the Kellogg government:

Department of Justice,
December 3, 1872

S. B. Packard, Esq.,
    United States Marshal,
        New Orleans, Louisiana.

You are to enforce the decrees and mandates of United States Courts, no matter by whom resisted, and General Emery will furnish you with all necessary troops for that purpose.

GEORGE H. WILLIAMS
Attorney General

The United States Marshal obeyed the Judge's order to the

letter and at two o'clock on the morning of the 6th day of December, 1872, with two companies of United States troops, he took possession of the State House of Louisiana and held it until the entire scheme for the overthrow of the existing State Government and the setting-up of the Kellogg usurpation had been carried out.

The next dispatches are as follows:

New Orleans,
Attorney-General Williams,   December 6, 1872.
    Washington, D. C.

Returning Board provided by election law of 'seventy, under which election was held, and which United States court sustains, promulgated in official journal this morning result of election of Legislature: House stands seventy-seven Republicans, thirty-two Democratic; Senate twenty-eight Republicans, eight Democratic. Board counted ballots attached to affidavits of colored persons wrongfully prevented from voting, filed with chief supervisor.

(*Signed*)   S. B. PACKARD
United States Marshal

New Orleans,
December 6, 1872.
President Grant:

Marshal Packard took possession of State House this morning at an early hour, with military posse, in obedience to a mandate of Circuit Court, to prevent illegal assemblage of persons under guise of authority of Warmoth's Returning Board, in violation of injunction of Circuit Court. Decree of court just rendered declares Warmoth's Returning Board illegal, and orders the returns of the election to be forthwith placed before the legal board. This board will probably soon declare the result of the election of officers of State and Legislature, which will meet in State House with protection of court. The decree was sweeping in its provisions, and if enforced will save the Republican majority and give Louisiana a Republican Legislature and State Government, and check Warmoth in his usurpations. Warmoth's Democratic supporters are becoming disgusted with him, and charging that his usurpations are ruining their cause.

(*Signed*)   Jas. F. CASEY

At twelve o'clock on December 9th, the hour fixed for the meeting of the Legislature, no one was admitted to the State

House except upon the order of the United States Marshal, Packard, Chairman of the Kellogg Republican State Committee. And instead of the Legislature, whose members had been declared elected by the legal Returning Board and recognized by the Governor of the State, certain persons declared to have been elected by the so-called Lynch Returning Board and named in a decree of Judge Durell were admitted to the State House, which proceeded to organize a bogus Legislature with barely a quorum of its alleged members in either House being present.

This bogus House of Representatives, without official and formal notice to the Governor, as required by law, and without any investigation by a committee, as specifically required by law, immediately and hurriedly adopted a resolution impeaching the Governor for "high crimes and misdemeanors."

The House at once appointed a Committee to present the resolution of impeachment to the bogus Senate, as shown by the following proceedings:

Senate Chamber,
December 9th, 1872.

Mr. Hahn, Chairman of a Committee from the House of Representatives, submitted the following resolution from the House of Representatives for the consideration of the Senate:

Mr. President:

In obedience to the order of the House of Representatives, we appear before you in the name of the House of Representatives and all of the people of the State of Louisiana; we do impeach Henry Clay Warmoth, Governor of the State of Louisiana, of high crimes and misdemeanors in office; we further inform the Senate that the House of Representatives will in due time exhibit particular articles of impeachment against him and make good the same; and in their name we demand that the Senate take order for the appearance of the said Henry Clay Warmoth to answer said impeachment.

(Signed)   MICHAEL HAHN
Chairman.
A. C. BICKHAM
A. WILLIAMS
C. W. KEATING.

STORMY DAYS IN LOUISIANA

The bogus Senate immediately organized as a court of impeachment, all of which proceedings were inaugurated and carried through within six hours after the meeting of this bogus assembly.

Under our Constitution the filing of an impeachment by the House of Representatives against an officer immediately suspends him from office, and Lieutenant-Governor Pinchback, taking official notice of the proceedings, at once broke into the Governor's office, took possession and telegraphed the fact to the President.

New Orleans,
December 9, 1872.

President Grant:

We have the honor to transmit to Your Excellency the following concurrent resolution of both Houses of the General Assembly and to request an early reply:

Whereas the General Assembly is now convened, in compliance with the call of the Governor, and certain ill-disposed persons are reported to be forming combinations to disturb the public peace and defy the lawful authority, and the State is threatened with violence: Therefore,

Be it resolved by the Senate and House of Representatives of the State of Louisiana in General Assembly convened, That the President of the United States be requested to afford the protection guaranteed each State by the Constitution of the United States when threatened with domestic violence, and that the presiding officers of the General Assembly transmit this resolution immediately, by telegraph or otherwise, to the President of the United States.

Adopted in General Assembly convened this 9th day of December, A.D. 1872.

(*Signed*) P. B. S. PINCHBACK
Lieutenant-Governor and President of the Senate.
CHAS. W. LOWELL
Speaker of the House of Representatives.

New Orleans,
December 9, 1872.

President Grant:

Having taken the oath of office and being in the possession of the gubernatorial office, it devolves upon me to urge the necessity of a

[213]

favorable consideration of the request of the General Assembly as conveyed in the concurrent resolution of this day telegraphed to you requesting the protection of the United States Government. Be pleased to send the necessary orders to General Emery. This seems to me a necessary measure of precaution although all is quiet here.

(*Signed*)   P. B. S. PINCHBACK
Lieutenant-Governor, Acting Governor of Louisiana.

Other dispatches are as follows:

New Orleans,
December 9, 1872.

Hon. Geo. H. Williams, Attorney-General,
Washington, D. C.
Returning Board has officially promulgated in official Journal this morning the result of the election of State officers. Kellogg's majority eighteen thousand eight hundred and sixty-one.

(*Signed*)   S. B. PACKARD
United States Marshal.

New Orleans,
December 9, 1872.

Hon. Geo. H. Williams, Attorney-General:
Senate, by vote of seventeen to five, have resolved into high court of impeachment. Senator Harris elected President of the Senate, Lieutenant-Governor Pinchback is now Governor.

(*Signed*)   S. B. PACKARD
United States Marshal.

New Orleans,
December 9, 1872.

Hon. Geo. H. Williams, Attorney-General:
Governor Warmoth has been impeached by vote of fifty-eight to six. Warmoth's Legislature returned by his board has made no pretense of a session.

(*Signed*)   S. B. PACKARD
United States Marshal.

New Orleans,
December 9, 1872.

Hon. Geo. H. Williams, Attorney-General,
Washington, D. C.
Lieutenant-Governor Pinchback qualified and took possession of the Governor's office tonight. Senate organized as high court of impeach-

ment, Chief-Justice Ludeling presiding, and adjourned to meet Monday next. It is believed that all the Democrats, members of the General Assembly, will qualify and take seats tomorrow.

(*Signed*) S. B. PACKARD
United States Marshal.

United States Senator Trumbull of the subsequently appointed Senate Committee comments as follows:

"While these revolutionary proceedings were being enacted, Judge Durell was busy fulminating new injunctions and restraining orders, and calling Governor Warmoth and his associates of the legal Returning Board before him to answer for alleged contempts of his void orders."

The Pinchback administration and Legislature thus set up was so entirely without the moral support and respect of the people that it was in great danger of falling to pieces, unless it could get the further support of the Federal administration, backed by a larger military force. So well was this understood that Pinchback and United States officials at New Orleans kept the telegraph busy calling on the President for help and additional forces. The two batteries and eighty-six men under Captain Jackson were not deemed sufficient to protect Pinchback and his Legislature from the just indignation of an outraged people. Hence the cries for help which were continually being sent to Washington. The following are specimens of some of these cries:

New Orleans, Louisiana,
December 11, 1872.

Hon. Geo. H. Williams, Attorney-General:

I have the honor to acknowledge the receipt of your dispatch. May I suggest that the commanding General be authorized to furnish troops upon my requisition upon him for the protection of the Legislature and the gubernatorial office. The moral effect would be great, and in my judgment would tend greatly to allay any trouble likely to grow out of the recent inflammatory proclamation of Warmoth. I beg you to believe that I will act in all things with discretion.

(*Signed*) P. B. S. PINCHBACK
Lieutenant-Governor, Acting Governor

[215]

WAR, POLITICS AND RECONSTRUCTION

New Orleans,
December 11, 1872.

President Grant:

Parties interested in the success of the Democratic Party, particularly *The New Orleans Times,* are making desperate efforts to array the people against us. Old citizens are dragooned into an opposition they do not feel, and pressure is hourly growing; our members are poor and adversaries are rich, and offers were made that are difficult for them to withstand. There is danger that they will break our quorum. The delay in placing troops at disposal of Governor Pinchback, in accordance with joint resolution of Monday, is disheartening our friends and cheering our enemies. If requisition of Legislature is complied with, all difficulty will be dissipated, the party saved, and everything go on smoothly. If this is done, the tide will be turned at once in our favor. The real underlying sentiment is with us, if it can but be encouraged. Governor Pinchback acting with great discretion, as is the Legislature, and they will so continue.

(*Signed*) JAS. F. CASEY
Collector.

New Orleans,
December 11, 1872.

Hon. Geo. Williams:

If President in some way indicates recognition, Governor Pinchback and Legislature would settle everything. Our friends here acting discreetly.

(*Signed*) W. P. KELLOGG

New Orleans,
December 11, 1872.

President Grant:

Democratic members of Legislature taking their seats. Most, if not all, will do so in next few days. Important that you immediately recognize Governor Pinchback's Legislature in some manner, either by instructing General Emery to comply with any requisition by Governor Pinchback, under joint resolution of Legislature of Monday, or otherwise. This would quiet matters much. I earnestly urge this and ask a reply.

(*Signed*) JAMES F. CASEY

[216]

STORMY DAYS IN LOUISIANA

President Grant:

New Orleans,
December 12, 1872.

The condition of affairs is this: The United States circuit court has decided which is the legal board of canvassers. Upon the basis of that decision a Legislature has been organized in strict conformity with the laws of the State, Warmoth impeached, and thus Pinchback, as provided by the Constitution, became acting Governor. The Chief Justice of the Supreme Court organized the Senate into a court of impeachment, and Associate Justice Talliaferro administered oath to Governor Pinchback. The Legislature, fully organized, has proceeded in regular routine of business since Monday. Notwithstanding this, Warmoth has organized a pretended Legislature, and it is proceeding with pretended Legislation. A conflict between these two organizations may occur at any time, and in my opinion there is no safety for the legal government, unless the Federal troops are given in compliance with the requisition of the Legislature. The Supreme Court is known to be in sympathy with the Republican State Government. If a decided recognition of Governor Pinchback and the legal Legislature were made, in my judgment it would settle the whole matter. General Longstreet has been appointed by Governor Pinchback as Adjutant-General of State Militia.

(*Signed*) JAMES F. CASEY.

In reply to these appeals for help the Attorney-General answered as follows:

Department of Justice,
December 12, 1872.

Acting Governor Pinchback,
New Orleans, Louisiana:

Let it be understood that you are recognized by the President as the lawful executive of Louisiana, and that the body assembled at Mechanics' Institute is the lawful Legislature of the State, and it is suggested that you make proclamation to that effect, and also that all necessary assistance will be given to you and the Legislature herein recognized to protect the State from disorder and violence.

(*Signed*) GEO. H. WILLIAMS
Attorney-General

The following telegrams were sent to the President by the friends of the State government which was being subverted:

[217]

WAR, POLITICS AND RECONSTRUCTION

New Orleans,
December 11, 1872.

The President of the United States:

Under an order from the Judge of the United States District Court investing John Lynch, James Longstreet, Jacob Hawkins, and others, with the powers and duties of returning-officers under State election law, and charging them with the duty of completing the legal returns and declaring the result in accordance therewith, those persons have promulgated results based upon no returns whatever, and no evidence except *ex parte* statements. They have constructed a pretended General Assembly, composed mainly of candidates defeated at the election, and those candidates protected by United States military forces have taken possession of the State House, and have organized a pretended Legislature, which today has passed pretended articles of impeachment against the Governor; in pursuance of which, the person claiming to be a Lieutenant-Governor, but whose term had expired, proclaimed himself acting Governor, broke into the executive office under the protection of United States soldiers, and took possession of the archives. In the mean time the General Assembly has met at the City Hall and organized for business, with sixty members in the house and twenty-one in the Senate, being more than a quorum of both bodies. I ask and believe that no violent action be taken, and no force used by the Government, at least until the Supreme Court shall have passed final judgment on the case. A full statement of the facts will be laid before you and the Congress in a few days.

(*Signed*) H. C. WARMOTH
Governor of Louisiana.

New Orleans,
Dec. 12th, 1872.

His Excellency U. S. Grant,
President United States:

Claiming to be governor-elect of this State, I beg you, in the name of all justice, to suspend recognition of either of the dual governments now in operation here until there can be laid before you all facts, and both sides, touching legitimacy of Pinchback government and its Legislature. Simply ask to be heard, through committee of many of our best citizens on eve of departure for Washington, before you recognize the one or the other of said governments. I do not believe we will be condemned before we are fully heard.

(*Signed*) JNO. MCENERY

STORMY DAYS IN LOUISIANA

New Orleans,
December 12, 1872.

His Excellency U. S. Grant,
    President of the United States:

Sir: As chairman of a committee of citizens appointed under authority of a mass meeting recently held in this city, I am instructed to inform you that said committee is about to leave here for Washington to lay before you and the Congress of the United States the facts of the political difficulties at present existing in this State, and further earnestly to request you to delay executive action in the premises until after the arrival and hearing of said committee, which is composed of business and professional men without regard to past political affiliations.

(*Signed*)   THOMAS A. ADAMS
Chairman

To these respectful appeals on behalf of the legitimate Governor and people of Louisiana, seeking to be heard before a usurping executive and Legislature should be forced upon them, the President, through the Attorney-General and War Department, returned the following replies:

Department of Justice,
December 13, 1872.

Hon. John McEnery,
    New Orleans, Louisiana:

Your visit with a hundred citizens will be unavailing so far as the President is concerned. His decision is made and will not be changed, and the sooner it is acquiesced in the sooner good order and peace will be restored.

(*Signed*)   GEO. H. WILLIAMS
Attorney-General

Washington,
December 14, 1872.

General W. H. Emery, U. S. A.,
    Commanding New Orleans, Louisiana:

You may use all necessary force to preserve the peace, and will recognize the authority of Governor Pinchback. By order of the President.

(*Signed*)   E. D. TOWNSEND
Adjutant-General

I cannot better state the history of the case than by quoting from the report of Senator Lyman Trumbull, a member of the Senate Committee, who investigated the proceedings of this controversy.

This pretended Legislature, made up of persons returned as members by the Lynch board, perfected its organizations, impeached the Governor, suspended him from office, and installed Pinchback in his place. All this was done on the same day and within a few hours, and that, too, in disregard of a statute of the State, which as stated to the committee, provides that the officer sought to be impeached shall be summoned before a committee of the House of Representatives; shall have permission to cross-examine witnesses that are brought against him; shall have citation of the witnesses he may desire to summon; that the House of Representatives shall act only in case the Committee report in favor of the impeachment; that if the committee report adversely to it, that is itself an acquittal, and the officer cannot ever be arraigned on the charges then reported on. No such proceedings were had in this case.

It may not be amiss to remark in this connection that each of the members of the Lynch board was immediately rewarded by Pinchback with a lucrative office, except Lynch, and his son was given an appointment.

These twenty telegrams tell the whole story, and show that the conspiracy to overthrow the State Government of Louisiana was organized in Washington, and that President Grant and Attorney-General Williams had agreed beforehand to aid and protect the conspirators before their villainous scheme was launched upon the people; and the stubborn refusal of President Grant to receive one hundred eminent citizens or to consider their protest condemns him as the chief spirit of the whole revolutionary movement.

CHAPTER VII

THE controversy having been decided in favor of the Kellogg usurpation by the President, and he having most peremptorily refused the people a hearing, nothing was left but to appeal from the President to the Congress of the United States. It was in the power of Congress to annul the action of the President, in one of two ways.

If the two Houses of Congress should adopt a resolution recognizing either the one or the other State Government that would be one way.

If the United States Senate should seat the person chosen by the Legislature of either one of the Governments, and the House of Representatives acquiesced in the movement, it would be such a recognition of the State Government as would bind the President and all departments of the United States Government. The final contest before the Senate was as to whether General W. L. McMillan, who was elected by the McEnery Legislature, or ex-Lieutenant-Governor P. B. S. Pinchback, who was elected by the Kellogg Legislature, should be seated. The credentials of both contestants were laid before the Senate, and they were referred to the Committee on Privileges and Elections for investigation and report. The investigation consumed several months. It was long drawn out. The majority report was signed by Senators Carpenter of Wisconsin, Logan of Illinois, Anthony of Rhode Island, and Alcorn of Mississippi.

All members of the Committee united in condemning the proceedings of United States Judge Durell from beginning to end, and declared that the United States Court was without jurisdiction; they violently denounced his orders, and the use of United States troops in the seizing of the State House by the United States Marshal, and the setting-up of the Kellogg Government, as the following extracts from their report will convince the reader.

I represented the cause of the people and the McEnery Government before the Senate Committee. I spent several months in Washington in this important service. I extract the following from the Senate Committee's report:

THE MAJORITY REPORT

The Committee agreed that these Boards for convenience of designation would hereafter be called the "Warmoth Board" and the "Lynch Boards," the legality of which was in contest before the Courts under the law of 1870.

Referring to Judge Durell's injunction against the Warmoth Board, the Committee said:

Thereupon, Governor Warmoth took from his safe a bill which had been passed by the Legislature in the previous spring, but never approved by him so as to become a law, and on the 20th of November, 1872, gave it his approval. This law abolished the Returning Board created by the Act of 1870.

Under this law Governor Warmoth proceeded to fill the Board provided for by the Act of November 20th by appointing men by the names of De Feriet, Wiltz, Isabel, Austin and Taylor, in pursuance of the authority conferred upon him by Article 60 of the Constitution, to fill vacancies happening in the vacation of the Legislature.

The Committee then said:

We now come to the saddest chapter in this melancholy business— the interference of Federal authority with the affairs of the State of Louisiana.

The Fifteenth Amendment of the Constitution provides as follows:
Section 1. The right of citizens of the United States to vote shall not be denied or abridged by the United States, or by any State, on account of race, color, or previous condition of servitude.

Section 2. The Congress shall have power to enforce this article by appropriate legislation.

STORMY DAYS IN LOUISIANA

The subject of suffrage belongs entirely to the States, and must be regulated by them exclusively, with the single exception created by this amendment, that no State can deny to a citizen of the United States the right to vote on account of race, color, or previous condition of servitude; and the extent of the power of Congress over the subject is to see to it that the States do not violate this provision. Congress has the undoubted power to enact such laws as are necessary and proper to secure to the colored citizen his right to vote upon the same terms and conditions, and with the same effect, as the right is enjoyed and exercised by white citizens; and, speaking of the case before us, this is the extent of jurisdiction possessed by the National Government in regard to State elections.

Therefore, a contest between two citizens of the same State in relation to the office of Governor or other State office, cannot be waged in a Federal Court, except upon the ground that the contestant has been defeated or deprived of his election by reason of the denial to any citizen or citizens of the right to vote on account of race, color, or previous condition of servitude. If the contestant has been defeated in consequence of a denial to citizens of the right to vote on account of their belonging to a particular political party, or a particular church, or for any reason except race, color, or previous condition of servitude, no Federal court has power to hear and determine it.

Again:

The utmost which the [Federal] court had authority to do upon this bill was to restrain the destruction of the returns and documents, to preserve which the bill was filed. They were State records, and the Federal court has no right to take possession of them. The bill did not ask the court to do so, but only to require copies to be filed. But the court issued the following restraining order. . . .

After quoting the void orders of Judge Durell the Committee's majority report further, said:

It is impossible to conceive of a more irregular, illegal, and in every way inexcusable act on the part of a judge. Conceding the power of the court to make such an order, the judge, out of court, had no more authority to make it than had the marshal. It has not even the form of judicial process. It was not sealed, nor was it signed by the clerk, and had no more legal effect than an order issued by any private citizen.

[223]

Again:

The De Feriet board, therefore, had color of official existence. Their canvass was completed, and the result promulgated under color of the State law, and it is clear that this gave the Federal court no more right to seize the State House than to seize this Capitol.

The marshal, on receiving this pretended order, called for a detachment of United States troops to act as a *posse comitatus*, seized the State House at 2 A.M. of December 6, and held it for weeks.

After quoting the decisions Judge Durell issued, trying to justify his course, the Committee reported as follows:

It is somewhat remarkable that in this opinion the judge makes no allusion to the fact that the State House was then in possession of Federal troops, under an order issued by him, out of court, the night before. The opinion materially misstates the allegations of the bill, and wholly ignores the fact that, under the act of November 20, the Governor had appointed a new canvassing board which had, in fact, canvassed the votes; of all of which he was aware, because the proclamation of the Governor officially promulgating these facts was embodied in the order for seizing the State House, made by the judge the night before. The judge also declares that about four thousand affidavits sustain the averments of the bill.

Your committee have examined many of these affidavits, and it is admitted that none of them contain the statement that right of registration or right of voting was denied on account of race, color, or previous condition of servitude.

Again:

In the opinion of your committee there can be no doubt concerning the validity of the act of November 20—that it transferred the duty of canvassing the returns of the last election to the board to be elected under the provisions of the act. The act provided for such election by the Senate, and, taking effect in the vacation of the Legislature, created offices to be filled thereafter by the Senate. This is what is styled in that State an original vacancy, which, happening in the vacation of the Legislature, the Governor is authorized to fill by appointment; and it is said that the courts of that State have repeatedly recognized the right of the Governor to make such appointments.

Viewed in any light in which your committee can consider them, the orders and injunctions made and granted by Judge Durell in this cause are most reprehensible, erroneous in point of law, and wholly void for want of jurisdiction; and your committee must express their sorrow and humiliation that a judge of the United States should have so proceeded in such flagrant disregard of his duty, and have so far overstepped the limits of Federal jurisdiction.

Speaking of the canvass of the so-called Lynch Board, the Committee said:

There is nothing in all the comedy of blunders and frauds under consideration more indefensible than the pretended canvass of this Board.

The following are some of the objections to the validity of their proceedings.

1. The Board had been abolished by the act of November 20.

2. The Board was under valid and existing injunctions restraining it from acting at all, and an injunction in the Armstead case restraining it from making any canvass not based upon the official returns of the election.

3. Conceding the Board was in existence, and had full authority to canvass the returns, it had no returns to canvass.

It was testified before your committee by Mr. Bovee himself, who participated in this canvass by the Lynch Board, that they were determined to have a Republican Legislature, and made their canvass to that end. The testimony abundantly establishes the fraudulent character of their canvass. In some cases they had what were supposed to be copies of the original returns, in other cases they had nothing but newspaper statements, and in other cases, where they had nothing whatever to act upon, they made an estimate based upon their knowledge of the political complexion of the Parish, of what the vote ought to have been. They also counted a large number of affidavits purporting to be sworn to by voters who had been wrongfully denied registration or the right to vote, many of which affidavits they must have known to be forgeries. It was testified by one witness that he forged over a thousand affidavits, and delivered them to the Lynch Board while it was in session. It is quite unnecessary to waste time in considering this part of the case; for no person can examine the testimony ever so cursorily without seeing that this pretended canvass had no semblance of integrity.

But for the interference of Judge Durell in the matter of this State election, a matter wholly beyond his jurisdiction, the McEnery government would today have been the *de facto* government of the State. Judge Durell interposed the Army of the United States between the people of Louisiana and the only government which has the semblance of regularity, and the result of this has been to establish the Kellogg government, so far as that State now has any government. For the United States to interfere in a State election, and, by the employment of troops, set up a Governor and Legislature without a shadow of right, and then to refuse redress of the wrong, upon the ground that to grant relief would be interfering with the rights of the State, is a proposition difficult to utter with a grave countenance.

Again:

Indeed, it is impossible not to see that this bill was filed, and the restraining order thereon was issued, for the sole purpose of accomplishing what no Federal court has the jurisdiction to do, the organization of a State Legislature.

And your committee cannot refrain from expressing their astonishment that any judge of the United States should thus unwarrantably have interfered with a State government, and know no language too strong to express their condemnation of such a proceeding.

It is the opinion of your committee that but for the unjustifiable interference of Judge Durell, whose orders were executed by United States troops, the canvass made by the De Feriet Board and promulgated by the Governor, declaring McEnery to have been elected, and the Legislature, would have been acquiesced in by the people, and that government would have entered quietly upon the exercise of the sovereign power of the State. But the proceedings of Judge Durell, and the support given to him by United States troops, resulted in establishing the authority *de facto* of Kellogg and his associates in State offices, and of the persons declared by the Lynch Board to be elected to the Legislature. We have already seen that the proceedings of that Board cannot be sustained without disregarding all the principles of law applicable to the subject, and ignoring the distinction between good faith and fraud.

Your committee are, therefore, led to the conclusion that, if the election held in November, 1872, be not absolutely void for frauds committed therein, McEnery and his associates in State offices, and the persons certified as members of the Legislature by the De Feriet board, ought to be recognized as the legal government of the State. Considering all the facts established before your committee, there seems no escape from the alternative that the McEnery government must be recognized by Congress or Congress must provide for a re-election.

The McEnery government, so-called, approaches more nearly a government *de jure,* and the Kellogg government a government *de facto.*

The Kellogg government is in possession of the State House, the seal, archives, and records of the State, and its empty treasury. There are two bodies of men in that State, one claiming to be the Senate and the other the House of Representatives, who recognize Kellogg and his associates as the officers of the State. But there is not, and never has been, a quorum of both houses who have any pretence of having been elected to their seats. This pretended Legislature is daily passing laws, and Kellogg is approving or vetoing them. This is the Legislature which pretended to elect Ray to fill the unexpired portion of Kellogg's term in the Senate. McEnery and his associates claim to be the rightful officers of the State, and two other bodies of men claim to be the Senate and House of Representatives of the State. And this is the Legislature which pretended to elect McMillan to fill Kellogg's unexpired term in the Senate.

Again:

The question we are considering is not a judicial question, and no judicial court can determine it. The question is political in its character, and, so far as the United States have to deal with it, must be determined by the political department of this Government. We must therefore investigate the facts, and no decision of any branch of a pretended State Government can stop us in this inquiry.

The people of the State are about equally divided in sentiment in regard to these two pretended governments. The people of New Orleans, which is the seat of government, support the McEnery government, two to one; and it is believed that if Federal support were withdrawn from the Kellogg government it would be immediately supplanted by the McEnery government. The people of the State, as a body, neither support nor submit to either government. Neither government can collect taxes, for the people have no assurance that payment to one will prevent collection by the other government. Business is interrupted, and public confidence destroyed; and should Congress adjourn without making provisions for the case, one of two things must result: Either collision and bloodshed between the adher-

WAR, POLITICS AND RECONSTRUCTION

ents of the two governments, or the President must continue the support of the Federal authority to the Kellogg government. The alternative of civil war or the maintenance by military power of a State government not elected is exceedingly embarrassing; and in the opinion of your committee the best solution of this difficulty is for Congress to order a re-election, and provide for holding it under authority of the United States; to the end that a government may be elected by the people, to which they will submit, or which in case of disturbance the United States can honestly maintain.

Therefore your committee recommend the adoption of the following resolutions:

1. That there is no State government at present existing in the State of Louisiana.

2. That neither John Ray nor W. L. McMillan is entitled to a seat in the Senate, neither having been elected by the Legislature of the State of Louisiana.

And your committee recommend the passage of the bill herewith reported.

(*Signed*)   MATT. H. CARPENTER
JOHN A. LOGAN
J. L. ALCORN
H. B. ANTHONY

Senator Lyman Trumbull, of Illinois, a member of the Committee, in a separate report said in part:

The history of the world does not furnish a more palpable instance of usurpation than that by which Pinchback was made governor, and the persons returned by the Lynch Board the Legislature of Louisiana; nor can a parallel be found for the unfeeling and despotic answers sent by order of the President to the respectful appeals of the people of Louisiana. This pretended Legislature, installed in power by the aid of the United States Army, in pursuance of a void order of the United States district judge, proceeded to elect John Ray to represent the State of Louisiana in the Senate of the United States; and it is said that the Senate must receive him because the Supreme Court of Louisiana has decided the Pinchback Legislature to be the rightful Legislature of the State, and that the Senate is bound to follow the decision of the State Court as to what constitutes its Legislature. . . .

It is, however, said by a majority of the committee that the election of November 4 was so tainted with fraud as to render it wholly void, and they recommend the passage of a law for holding a new election under the authority of Congress.

If it were admitted, as it is not, that Congress has authority to inquire into the fairness and regularity of a State election, it is denied that there was any such fraud in the late Louisiana election as would justify setting it aside. It was confessedly one of the most quiet and peaceful elections ever held in the State, and the evidence shows that it was substantially free and fair.

The vote polled was twenty thousand larger than ever before cast in the State, and against more than two-thirds of it no complaint of unfairness is ever alleged. . . .

It has been said that the colored voters were all Republicans, that the colored population of the State outnumbers the whites, and that therefore if the election had been fair the Republican ticket must have succeeded; but the census of 1870 shows that there were in the State one hundred and fifty-three more white than colored males over twenty-one years of age; and it is also in evidence that from eight to ten thousand colored persons voted the fusion ticket, while the number of whites who voted the Republican ticket is not believed to have exceeded half that number.

That fraud was practised in some of the Parishes, that irregularities existed in others, may be admitted; and still, in the absence of any legitimate evidence to establish those frauds, or of any sort of complaint even against the fairness of the election in more than two-thirds of the State, the undersigned cannot admit that such a case exists as would authorize the interference of Congress with the election in any form; and his conclusion is that, by the admission of McMillan to his seat in the Senate, and the recognition thereby of the McEnery Legislature as the legitimate Legislature of the State, the peace of Louisiana will be speedily restored, and effect given to the fairly expressed will of her people.

(*Signed*) Lyman Trumbull

In his separate report of the Committee, Senator Joshua Hill, of Georgia, said:

No one doubts that but for the interposition of a judge of the United States district court the returns of the election would have been counted by a board of canvassers under the laws of the State, and that a result would have been reached, at least, with all the appearances of regularity, in which a majority of the people would have acquiesced. Shall the unauthorized act of this official, condemned as it is by all legal minds, be permitted of itself to reverse the expressed will of a majority of the voters of Louisiana, or at least a majority of those that voted? Surely, it cannot be a sound principle in politics or ethics that an admitted usurpation can create anything more than a government *de facto*. To assert that it may bring into existence by its mere recognition a government that lives, moves, and has its being solely by such adoption, is to declare that the usurping tribunal is supreme, and its decisions and orders are irreversible. What boots it to rebuke the illegal and tyrannical assumptions of a judge if his orders and decrees must have all the effect he designed to give them? Of what consequence is it that his violations of law should be reviewed and censured, if the effect is the same as though he had not exceeded his jurisdiction and abused the authority of his office? It would seem to be an act of supererogation to pause to wonder at the fatuity that dictated his course, if its end and aim are to stand as facts accomplished. In the light of policy, it would seem better in deciding that a government foully and fraudulently set up by the fiat of a judge shall stand, because it is a *de facto* government; that no discredit should be cast upon the integrity or intelligence of the magistrate. It certainly cannot commend a State government to those who are to live under it, to inform them that the National Legislature, after a thorough examination into the history of its origin, have ascertained that it was born of fraud and arrogated power, and but for these could never have had existence.

The only member of the Committee on Privileges and Elections who attempted to excuse the usurpation of President Grant in setting up the Kellogg government was Senator Morton of Indiana. Even he, with every other member of the Committee, condemned in the strongest terms the whole proceeding of Judge Durell of the United States Court, and of the United States Marshal and the United States troops in seizing the State House and setting up the Kellogg government.

In a separate opinion, Senator Morton says:

The conduct of Judge Durell, sitting in the circuit court of the United States, cannot be justified or defended. He grossly exceeded his jurisdiction, and assumed the exercise of powers to which he could lay no claim. . . .

His order issued in the Kellogg case to the United States marshal to take possession of the State House for the purpose of preventing unlawful assemblages, under which the marshal called to his aid a portion of the Army of the United States, as a *posse comitatus,* can only be characterized as a gross usurpation.

President Grant took such a personal interest in the contest that he called the Senate Committee of Privileges and Elections before him and insisted that it support him.

Senators Morton, Carpenter, Logan, Anthony, and Alcorn were all intimate personal and political friends of President Grant. Their influence and power at home depended greatly upon their standing with the President and their ability to control the patronage and favors of the administration. They knew the wilful and arbitrary nature of General Grant, who bitterly resented the failure of the State of Louisiana to give him its electoral vote. His revenge was embodied in his organized plan to overthrow the State Government. He was antagonistic to me personally; he supported Judge Durell, his brother-in-law Collector Casey, and United States Marshal Packard in the seizing of the State House in the middle of the night of December 5th; and he furnished the troops with which to hold the building for four weeks until I was overthrown and his partisans were installed as the government of the State. This military support was specifically promised in the dispatch of Attorney-General Williams, three days before the seizing of the State House took place.

These gentlemen of the Committee condemned Judge Durell for his every act; they condemned the United States Marshal; they condemned the use of the United States troops for seizing and holding the State House; they condemned everybody, but they did not dare to condemn or even criticize President Grant or Attorney-General Williams, who had organized the whole scheme of revolution and carried it through.

These partisan Senators were forced to devise some scheme,

some theory, some excuse, to help the President out of the dreadful mess he and his Attorney General had brought about in Louisiana; so they resorted to a charge that the State election was fraudulent. This they did without any evidence whatever, except the claims of defeated candidates. There was no proof. Even United States Marshal Packard testified that "the election was generally peaceable, orderly and fair." That there were a few irregularities reported in several Parishes may have been true, but the Senate Committee had no evidence before it showing frauds of any kind. They accepted the oral statements of Kellogg and his coadjutors that the negroes were in a large majority in the State; that they all voted for him and his ticket, and that but for fraud he would have been elected.

Therefore, the recommendation of these committee men that a new election should be held in Louisiana was merely a maneuver to drag the contest along and wear the people out. They could not afford to antagonize the President.

As Senator Carpenter said to me: *"We can't recognize the Kellogg usurpation and we won't recognize the McEnery Government."*

Hence this bill for a new election under Federal auspices. No one in Congress favored it. There was but one speech made in favor of the bill and that was made by Senator Carpenter, who declared that it had to be passed, or the McEnery Government would have to be recognized.

In his speech he admitted that the election was one of the quietest and most peaceable ever held in the State, but he asserted that "the Governor [Warmoth] resorted to craft rather than violence," and he then proceeded to describe in the following words the man whose craft had won the election for McEnery:

"There is in Louisiana a very remarkable young man, dignified in mien, of elegant presence and agreeable conversation; a man full of resources, political and social, gallant, daring, and with a genius for politics; such a man as would rise to power in any great civil disturbance, embodying in himself the elements of revolution, and delighting in the exercise of his natural gifts in the midst of political excitement."

Senator Morton said:

"I recommend masterly inactivity. I say let that government alone, and if Congress adjourns and leaves it just where it is now, all will be well. If McEnery attempts to make any trouble, Governor Kellogg is able to take care of him without any assistance from the Government of the United States; but if he requires it he will get it. The President has said he would give it."

As Senator Morton was speaking for the President, Congress adjourned without action on the Louisiana contest, leaving everything in the hands of the President. Congress did adjourn session after session without taking any action; in fact, it never did take action, but left the people in a state of anarchy for over four years.

This delay cost the State of Louisiana millions of dollars, hundreds of human lives, and five years of anarchy; and it resulted in such bitterness that the colored people of the South lost all of their civil and political rights and have not regained them even to this day.

An interesting incident occurred in Washington during this contest before Congress which is worthy of record. General George A. Sheridan (Congressman-at-Large, elected on the McEnery ticket) and I occupied rooms on F Street for several months. The contest over the recognition of the Kellogg government by the Senate had progressed to the point where Senator Morton, Chairman of the Committee on Privileges and Election, made up his mind that he had enough votes to seat P. B. S. Pinchback, who claimed the seat, having been elected by the Kellogg Legislature. So Senator Morton made a motion, but without the authority of his committee, that Pinchback should be seated, and the day was fixed in the Senate for the consideration of the question.

On January 19, 1873, one day before this date, Captain E. E.

Norton, one of the chief conspirators who had influenced Judge Durell in his course, and who had been promised the seat in the United States Senate, called upon General Sheridan and me at our rooms. He came about ten o'clock in the morning and spent nearly the whole day with us, during which time he carefully went over and stated in great detail all of the facts by which Judge Durell had been induced to take jurisdiction of the Kellogg case and to set up the Kellogg government. He told us that the plan to overthrow me and to set up the Kellogg government had been formed in Washington and that the President and the Attorney General had promised military support to execute the Judge's orders. He said these facts were made known to Judge Durell before he would reluctantly consent to take jurisdiction of the case. He told us of the agreement that Billings should be the successor of Durell, and that he (Norton) should have the seat in the Senate made vacant by the election of Kellogg to the governorship. He told us particularly of an interview between himself, Mr. Kellogg, and Mr. Pinchback. He told us that a caucus was to be held by the Legislature on a certain night to select the nominee for the senatorship; that it was known that Pinchback was a candidate and that they feared he might secure the nomination. Kellogg sent for Pinchback and told him of the agreement that had been made that Norton should have this seat in the Senate. Pinchback pretended that he did not know of any such agreement, and besides, that he was not bound by it any way.

Then Kellogg told Pinchback that Judge Durell had set up the government and that he had the power to unseat it, and that unless the agreement with Norton was carried out, he feared for the result; whereupon Pinchback stated that he had already spent ten thousand dollars in his canvass for this seat in the Senate, and that he could not afford to lose the money. But Kellogg said that he had no doubt but that Captain Norton would make good to him his expenses up to that time. So

Pinchback agreed to accept the advice of Mr. Kellogg, and to withdraw his candidacy in favor of Norton; and Norton sent out and got ten one-thousand-dollar bills, which he handed over to Pinchback, and the latter promised to go to the caucus and secure the nomination of Norton.

Pinchback attended the caucus but, instead of Norton's being nominated for the seat in the Senate, Pinchback was nominated, and Captain Norton told us that some time elapsed before he was able to recover his money.

As I said before, Norton spent nearly the whole day with us. After he left I turned to Sheridan and said: "General, I know your personal relationship with Senator Morton. You have canvassed the State of Indiana for the Republican ticket several times and I know he will believe anything that you may tell him. I want you to go and take a bath and then we will dine and after dinner I want you to go to the Ebbitt House where Senator Morton lives and tell him that you have an important communication to make to him and that you want him to lock all doors until you finish. Then tell Morton this whole story from beginning to end."

General Sheridan took my advice, called upon Senator Morton, and went over the whole case as related to us by Captain Norton. When he was through Senator Morton said to General Sheridan: "How can I verify these facts?"

Sheridan replied: "Senator Morton, you are a lawyer and you have had great experience in examining witnesses. I suggest to you that you send for Pinchback and say to him in a manner you well know, 'Governor, I want you to tell me all about how you defeated that fellow Norton for his nomination to the Senate.' I know Pinchback well enough to know that his vanity is such that he will be delighted to tell you of the trick that he put over on Kellogg and Norton."

The case was fixed in the Senate for 11 A.M. the day following. Senator Morton's seat was in the front row on the main aisle. Looking behind him he discovered Pinchback seated on a sofa in the rear. Taking his two canes, one in each hand, Senator Morton arose and hobbled back to the cloak-room. As he did so, he passed Pinchback and motioned him to follow. In a most pleasant manner he asked Pinchback to tell him the whole story, which Pinchback did. When he had finished, Morton brought his lower jaw up tight against the upper one and, gathering up his canes, walked back to his seat. And when the hour of eleven arrived, he moved that the case of the State of Louisiana and of P. B. S. Pinchback claiming to be a Senator-elect be referred back to the Committee on Privileges and Elections. That was really and in fact the end of Pinchback's ever being a Senator of the United States.

After a lapse of three sessions of Congress, Senator Morton made a motion that P. B. S. Pinchback be seated as a Senator from the State of Louisiana, but Senator Edmonds of Vermont moved to amend the motion by inserting the word "not" after the word "be," and the amendment was adopted by a vote of 32 to 29. This was the end of Pinchback's fight to be a Senator, and it was a distinct refusal of the Senate to recognize the Kellogg government.

Pinchback also claimed to have been elected Congressman-at-Large on the Kellogg ticket, and presented to the House of Representatives a certificate to that effect, signed by W. P. Kellogg. The Committee on Elections after a full examination reported in favor of the seating of General George A. Sheridan, who was elected on the McEnery ticket, his credentials being signed by John McEnery as Governor.

The House of Representatives did the very unusual thing of allowing both contestants to speak in favor of their claims before the House of Representatives in open session. Both Pinchback and Sheridan addressed the House, whereupon a vote was taken and Sheridan was seated as the Congressman-at-Large from Louisiana, elected on the McEnery ticket. So the Senate refused to recognize Kellogg and his government, and while not seating the Senator elected by the McEnery Legislature, left the question still in the hands of the President. But the House of Representatives by a large majority seated the Congressman-at-Large, elected on the same ticket with McEnery, thereby recognizing McEnery's state government.

Yet after all of these events, and with a full history of the whole case before him, the President continued to uphold and support Kellogg and his usurpation, and he did it to the end.

In face of the fact that the Senate Committee on Privileges and Elections had unanimously declared that Judge Durell of the United States Circuit Court, who had seized the State House with United States troops and set up the Kellogg Government, was totally without jurisdiction and condemned his conduct in the plainest and strongest terms; in face of the action of the United States Senate in rejecting the claims of the man elected by the Kellogg Legislature to a seat in the Senate; in face of the fact that the House of Representatives had seated General George A. Sheridan as the member-at-large from the State of Louisiana, elected on the ticket with Governor McEnery and *repudiated* the certificate of Kellogg that P. B. S. Pinchback had been elected on the ticket with him; in face of the unanimous voice of the press of the nation that the Kellogg Government was a usurpation—General Grant was able to delay action, drag the contest along, and hold up a decision by Congress for four years, till the end of his term of office, all of which time he maintained Kellogg and his usurpation in control of the State, by furnishing the army and garrisoning the State with troops.

At the end of General Grant's term came the Presidential election of 1876, and also the election of a Governor, State officers, and a Legislature in the State of Louisiana. Kellogg being recognized as the *de facto* Governor of Louisiana by the President and supported by the troops of the United States, he, of course, conducted the State election. At will, he controlled the nomination of the candidates on the Republican State ticket. He nominated United States Marshal S. B. Packard as his candidate for Governor, and C. C. Antoine, a negro, as his candidate for Lieutenant-Governor. The Greeley and Brown Liberal Party of 1872 had disbanded or disappeared. The "Last Ditch" Democrats put forth a State ticket with General Francis T. Nichols for Governor and Lewis A. Wiltz for Lieutenant-Governor. The contest was a bitter one and not creditable to either party. Both parties practised trickery, and the Democrats resorted to intimidation and violence in some of the Parishes, which gave Kellogg's Returning Board an excuse for throwing out the returns from certain polls in those Parishes. It became a national scandal.

The Republicans sent down a party of prominent gentlemen, among them Senator John Sherman, General James A. Garfield of Ohio, and General Lew Wallace of Indiana. The Democratic delegation contained, among others, Henry Watterson of the *Courier-Journal,* Ex-Speaker of the House of Representatives, Samuel J. Randall of Pennsylvania, and General John M. Palmer of Illinois, to watch the count of the votes of the Returning Board. The Republican delegation approved and defended the action of the Returning Board, while the Democratic delegation disapproved and condemned its action. The certificate of election was given by Kellogg to the Hayes and Wheeler electors. The election was very close, and its result was finally decided in favor of Hayes and Wheeler by one vote majority, and Louisiana furnished that vote.

Controversy over the election came near to precipitating civil war; but for the concession that was granted by the Grant and Hayes forces to Louisiana, South Carolina, and Florida, it would have resulted in a conflict. Hayes and Wheeler became President and Vice-President, but the Democrats were conceded the State governments of Louisiana, South Carolina, and Florida;

so the conflict was avoided and peace was preserved in the nation.

Kellogg and Packard attempted to hold on to the State Government of Louisiana. Being a member of the Legislature, I had access to both the Nichols and the Packard Legislatures. I was a witness to the disintegration of the Packard Legislature and finally had the satisfaction to see Kellogg and Packard overthrown. Kellogg had to be bought off with the seat in the United States Senate. Packard was bought off with an appointment by President Hayes to the consul-generalship at Liverpool. Pinchback was bought off with the appointment of his brother to a tax-collectorship by Governor Nichols; and $60,000 from the Louisiana Lottery Company helped to satisfy a number of other members of the Packard Legislature to move over to the Nichols Legislature and give it a legal quorum. Governor Nichols and his Legislature became the masters of the State of Louisiana and the Democratic party has continued its control of the State from that day to this, now fifty-three years.

In our efforts to induce Congress to recognize the McEnery Government, we had great difficulty in keeping the violent element in our State in order. The outrage upon the people was so stupendous and the establishment and maintenance of the Kellogg Government by force aroused such bitter resentment that it is to the credit of the masses of the people of Louisiana that they bore it as well as they did. But unfortunately we had one element that we could not control; that was some of the fiery newspaper editors.

For example, *The New Orleans Bulletin,* an evening paper published in the city of New Orleans, took it upon itself to repudiate every pledge that the Liberal Party, the Democratic Party, and the Reform Party had made in their Conventions, acting separately, and later jointly, to the colored people of the State as to their civil and political rights. All three of the conservative parties had stressed their obligations to sustain and protect the colored people in their civil and political rights. Governor McEnery, Lieutenant-Governor Penn and every one of us who made the canvass for our ticket took great pains to pledge the colored people that we would sustain and protect them in all of their civil and political rights.

The Reform Party, headed by Gen. G. T. Beauregard, Jas. I. Day, Gen. Randall L. Gibson, I. N. Marks, Chas. H. Thompson, W. M. Randolph, Geo. Williamson, and many other very important and distinguished white men, together with the written approval of several thousand of our best citizens, went so far as to declare in their platform as follows:

Be it therefore resolved:

1. That henceforth we dedicate ourselves to the unification of our people.

2. That by "our people" we mean all men, of whatever race, color or religion, who are citizens of Louisiana, who are willing to work for her prosperity.

3. That we shall advocate by speech, pen, and deed, the equal and impartial exercise by every citizen of Louisiana of every civil and political right guaranteed by the Constitution and laws of the United States, and by the laws of honor, brotherhood, and fair dealing.

4. That we shall maintain and advocate the right of every citizen of Louisiana and of every citizen of the United States to frequent at will all places of public resort, and to travel at will on all vehicles or public conveyances, upon terms of perfect equality with any and every other citizen; and we pledge ourselves, so far as our influence, counsel and example may go, to make this right a live and practical right, and that there may be no misunderstanding of our views on this point:

(a) We shall recommend to the proprietors of all places of licensed public resort in the State of Louisiana the opening of said places to the patronage of both races inhabiting our State.

(b) And we shall further recommend that all railroads, steamboats, steamships, and other public conveyances pursue the same policy.

(c) We shall further recommend that our banks, insurance offices, and other public corporations recognize and concede to our fellow-citizens, where they are stockholders in such institutions, the right of being represented in the direction thereof.

(d) We shall further recommend that hereafter no distinction shall exist among citizens of Louisiana in any of our public schools, or State institutions of education, or in any other public institution supported by the State, city or Parish.

(e) We shall also recommend that the proprietors of all foundries, factories, and other industrial establishments, in employing mechanics or workmen, make no distinction between the two races.

But in the midst of our contest before Congress this newspaper came out in an article headed:

Political Equality

Having succeeded in obtaining the purification of the public schools, the inviolability of the places of public amusement and resort, we have now but one duty to perform, and that is to secure a return to the system of the "Star" cars on our street railways.

Colored people had previously not been allowed to ride on any street-car that did not have a large star painted on its sides. The feeling of the people was such that *The New Orleans Picayune* interviewed Governor McEnery, Lieutenant-Governor Penn, General Fred Ogden, Robt. H. Marr, and many other leaders of our fusion movement, who plainly disavowed this article and expressed their great regret at its publication, especially at this particular time when we felt that we were on the eve of winning our case before Congress. I had but recently returned from Washington, where I had spent several months in the interest of our cause, and I realized the great injury that would follow the re-publication of this article in the Northern press. So I wrote a respectful letter to the editor of the *Bulletin,* calling his attention to the pledges which each one of our political organizations had made separately—and later, after our fusion, all together—to the colored people.

I took my letter to the editor of the *Bulletin.* After reading it he told me he would ruin me if I published it. I laughingly told him to publish my letter and that I would take my chances on his being able to ruin me. He published my letter and followed it with a most scurrilous and vindictive editorial, attacking me politically and personally. Of course, I wrote an exceedingly caustic reply.

The result of this correspondence was a letter brought to me by Mr. Washington Marks and Mr. John Overton, noted duelists, demanding an abject apology for the statements I had made in my letter; I promptly refused. Within an hour after this demand I was served with a challenge from E. L. Jewell, editor of the *Bulletin,* to fight a duel; this I promptly accepted, and our respective friends arranged that we were to fight on the following Monday, over in the State of Mississippi, with pistols at ten paces.

The next day after this arrangement, about eleven o'clock, I was walking on Canal Street when I met Mr. Dan Byerly, the manager of the *Bulletin.* I had no quarrel with him; my fight was with the editor. I saw only his head and shoulders because he was following closely behind two young women somewhat shorter than himself. I was on the inside of the walk. As the women passed me I raised my hat in salutation to Mr. Byerly, when he struck me over the head with the heavy cane in his right hand, and followed it up twice, cutting open my head and stunning me for a moment. Having split his cane he threw it away and grabbed me and threw me down on the side of the banquette, my head and shoulders extending over into the street.

A friend of mine some time before had given me a pocket knife with one blade about four inches long, which I carried in my left coat-pocket. While on my back and with Byerly on top of me, I got out my knife and opened it and plunged it into him five or six times. Some policemen nearby seized him and pulled him off of me, and as he arose I planted my heels in his abdomen and drove him as far away as I could so as to be able to get up before I should be shot.

I was immediately arrested and placed in the old Parish Prison on Orleans Street, where I was kept for five days and nights. I was put in a room with a gambler by the name of Sam Williams, who had been tried and sentenced to be hanged for killing a woman. He was my companion for five days and nights.

The coroner's jury finally held an inquest and made their report, and I was brought before the court and discharged on the ground that I had acted clearly in self-defense. No indictment was ever preferred against me by the grand jury and I think that everybody justified me. That ended the duel.

I was visited while in prison by a large number of people, among them Governor McEnery, Lieutenant-Governor Penn, Mayor Wiltz, and Governor Kellogg, but the most comforting visitor that I had was dear old Bishop Wilmer of the Episcopal Church. I remember that he assured me that I was perfectly justified in defending myself from the attack of my assailant, but he said that he had one fault to find with me, and that was that if I had been a member of his church he would not have allowed me to accept the challenge to fight a duel. I jumped up, seized him by the hand and said to him: "My dear, dear Bishop, I shall join your church as soon as I get out of this jail!" It is not necessary for me to say here that I am a member of the Episcopal Church at this time.

The Grant leaders in the Republican Party hoped to be able to nominate him for a third term, but his second administration developed great hostility among the people, not the least of his acts being his brutal treatment of the people of Louisiana.

The opposition grew so powerful that the House of Representatives by a vote of 234 to 18 adopted a resolution denouncing his aspirations for a third term. The result was that his name was not even presented to the Republican Convention at Cincinnati in 1876. Rutherford B. Hayes, of Ohio, was nominated and elected.

But General Grant's friends at once began organizing for his nomination in 1880. In pursuance of this scheme, it was arranged that he should make a tour of the world, and the newspapers were kept full of the wonderful receptions he had extended to him everywhere. John Russell Young, a great newspaper man, accompanied him on his tour. President Hayes placed the great warship "Vandalia" at his disposal. His tour occupied over two years, and he visited nearly every place of interest in the world, all of which was duly recorded and published on the front pages in all the great newspapers of the United States.

He returned, arriving at San Francisco, California, on the 20th of September, 1879, only eight months before the meeting of the National Republican Convention in Chicago, on June 2nd, 1880. By this time, the stage was fully set for carrying his nomination by storm. Every politician who had held office under Grant and had lost such position was working for him; all of the capitalists, jobbers, and government contractors who had grown rich through his favors; the Army and Navy cliques and worn-out soldiers of the Civil War strained their lungs; and the Grant press screamed for his nomination. Millions of dollars were spent in organizing for propaganda and for obtaining delegates. The fight was fierce. It was led in the Convention by Senator Conkling of New York, General Logan of Illinois, J. A. J. Crosswell of Maryland, Geo. M. Boutwell of Massachusetts, and W. O. Bradley of Kentucky. There were several contested delegations, and it required three days and nights of hard work for the Committee on Credentials to hear the cases and to decide their claims.

The Grant adherents in Louisiana contested the seats of my delegation, but it was seated by the unanimous vote of the Committee, and also by the unanimous vote of the Convention.

The Convention sat up until midnight on the fourth day. It held day and night sessions. There never was such a contest, such excitement and bitterness in a National Republican Convention before or since. The speech presenting Grant's name to the Convention was made by Senator Roscoe Conkling of New York. It was a powerful and dramatic effort by a wonderful man and orator. He began his speech by saying:

> "And when asked what State he hails from,
> "Our sole reply shall be,
> "He hails from Appomattox,
> "And its famous apple-tree!"

No other words could have been so aptly used: they stirred and thrilled the heart of every delegate, those for him as well as those against him. The Convention and the crowded galleries responded with tremendous applause. Senator Conkling's address was the grandest speech he ever delivered. It had all of the skill and force of his tremendous nature. His whole soul was in it. He availed himself of every argument in favor of Grant; he appealed to every sentiment, to every emotion, with the consummate skill of the great orator that he was, and he was beyond question the greatest orator on the American platform at this time.

Senator Bradley of Kentucky seconded Grant's nomination with a splendid speech. John Sherman of Ohio and James G. Blaine of Maine were also candidates.

When the State of Ohio was called, General James R. Garfield arose to place before the Convention the name of John Sherman of Ohio. The fifteen thousand people who crowded that auditorium drew a long breath. The Grant followers believed that the speeches of Conkling and Bradley had won the day, and that General Grant's nomination was assured. The question in every mind was whether Garfield could turn the tide which had rushed so fiercely in favor of Grant.

General Garfield was himself a splendid man. His presence was most pleasing, more amiable than that of Conkling. His voice and manner were more kindly. His tones were gentler,

and full of conciliation. He began his address with these
words:

"Mr. President: I have witnessed the extraordinary scenes of this
Convention with deep solicitude. Nothing touches my heart more
quickly than a tribute of honor to a great and noble character; but as
I sat in my seat and witnessed this demonstration, this assemblage
seemed to me a human ocean in tempest. I have seen the sea lashed
into fury and tossed into spray, and its grandeur moves the soul of
the dullest man; but I remember that it is not the billows but the
calm level of the sea from which all heights and depths are measured.
When the storm has passed and the hour of calm settles on the ocean,
when the sunlight bathes its peaceful surface, then the astronomer and
the surveyor take the level from which they measure all terrestrial
heights and depths.

"Gentlemen of the Convention, your present temper may not mark
the healthful pulse of our people. When your enthusiasm has passed,
when the emotions of this hour have subsided, we shall find below
the storm and passion that calm level of public opinion from which
the thoughts of a mighty people are to be measured, and by which
their final action will be determined.

"Not here in this brilliant circle, where fifteen thousand men and
women are gathered, is the destiny of the Republic to be decreed for
the next four years. Not here, where I see the enthusiastic faces of
756 delegates, waiting to cast their lots into the urn and determine
the choice of the Republic; but by four millions of Republican fire-
sides where the thoughtful voters, with wives and children about them,
with calm thoughts of love of home and country, with the history of
the past, the hopes of the future, and reverence for the great men who
have adorned and blest our nation in the days gone by, burning in
their hearts—there, God prepares the verdict which will determine the
wisdom of our work tonight. Not in Chicago, in the heat of June,
but at the ballot-boxes of the Republic, in the quiet of November,
after the silence of deliberate judgment, will this question be settled.
And now, Gentlemen of the Convention, what do we want? (*A voice—
"We want Garfield!"*) Bear with me a moment. Hear me for my
cause. Be silent that you may hear."

From that moment Garfield's name was in the hearts and
on the lips of every delegate opposed to the nomination of General Grant, and after a struggle of three days and nights, and

with 36 different ballots, Garfield received 399 votes to 306 for Grant.

It was a great source of satisfaction to me that I was able to contribute to the defeat of Grant in his greatest ambition, in humiliation of the man who had done so much to humiliate and destroy the people of the State of Louisiana. I sat beside General Garfield and studied his face as the great honor was conferred on him, when State after State cast its votes for his nomination.

Senator Conkling was most bitterly disappointed. He said to me, in speaking of Garfield, that we had "dragged a candidate out from under an Army wagon." It is a lamentable fact that Senator Conkling's continued expressions of bitter hatred of both General Garfield and Secretary Blaine led a crazed follower of his to shoot the President of the United States to death in the open daylight in the Capital of the Nation.*

By 1888 the men who had brought the Republican Party in Louisiana to ruin in 1872 were gone. United States Marshal Packard, the head and front of all of the trouble, who had tried to succeed Kellogg as Governor in 1876 but failed, had been pensioned off by President Hayes to London as United States Consul in order to get rid of him. Colonel Casey, the President's brother-in-law, was gone—no one knew where.

The Republican Party was bereft of its leaders of 1872-74-76. The Democratic Party had been in power in the State and city since 1876—for twelve years. Governor Francis T. Nichols was Governor of the State from 1876 to 1880, when he was succeeded by Alfred Wiltz, who died soon after his election. His Lieutenant-Governor, Samuel D. McEnery, succeeded him and served out his term, and was later elected to succeed himself for another full term, being in office nearly eight years, bringing us up to 1888.

* President Garfield was assassinated by Charles Guiteau in Washington, D. C., July 2, 1881, and died Sept. 19, 1881.

The attempt of Governor McEnery in 1888 to succeed himself resulted in a very bitter contest in his own party. It began more than a year before the end of his second term. Meetings were held in many Parishes criticizing him in bitter terms. Governor McEnery mastered his party organization through his white supporters who controlled the large negro Parishes. Representation in their State Convention was based on population, and negroes were counted in the census though they were not allowed to register or vote at elections. This gave to the white leaders in the negro Parishes a preponderance of delegates in the Democratic State Convention. Former Governor Francis T. Nichols was agreed upon as Governor McEnery's opponent for the nomination. Edward D. White, who later became United States Senator and still later Chief Justice of the Supreme Court of the United States, was Governor Nichols' political campaign manager.

The powerful election machinery was all in the hands of Governor McEnery, and he was accused of using it unfairly in the interests of his friends and himself. The white men of the strong negro Parishes of the State were generally supporters of McEnery. He allowed them to control the ballot boxes. The white Parishes generally supported Nichols. The press of the State was divided in its support—*The Times Democrat* of New Orleans supported McEnery, but the *Picayune* supported Nichols. The columns of each paper were full of spirited editorials in favor of their respective candidates and against their opponents. *The Times Democrat,* of October 4th, said: "Nichols and his reformers have six weeks' time to explain what they are after."

A great meeting was held in the City of New Orleans in the Second Ward on the 22nd day of December, 1887. Governor McEnery was the principle speaker and he said, among other things:

"There have been loud complaints which have increased with increasing years in regard to the frauds at your elections, not only here but throughout the State of Louisiana, and they have gone beyond the limits of our State and have given our State an unenviable notoriety. So far as my administration of the election laws is concerned, I have listened to complaints and I propose in the future to do in a general way what I have done in a special case, to-wit: in the removal of E. A. Dureino, who is now a prominent reformer, for obtaining frauds in the election. And I pledge you here tonight that not only in this city of New Orleans, but throughout the State of Louisiana, I will see an honest and fair election; and I will see that every vote cast is counted as deposited and that no substitution of ballots is practised, but that the voice of all the voters in the State as deposited in the ballot box shall find expression and receive recognition, and that the officers elected shall be commissioned. To that end I will remove any registrar or returning officer in the city or State that I have reason to believe will aid in the suppression or changing of the popular will."

The editorial in *The Times Democrat*, December 23, 1887, said:

We would explain here that in the country Parishes the assessors are the registers of votes, having control of the registration, and that the returning officers have the power of naming the polling places and appointing the commissioners of election. We congratulate the people of Louisiana on the assurance of an absolutely fair and honest election in which the registration will be thoroughly purged of fraud and in which every vote will be counted as deposited.

Editorial, *Times Democrat*, December 30, 1887, said:

General Nichols will never forgive nor forget Tensas. It was in Tensas that the first cry against the State Administration was heard. It was his message against the white people of Tensas which made the Democrats of Louisiana distrust him and which encouraged Republicans to assault the State in Congress.

It was Tensas again which sent a solid McEnery delegation to the State Convention, which was so solidly opposed to Governor Nichols, for the reason we have already stated, that he could not get a man in the Parish to protest in his interest against the vote. General Nichols has no love for Tensas and does not hesitate to speak out against the Tensas Democrats.

At a large meeting in the Eighth Ward of the city of New Orleans, Governor Nichols replied to Governor McEnery. He said:

"If the supporters of Governor McEnery succeed, instead of one Tensas with 3800 alleged Democratic votes and only 400 white Democratic voters, giving a negro Parish 19 delegates to the Convention and overruling a dozen white Parishes, then there will be five or ten Tensas Parishes made, and the city and white Parishes will be thus controlled, until nothing short of a revolution could create a change."

Editorial in *The Times Democrat:*

Of the 58 Parishes in the State 36 have negro majorities and only 22 white. We cannot afford to repudiate, as General Nichols suggested, the vote of these 36 Parishes because there is a majority of negroes in them. Tensas, Concordia, East and West Feliciana, Caddo and De Soto are as necessary to our success as Washington, Vernon, Sabine and Winn.

The Democratic State Convention met at Baton Rouge on January 10, 1888. Intense bitterness was displayed on both sides. The great issue was the admission of the large delegations from the extra large negro Parishes. The Committee on Credentials was engaged for four days and nights in almost continuous sittings. The Nichols faction was finally able to turn out enough of the McEnery delegates from the large negro Parishes to give them a majority over McEnery.

General Nichols was nominated on the first ballot, receiving 289 votes against 183 for McEnery. The Convention adjourned in the worst humor, McEnery declaring, "Now you have *nominated* Nichols, *elect* him!"

Governor McEnery knew that there was only one way by which a Democratic State ticket could be elected and that was by employing what was known as the "Ouachita Plan," which he had devised and which in the end he employed to the limit in behalf of General Nichols, in spite of his pledges of a fair election.

This bitter contest between the two factions of the Democratic Party seemed to give the reorganized Republican Party an opening. There had grown up in the State within the past twelve years a large element of people who found it necessary to combat the free-trade tendencies of the national Democratic Party. The sugar and rice planters, the machinery manufacturers, the cotton and woolen mill owners and operatives, the railroad corporations, and many bankers and merchants were interested in the success of Republican principles. Under these influences and greatly encouraged by the split in the Democratic Party, the various Republican elements of the State united in holding a State Convention in the city of New Orleans on the 3rd day of January, 1888.

Every Parish in the State was fully represented. The Convention nominated the following ticket:

For Governor	Henry C. Warmoth of Plaquemines
For Lieutenant-Governor . .	Henry C. Minor of Terrebonne
For Secretary of State . . .	John F. Patty of St. Mary
For Attorney-General . . .	ex-Judge W. G. Wiley of Carroll
For Superintendent of Education	ex-Governor B. F. Flanders
For Auditor of Public Accounts	James Forsyth of Catahoula
For Treasurer	Andrew Hero of Orleans

Every candidate but two had been prominent with me in the Liberal Republican or Greeley-Brown movement of 1872. There was but one colored man on the ticket—John F. Patty—and he was a very respectable and popular man. There were in nearly every part of the State strong manifestations of earnest support of the ticket, and the fact reacted on the managers of the Nichols' ticket.

Before I accepted the nomination for Governor, I called upon Governor McEnery, together with my friend, General McMillan (who had been elected to the United States Senate by the McEnery Legislature in 1872), who at the time was a guest of the St. Charles Hotel. We expressed our sympathy for him in his defeat for the nomination for Governor and condoled with him on the ingratitude of political parties and political leaders, concluding our interview with an inquiry as to the seriousness of his public declarations and pledges made in his speeches for a fair and honest election. He asserted to us with much show of spirit that he not only meant what he said in his public declarations, but that I could rely upon it that I should have every vote put in any box for me counted and returned as cast. I cannot say that the Governor urged me to accept the Republican nomination for Governor, but his tone and manner convinced both General McMillan and me that he would not be unhappy if I should win the race and defeat General Nichols, of whom he spoke in most vituperative terms.

At any rate, we made up our minds that I should accept the nomination for Governor on the Republican ticket and make a vigorous campaign. I did accept the nomination, and we proceeded with the best and strongest campaign that I ever made in Louisiana.

There was at the time a bitter split in the Democratic Party of the city of New Orleans over the election of the Mayor and other City officials. Mr. W. S. Parkerson led an independent movement in favor of the election of Joseph Shakespeare and his ticket as against the regular ring Democratic ticket. The Republicans made a combination with Mr. Parkerson, and we gave his independent ticket the solid Republican vote of the city, and it was elected by a decided majority. Our consideration was mainly an agreement that the Parkerson faction should secure us a fair and full count of the votes in the support of our candidates for our State and Legislative ticket. It turned out that Mr. Parkerson was obliged to organize and arm a large force of men to guard and protect the ballot boxes from being overwhelmed by the violent element that the "ring ticket" had organized.

As the campaign progressed it became clear to Judge White (Governor Nichols' manager) and his leaders that something had to be done or they would be doomed to defeat. A fair election would be certain to give the Warmoth ticket the victory. Governor McEnery and his friends continued to sulk in their tents. So after a full discussion of the matter at Democratic Headquarters, it was determined to send Captain Richard Sinnott to Baton Rouge to see Governor McEnery and find out whether the Governor could not be induced to come down to New Orleans and meet General Nichols and his friends. It was a delicate job, but Captain Sinnott was a diplomat as well as a most aggressive and forceful man. His mission was successful. Governor McEnery reluctantly came to New Orleans with Captain Sinnott, who steered him around to the old "Varieties Club," under the old "Varieties Theatre," on Canal Street, where they happened to meet General Nichols, Judge White and some other friends. Not being present, I cannot give the details of the interview, but the public later learned that it was made as pleasant for the Governor as the good liquors and cigars of the club could make it, and it resulted in a big dinner that night up on the third floor of Moreau's Restaurant, where the big leaders of the party were present, and where eloquence, sympathy and fear of defeat, combined with good liquors, held the night until a late hour, and the Governor was carried to his hotel with the assurance of an appointment to the Supreme Court of the State for a term of twelve years. He in turn promised to see to it that every ballot box should be stuffed to the limit in favor of General Nichols and his ticket. All of the details of this combination gradually became known to me and my friends who were absent with me in the State making our campaign.

I went to the great Parish of Tensas to hold a meeting at the town of St. Joseph. This was a Parish in which I had not only a strong colored support, but nearly every leading Democrat in the Parish had, during the time I was Governor, held my commission to some office, and all of them had been with me in the Greeley-Brown fight in 1872. I had appointed my old friend, Charlie Cordill, Judge of the Parish. Among my first acts as Governor, I appointed Jim Gillespie Sheriff of Tensas Parish. I had appointed John Smyth on the Levee Board, and a number of important men on the Police Jury.

They met me at the landing of my steamboat and escorted me to the village hotel for lunch; they escorted me to the Court House where a very large meeting was held. Judge Cordill presided at this meeting and introduced me and also General Sheridan and General McMillan, as speakers. The meeting was most enthusiastic, Judge Cordill and all of his friends leading in the applause.

After the meeting was over, these gentlemen escorted us back to the hotel and gave us a most enjoyable dinner. Prohibition was not then the law of the land and after the turkey and wine and other good things had been served and the room was pretty well filled with smoke from our excellent cigars, I turned in my chair and thanked the gentlemen present for our reception and their kind and generous hospitality; and I made bold to ask the Judge what vote he thought I could count on in Tensas Parish. I noticed some confusion and detected, as I thought, some embarrassment, as the Judge looked at one, and then another, of his friends around the table. After a little delay, characterized by an impressive silence, the Judge took me by the hand and said:

"Governor Warmoth, all of us here are your friends. Several of us held your commission for important offices when you were the former Governor of the State. Tensas Parish has no complaint to make whatever against the Republican Party, or you, during your administration, but we had grave cause to complain of the Kellogg régime and the negroes who dictated things afterwards; and we do not think that we can afford to let another Republican be elected Governor of the State, and we do not believe that you will receive a single vote in this Parish."

This was a great shock to me and my campaign party. The result showed that my friend, Judge Cordill, was not mistaken, for I received only 113 votes in Tensas Parish, although 4,627 votes were returned for General Nichols. We learned from these gentlemen that it had been determined to count General Nichols in, whatever the vote should be.

After the trade was completed between Governor McEnery and General Nichols, a large meeting was held at the Washington Artillery Hall in New Orleans on March 8, 1888, at which Governor McEnery spoke. After giving a picture of Republican rule and its awful consequences, he said:

"Is there no danger of this conflict? Is there any danger of the negro ever again getting possession of the Government? Yes, and it is imminent. Warmoth is the central figure of the period of the negro domination. He is their idol—the demigod of the uneducated negro, who looks upon Warmoth as the Moses to lead him to the Promised Land.

"I have no opposition to make against Governor Warmoth's personal or private character. I have cited the testimony of accomplices who were actors in the sad drama of our history. They may not have told the truth as to him personally; but as to the acts of the party of which Governor Warmoth was the Chief, their evidence is trustworthy. Governor Warmoth is a product of that era and he is inseparable from it. As a private citizen his life has been exemplary, his ability invariably admitted, and his energy and progressiveness recognized."

Senator B. F. Jonas also spoke. He said:

"Whom have the Democratic Party to confront? If anything was needed to unite the Democratic Party it was the nomination of Warmoth, which to the Democrats would have the same effect as shaking a red flag in a mad bull's face.

"Warmoth has been for several years past a peaceable, successful and enterprising farmer in Plaquemines, where he lived under his own fig tree and waited until his past was forgotten. I like Warmoth personally. He is an energetic planter and an agreeable man, but when he comes and asks for public office, we ask him for his recommendations and character from his former political employer. Could he get this from the people of Louisiana? Could he get it from Governor Kellogg? Warmoth pleads his youth and ignorance as an excuse for his mistakes when he was Governor of Louisiana. Governor Warmoth never was youthful; he was born old."

A little later Governor McEnery was induced to take the stump and canvass the State for Governor Nichols. At a meeting in Natchitoches he made one of his characteristic speeches, in which he said:

"If Warmoth is elected, we shall have the Africanization of the State, and before I will consent to such a calamity I will wrap the State in revolution, and I now proclaim that I suspend the law, until the danger is over, from the Arkansas Line to the Gulf of Mexico."

Captain Jacks, a local attorney, followed Governor McEnery, and called the audience's attention to the declaration made by Governor McEnery. He said:

"You have heard the Governor of the State declare that he suspends the law from the Arkansas Line to the Gulf. All you have to do is to follow his advice and victory will perch upon our banners."

When I reached Homer in Claiborne Parish, the election officers showed me a letter from Governor McEnery, which read as follows:

Dear Sir:

Suspend the law until after the election; and see that a large Democratic majority is returned from your Parish. Warmoth is developing a very dangerous strength in the southern Parishes which must be overcome by a large Democratic majority in the Parishes north of Red River. You are expected to do your full duty in your Parish.

Very truly,

S. D. McEnery
Governor.

In the final count it became clear that Governor McEnery's orders to his election officers to see that large majorities should be returned for General Nichols were complied with to the letter. The election officers of Governor McEnery's home Parish (Ouachita) returned me only 5 votes, while it gave General Nichols 2,994 votes. Twenty-seven Parishes out of the 48 were returned as follows:

Parish	Warmoth	Nichols
Acadia	149	1688
Bienville	37	1923
Bossier	95	4213
Caddo	324	4802
Cameron	2	402
Concordia	145	4219
De Soto	74	1865
East Carroll	285	2680
East Feliciana	5	2276
Franklin	4	987
Jackson	7	963
Lincoln	..	1273
Livingston	191	766
Madison	..	3530
Morehouse	14	584
Natchitoches	225	3373
Ouachita	5	2994
Rapides	449	4678
Red River	78	1679
Richland	83	1287
Sabine	2	1441
Tensas	113	4627
Union	91	2369
Vernon	..	947
West Carroll	81	420
West Feliciana	377	2038
Winn	83	1196
	2959	59220

In 27 Parishes out of 48, Governor McEnery's election officers returned Warmoth only 2,959 votes, while they gave General Nichols 59,220 votes.

The total vote returned for Warmoth was 51,471, 11,109 of which were cast for me in the city of New Orleans, while 137,-257 votes, or a majority of 85,786, were returned for General Nichols. The total vote returned at this election was 188,728 votes, as against the largest vote ever returned before—120,000 votes. In other words, there were 68,728 more votes returned at this election than ever before in the history of the State.

The Ouachita Plan, devised by Governor McEnery, was: "Don't let negroes register or vote, but always count them for the Democratic ticket."

So much for Samuel D. McEnery's pledge for a fair, free, honest election.

Edward D. White, who managed the campaign for the nomination of General Nichols, was delighted at the result. The new Legislature elected Mr. White to the Senate of the United States; he was later appointed a Judge of the Supreme Court, and still later Chief-Justice of the Supreme Court of the United States.

Apropos of Judge White: United States Senator Donaldson Caffrey used to love to tell of the meeting he attended together with a number of other leading Nichols' supporters during the campaign of 1888. It was held at the Nichols Headquarters, Judge White presiding. He was informed by these leaders that if Governor McEnery adhered to his elaborate pledge of a fair, free, and honest election, General Nichols would be defeated, and that it was necessary to manipulate the ballot boxes liberally or Warmoth would certainly carry the State and be elected. They stated to Judge White that they had come to consult him as to what they should do under the circumstances. Senator Caffrey said that the Judge seemed to be very much embarrassed by these statements, but after a long and full discussion of the matter he finally said to his visitors: "Gentlemen, if you think it necessary for the election of General Nichols to manipulate the ballot boxes, go and do it, but don't let me know anything about it." It was this meeting of General Nichols' friends that resulted in the sending of Captain Richard Sinnott to Baton Rouge and the bringing of Governor McEnery down to New Orleans, and the great dinner up in the top rooms of Moreau's

Restaurant, at which Governor McEnery was promised a place on the Supreme Bench of the State, and made his agreement to "suspend the Law till the danger was over."

Governor Samuel D. McEnery was rewarded by General Nichols for his services by an appointment as one of the Judges of the State Supreme Court for a term of twelve years, and later he was chosen for a seat in the United States Senate for six years. Both Judge White and Governor McEnery earned their rewards. They would not allow the colored people to vote for me, but they counted them by the thousands for Governor Nichols. May the good God Almighty have mercy on their souls!

On May 30, 1877, I was married to Miss Sallie Durand, daughter of Mr. and Mrs. James M. Durand of Newark, New Jersey, and brought her to live with me in Louisiana. Time has passed very rapidly, for it is now more than fifty years since that happy event.

We have to show, as the result of our union, two sons and one daughter—Frank Sheridan, Reinette Lester, and Carroll Kennon.

Sallie Durand is a lineal descendant of Doctor Jean Durand, the famous "Little French Doctor" of colonial times, who was born in La Rochelle, France, in 1667. He was educated as a physician in the School of France, came to New York after the Revocation of the Edict of Nantes, and, after living in South Carolina, and in New Rochelle, New York, finally settled in Connecticut where he died, at Derby, March 24, 1727.

Sallie Durand is a grandniece of Asher B. Durand, the celebrated painter (of the Hudson School) whose work hangs in the Metropolitan Museum, and that his talent did not die with him is shown by many interesting charcoal sketches by my wife, and by the fact that our granddaughter, Elsie, daughter of our son, Frank S. Warmoth, is at present an art student of no small promise in a New York school.

Soon after our marriage in 1877, my wife and I established our home at the Magnolia Plantation in the Parish of Plaquemines. I had already acquired an interest in the plantation with my friend, the Hon. Effingham Lawrence, its owner, and his death necessitated my buying out the interest of his heirs and becoming the sole owner.

We organized the Magnolia Sugar Refining Company and consolidated seven other plantations in our neighborhood with our company. We built a railroad from New Orleans through these plantations, connecting them with our factory. We introduced the diffusion process in place of the roller mills, and by it increased our production of sugar from the cane very greatly. We developed the industry to the highest point possible and continued it until after we had been obliged to sell two crops for 2½¢ a pound, which had cost us 3½¢ to make. We then made up our minds that we could not compete with Germany, France, and especially Cuba, San Domingo, and the tropics, in the production of sugar. So we sold off all our plantations and all of our machinery, saving only our home place, "Magnolia," paid our debts and quit the business. Since then I have tried to live a quiet and peaceful life in the city of New Orleans.

We had a most interesting and eventful life on the plantation. There was probably nothing in Louisiana more alluring and charming than life on a sugar plantation. We had a beautiful home, wonderfully fertile lands, excellent and abundant labor, and a small but efficient sugar factory, all of which I sought to develop to its highest efficiency.

In 1884 I made a trip to France and Germany, in company with Dr. G. L. Spencer of the Department of Agriculture, to study the sugar industry of those countries. President Arthur

SALLY D. WARMOTH

had his Secretary of State write the following letter to our representatives abroad:

Department of State,
Washington, July 19, 1884.
To the Diplomatic and Consular Officers of the United States, Abroad.
Gentlemen:

At the instance of the President, I take pleasure in introducing to your acquaintance the Honorable H. C. Warmoth, ex-Governor of Louisiana, who is about to depart for Europe in the interest of the United States, to investigate the beet-sugar industry, and in whose behalf I bespeak such courteous attentions as you can properly render, not inconsistent with your official duties, during his sojourn there.

I am, Gentlemen,

Your obedient servant,
(*Signed*)   FRED T. FRELINGHUYSEN

So I went to these countries actually as a representative of the United States Government, and was extended the greatest courtesies by all the people with whom I came into contact. I learned a great many things from this mission, especially about the manufacture of sugar, and when I returned from my trip, the administration at Washington, upon my recommendation, established a sugar experimental station on Magnolia Plantation, placing Dr. Henry W. Wuley and a number of other scientific experts in charge.

We kept open house and entertained about all of the important sugar people of the State and of the United States who visited us at one time or another.

The Democratic Congress, together with President Cleveland, cut down the duty on foreign sugars so low that it came near to bankrupting every sugar planter in Louisiana. After the election of McKinley and Roosevelt, together with a Republican Congress, the sugar planters of Louisiana determined to make a vigorous fight for a higher duty on foreign sugars, and also for a bounty of $5,000,000 to reimburse them in part for the losses they had sustained during the past four years.

I was selected by the Sugar Planters' Organization to conduct the fight before Congress. It is a long story. We succeeded after a hard fight on the last night of the session.

To show that my services were recognized, I append the following telegram from Mr. W. B. Bloomfield and Colonel J. D. Hill of the Sugar Planters' Committee:

New Orleans,
March 3, 1895.

Governor H. C. Warmoth,
    Arlington Hotel,
       Washington, D. C.

Congratulate you upon your splendid victory, and we are heartily thankful for all of the services you have rendered.

(*Signed*) BLOOMFIELD and HILL

On March 8, 1890, President Benjamin Harrison appointed me Collector of Customs for the Port of New Orleans. There were a great many applications for positions in the Custom House and the applicants were very persistent in pressing their claims upon the Collector for appointment. There were many more applicants than there were positions in the service. I was anxious, of course, to have a trained and competent organization, and I found such already installed in the building; and I could not well, in justice to the service and my own duty, put them out and replace them by untrained though deserving Republican politicians.

The Civil Service Law had gone into effect some time before and the President had appointed a Civil Service Commission, of which the Hon. Theodore Roosevelt was the Chairman and Colonel Lyman a member.

I disappointed so many applicants that a fierce war was inaugurated against me and a petition was prepared and was signed by a number of applicants and supported by Colonel H.

Dudley Coleman, who represented the Second Congressional District in Congress. I was charged with having violated the Civil Service rules established by the Commission. The war on me was fierce. So one day who should walk into my office but Colonel Theodore Roosevelt, accompanied by Colonel Lyman, who, I believe, was Secretary of the Civil Service Commission. I received them cordially and asked them to be seated, and after some preliminary conversation, Colonel Roosevelt handed me a paper that turned out to be the charges which had been preferred against me.

I opened the paper and looked over the charges, and the further I went the madder I got; so finally turning upon Colonel Roosevelt, with a great deal of spirit, I said:

"Mr. Roosevelt, President Harrison has put me here to run this Custom House and I'll be damned if I don't intend to do it in my own way, and you fellows can go to hell!"

Colonel Roosevelt jumped up and said: "We haven't done you any harm yet, have we?"

"Yes," I said. "You have done me a damned sight of harm by paying any attention to these politicians who want me to fill this Custom House with their henchmen."

Colonel Roosevelt turned to Lyman and said: "Lyman, things are different down here from what they are up in our country; we want to take into consideration the conditions existing down here. You stay here and investigate this matter. I am going to Texas tonight to shoot hogs." With that, he bade me good-day.

It was the end of the week, and I took Colonel Lyman down to my Magnolia plantation to spend Sunday with my family. Lyman returned to Washington and reported that the charges were all false, or frivolous, that I was running the Custom House according to the rules of the Civil Service; and when Roosevelt got back from shooting hogs in Texas, he signed the report. And that was the end of the matter.

I guess I am the only man who ever gave Theodore Roosevelt a "cussing" and got away with it.

I served as Collector until June 27, 1893—for over three years, when President Cleveland removed me to appoint a Democrat.

The readers of the literature of the era of the "Carpet-bag" government of Louisiana will be impressed by the story of the burdensome taxes which that government imposed on the impoverished people of Louisiana.

All taxes are burdensome and people do not like to have to pay them. In fact, there were no taxes collected from the people for the years 1861, 1862, 1863, 1864, 1865, and 1866. Six years of war and anarchy paid no taxes. In the meantime the expenses of the Government accumulated. The Confederate State Government, the Hahn Government of 1864, and the Wells Government of 1866, all carried on by flooding the people with "State Notes." The State Notes issued by the Confederate Government became valueless after the War ended. The State Notes issued by the Hahn and the Wells Governments were not repudiated by the Carpet-bag government of 1868, but were provided for and made payable for any back taxes, and the collection was extended for two years. So that the people were not so badly burdened, because they could purchase those State Notes and the unpaid coupons on bonds on the market at from 20¢ to 25¢ on the dollar.

The Revenue Act of 1868 levied "a tax of one-fourth of one per cent on all property of the State for the purpose of supporting the Government of the State; to pay the public debt and promote the public interest thereof."

The Act of 1869 levied the same rate of taxation.
The Act of 1870 reduced the rate to four mills.
The Act of 1871 fixed the rate at four mills.
The Act of 1872 fixed the rate at four mills.

The taxable property of the State in 1860 was $470,164,-963.00. In 1870 it had fallen to $250,063,359.83. The reader will see that the Carpet-bag Government was not oppressive in the rate of taxation. In 1927 and 1928 it was 8¾ mills on the dollar as against the rate of 1870, 1871, 1872 of only 4 mills. The assessed value of the property of the State in 1870 was $250,063,359.83. The assessed value is today $1,717,877,-125.00. The State debt in 1872 was less than $25,000,000.00—today it is $57,319,420.00.

Young men and women with ambition and political aspirations may well take cognizance of one fact: Gratitude is practically unknown among politicians. I state the fact as something important to be known and not as a thrust or a lamentation. Take my case as an example. Nearly every one of the men who entered into the movement of 1872 to overthrow me and put me into the hands of my adversaries was under special obligations to me.

One of my first appointments after I became Governor was that of S. B. Packard to the office of Register of Conveyances for the Parish of Orleans, a lucrative position, and I joined in the movement to have him appointed United States Marshal for the Eastern District of Louisiana.

P. B. S. Pinchback, I practically appointed to be Lieutenant-Governor of the State, and came nearly to wrecking myself with my friends in doing so.

John T. Ludeling, I appointed Chief Justice of the Supreme Court of the State of Louisiana.

General James Longstreet, I appointed Adjutant-General of the State Militia.

Senator John Lynch of the famous Returning Board—upon him I showered many favors.

General Herron, I appointed Tax Collector of the Fourth District of New Orleans, and afterward Secretary of State, and when he was in serious trouble as Tax Collector, assisted him financially and with means for which I was never repaid.

Judge Dibble, I appointed to the most important judgeship in the city of New Orleans.

Collector Casey, I saved from removal as Collector of Customs when every Republican leader in the State was after his scalp.

To George W. Carter I gave an important and lucrative office, and I later created the Parish of Cameron, making it so he could come as its Representative in the Legislature of the State.

In the big crisis of my life every man named above deserted me and sought my destruction. In view of such experience, am I other than human in saying to others who may follow me that politicians are without gratitude?

THE NEGRO RACE

THE conduct of the negro people during the Reconstruction Period needs to be spoken of here. Suddenly freed from abject slavery, admitted to the elective franchise and even to high official station, they hardly knew what to do with themselves. They were in an embarrassing situation; and that they stumbled and sometimes fell is not strange. The step from the auction block, the slave-driver's rigid discipline, ruthless and severe punishment for minor delinquencies, and capital punishment for offences not ordinarily regarded as grave when committed by others—to offices in which they executed the laws, and arrested and punished their former masters for violation of the law, was enough to turn the heads of a people of a much higher civilization.

In face of it all, it must be said in justice to the Black Race that they always showed great affection and regard for their old and young masters in their official relations. Their hands and their hearts were ever open to the consideration of any request that was made of them as officers of the government; and, after the first shock of freedom, and after the white people came to realize and accept these new and startling changes in their relation to these people, there grew up a more kindly feeling between the two groups; and I believe that with increasing intelligence, patience, and the work of time these relations will be strengthened to the good of both races.

Of the devotion and kindness of thousands of black men and women to their masters, mistresses, and little children the historian, novelist, and poet have written eloquently. There never was a race which, under such trying circumstances, was more patient or more docile. They are now largely what the white race has made of them. Let me not shock my readers when I say that there was never a more lovable people than the black men and women; and the white masters in general showed a tender love for their black slaves.

We must protect the negro in his political and civil rights; educate, encourage, and show him our friendship by justice, human charity, and brotherhood; and his love will respond to ours in "measure overflowing, full." *Love rules the world,* when it is ruled right. *Love works miracles.* It will solve our race problem, and only Love *can* solve it, as it must solve all of our human problems.

I knew the black people as slaves. I knew them as they were freed by Mr. Lincoln. I knew them in their first efforts to exercise their freedom; and I knew how weak and awkward they often were in attempting to imitate their white rulers who had had advantages of training. I know they made mistakes; but they were often the mistakes, the follies, and the crimes of their white associates—no greater in number, and no worse, than those of their white leaders.

With all their weaknesses, the members of the African race in America are to be congratulated. As the Children of Israel had to pass through the Red Sea, and their descendants have suffered long ages of proscription and persecution to this day;

so the American negro has waded through a sea of blood to his Promised Iand. He will make good—he has made good. He is one of the greatest assets of the South today. His brain, his muscle, his native intelligence under the leadership of and association with the white man, have made the South blossom as the rose.

Having been born on May 9, 1842, in the State of Illinois, emigrating to the State of Missouri when a boy, with a few law books and only a twenty-dollar gold piece in my pocket; having made many friends on the top of the Ozark Mountains, and being admitted to practise law in the State of Missouri when but eighteen years of age; having been appointed County Attorney by the County Court of Laclede County soon after, and later appointed District Attorney of the 18th Judicial District of the State of Missouri by Governor Hamilton R. Gamble, again later a Colonel of Missouri State Militia, a little later still a Brigadier-General of Militia, and afterward Lieutenant-Colonel of the 32nd Missouri Regiment of Volunteers; having fought our way from St. Louis, Missouri, down to Vicksburg, Mississippi, under General Sherman; been licked at Chickasaw Bayou, and with my regiment participated in the capture of Arkansas Post, taking General Churchill and seven thousand prisoners; having a little later been detailed on the staff of Major-General John A. McClernand, commanding the Thirteenth Army Corps, and participating in all of the battles around and in the rear of Vicksburg; having been wounded at Vicksburg on May 22nd, I suffered dismissal from the Army resulting from the quarrel between Generals Grant and McClernand. I was restored to the service by President Lincoln on the recommendation of the Judge Advocate General of the Army of the United States, in which he concluded his report as follows:

In short, it is believed that few young men in the service can present a fairer or more honorable record, and in view of the manifest injustice which has been done Lieutenant-Colonel Warmoth, and of his evident value to the service, it is recommended that the special order dismissing him be at once revoked, so that he be placed, as to his rank, pay, etc., in precisely the position which he would have occupied had he not been dismissed.

Having later participated as Commander of my regiment in the campaign from Memphis and in all of the battles, including the capture of Lookout Mountain, Rossville Gap and Missionary Ridge; having later been redetailed on the staff of Major-General McClernand, who had been restored to his command of the Thirteenth Army Corps, and having served as Judge Advocate on his staff in the State of Texas and later on Red River, Louisiana, I was next appointed by General Banks, Judge of the United States Military Provost Court at New Orleans for the Department of the Gulf, and after the War settled in New Orleans to practise law.

I was Governor of the State for four years, from 1868 to 1872; a member of the Legislature of 1876 and a member of the Constitutional Convention of 1879; was nominated by the reorganized Republican Party as its candidate for Governor against ex-Governor Francis T. Nichols in 1888, which caused Governor S. D. McEnery to "suspend the law till the danger of my election should be over," and to instruct his election officers to see that large Democratic majorities should be returned against me. In spite of these orders I was actually allowed 51,471 votes, while Governor Nichols was given 137,257 votes, or 85,786 majority, taken chiefly from the larger negro Parishes, and counting nearly 70,000 more votes than at any previous election ever held in the State. Appointed Collector of Customs for the Port of New Orleans by President Harrison in 1890, I served three years, until President Grover Cleveland removed me to appoint a Democrat. Having fought all these battles incident to public life, openly and squarely, in the most spirited State in the Union and through a most turbulent era, and having experienced about all the triumphs and defeats incident to such life, and having not a drop of any other than Southern blood in my veins, I think I may say, at eighty-seven years of age, that I was never a "Louisiana Carpet-bagger," though I might, in common parlance, be termed a "scallawag."

APPENDIX A

AN ORDINANCE

To dissolve the union between the State of Louisiana and other States united with her, under the compact entitled "The Constitution of the United States of America." We, the people of the State of Louisiana in Convention assembled, do declare and ordain, and it is hereby declared and ordained, That the Ordinance passed by us in Convention on the 23rd day of November, eighteen hundred and eleven, whereby the Constitution of the United States of America, and the amendments of the said Constitution, were adopted; and all Laws and Ordinances by which the State of Louisiana became a member of the Federal Union, be and the same are hereby repealed and abrogated; and that the union now subsisting between Louisiana and the other States, under the name of "The United States of America," is hereby dissolved.

We do further declare and ordain: That the State of Louisiana hereby resume all rights and powers heretofore delegated to the Government of the United States of America; That her citizens are absolved from all allegiance to said Government; and that she is in full possession and exercise of all those rights of sovereignty which appertain to a free and independent state.

We do further declare and ordain: That all rights required and vested under the Constitution of the United States, or any Act of Congress, or Treaty, or under any Law of this State and not incompatible with this Ordinance, shall remain in force and have the same effect as if this Ordinance had not been passed.

APPENDIX B

It is within the knowledge of all citizens resident here before the War, that for years preceding the Rebellion, elections in the Parish of Orleans were a cruel mockery of free government. Bands of organized desperadoes, immediately preceding and during an election, committed every species of outrage upon peaceful and unoffending citizens, to intimidate them from the exercise of the inestimable privilege of free men, the elective franchise. A registry of 14,000 names, in the days alluded to, could scarcely furnish one-fourth of that number of legal votes at the polls, although six or seven thousand votes were usually returned as cast. To guard against the possibility of a return to such a condition of affairs, many citizens of integrity, intelligence, and loyalty to the Union, who believe that a new danger will now be added to the pre-existing ones, in the expected rapid increase of population, advise a reconsideration of the electoral qualification in all municipal elections for the future; holding that experience has shown conclusively that they cannot be confused with the political contests of the times with safety to the true interests of the country. This view is worthy of respectful consideration.

APPENDIX C (Hebert, 1856)

"That the repetition of such outrages would tarnish our national character, and sink us to the level of the anarchical governments of Spanish America; that before the occurrence of those great public crimes, the hideous enormity of which he could not describe and which were committed with impunity in mid-daylight and in the presence of hundreds of persons, no one could have admitted even the possibility that a bloodthirsty mob could have contemplated to over-awe any portion of the people of this State in the exercise of their most valuable rights; but that which would then have been denied, even as a possibility, is now an historical fact."

APPENDIX D (Wickliffe, 1857)

"It is well known that at the last two general elections, many of the streets and approaches to the polls were completely in the hands of organized ruffians, who committed acts of violence on multitudes of our naturalized fellow-citizens who dared venture to exercise the right of suffrage. Thus nearly one-third of the registered voters of New Orleans have been deterred from exercising their highest and most sacred prerogative. The suppression of such elections is an open and palpable fraud on the people, and I recommend you to adopt such measures as shall effectually prevent the true will of the majority from being totally silenced."

APPENDIX E (N. O. Delta, May 6, 1860)

For seven years the world knows that this city, in all of its departments, Judicial, Legislative, and Executive, has been at the absolute disposal of the most godless, brutal, ignorant and ruthless ruffianism the world has ever heard of since the days of the great Roman conspirator. By means of a secret organization, emanating from that

APPENDIX

fecund source of political infamy, New England, and named Know-Nothingism or Sammyism from boasted exclusive devotion of the fraternity to the United States, our City, far from being the abode of decency, of liberality, generosity, and justice, is a sanctum for crime. The ministers of the Law, nominees of bloodstained, vulgar, ribald caballeros and licensed murderers, shed innocent blood on the most public thoroughfares with impunity; witnesses of the most atrocious crimes are either spirited away, bought off, or intimidated from testifying; perjured associates are retained to prove alibis, and ready bail is always procurable for the immediate use of those whom it is not immediately prudent to enlarge otherwise. The electoral system is a farce; and fraud, the knife, the sling-shot, the brass knuckles deterring, while the shame is being enacted, who shall occupy and administer the offices of the municipality, and the Commonwealth?

Can our condition surprise any man?

APPENDIX F
ORDINANCE
Relative to the Police of Recently Emancipated Negroes or Freedmen, Within the Corporate Limits of the Town of Opelousas

Whereas the relations formerly subsisting between master and slave have become changed by the action of the controlling authorities; and whereas it is necessary to provide for the proper policing and government of the recently emancipated negroes or freedmen, in their new relations to the municipal authorities;

Sect. 1. Be it therefore ordained by the Board of Police of the Town of Opelousas: That no negro or freedman shall be allowed to come within the limits of the Town of Opelousas without special permission from his employer specifying the object of his visit and the time necessary for the accomplishment of the same. Whoever shall violate this provision shall suffer imprisonment and two days' work on the public streets, or shall pay a fine of two dollars and fifty cents.

Sect. 2. Be it further ordained that every negro or freedman who shall be found on the streets of Opelousas after 10 o'clock at night without a written pass or permit from his employer, shall be imprisoned and compelled to work five days on the public streets, or pay a fine of five dollars.

Sect. 3. No negro or freedman shall be permitted to rent or keep a house within the limits of the town under any circumstances, and any one thus offending shall be ejected, and compelled to find an employer or leave the town within twenty-four hours. The lessor or furnisher of the house leased or kept as above shall pay a fine of ten dollars for each offence.

APPENDIX

Sect. 4. No negro or freedman shall reside within the limits of the Town of Opelousas who is not in the regular service of some white person or former owner, who shall be held responsible for the conduct of said freedman. But said employer or former owner may permit said freedman to hire his time, by special permission in writing, which permission shall not extend over twenty-four hours at any one time. Any one violating the provisions of this section shall be imprisoned and compelled to work for two days in the public streets, or pay a fine of five dollars.

Sect. 5. No public meetings or congregations of negroes or freedmen shall be allowed within the limits of the Town of Opelousas, under any circumstances or for any purpose, without the permission of the Mayor or President of the Board. This prohibition is not intended, however, to prevent freedmen from attending the usual church services conducted by established ministers of religion. Every freedman violating this law shall be imprisoned and made to work five days on the public streets.

Sect. 6. No negro or freedman shall be permitted to preach, exhort, or otherwise declaim to congregations of colored people without a special permission from the Mayor or President of the Board of Police, under the penalty of a fine of ten dollars or twenty days' work on the public streets.

Sect. 7. No freedman who is not in the military service shall be allowed to carry fire-arms or any kind of weapons within the limits of the Town of Opelousas, without the special permission of his employer, in writing, and approved by the Mayor or President of the Board of Police. Any one thus offending shall forfeit his weapons and shall be imprisoned and made to work five days on the public streets or pay a fine of five dollars in lieu of said work.

Sect. 8. No freedman shall sell, barter or exchange any articles or merchandise of traffic within the limits of Opelousas, without permission from his employer or the Mayor or President of the Board, under the penalty of the forfeiture of said articles, and imprisonment and one day's labor, or a fine of one dollar in lieu of said work.

Sect. 9. Any freedman found drunk within the limits of the Town shall be imprisoned and made to labor five days on the public streets, or pay five dollars in lieu of said labor.

Sect. 10. Any freedman not residing in Opelousas, who shall be found within its corporate limits after the hour of 3 o'clock P.M., on Sunday, without a special written permission from his employer or the Mayor, shall be arrested and imprisoned and made to work two days on the public streets, or pay two dollars in lieu of said work.

Sect. 11. All the foregoing provisions apply to freedmen and freedwomen, or both sexes.

[274]

APPENDIX

Sect. 12. It shall be the special duty of the Mayor or President of the Board to see that all the provisions of this ordinance are faithfully executed.

Sect. 13. Be it further ordained, that this ordinance is to take effect from and after its first publication.

Ordained the 3rd day of July, 1865.

(*Signed*) E. D. ESTILLETTE,
President of the Board of Police

(*Signed*)
JOS. D. RICHARD, *Clerk*

APPENDIX G

ORDINANCE

Relative to the Police of Negroes or Colored Persons Within the Corporate Limits of the Town of Franklin

Sect. 1. BE IT ORDAINED BY THE MAYOR AND COUNCIL OF THE TOWN OF FRANKLIN that no negro or colored person shall be allowed to come within the limits of said town without special permission from his employer, specifying the object of his visit and the time necessary for the accomplishment of the same. Whoever shall violate this provision shall suffer imprisonment and two days' work on the public street, or shall pay a fine of two dollars and a half.

Sect. 2. Be it further ordained, &c., That every negro or colored person who shall be found on the streets of Franklin after ten o'clock at night without a written pass or permit from his or her employer, shall be imprisoned and compelled to work five days on the public streets or pay a fine of five dollars.

Sect. 3. No negro or colored person shall be permitted to rent or keep a house within the limits of the town under any circumstances; and any one thus offending shall be ejected and compelled to find an employer, or leave the town within twenty-four hours. The lessor or furnisher of the house kept as above shall pay a fine of ten dollars for each offence: PROVIDED, That the provisions of this section shall not apply to any free negro or colored person who was residing in the town of Franklin prior to the 1st January (1865) last.

Sect. 4. No negro or colored person shall reside within the limits of the town of Franklin who is not in the regular service of some white person or former owner, who shall be held responsible for the conduct of said negro or colored person; but said employer or former owner may permit said negro or colored person to hire his or their time by special permission in writing, which permission shall not extend to over twenty-five hours at any one time. Any negro or colored person violating the provisions of this section shall be imprisoned and forced to work for two days on the public streets: PROVIDED, That the provisions of this section shall not apply to negroes or colored persons heretofore free.

Sect. 5. No public meetings or congregations of negroes or colored persons shall be allowed within the limits of the town of Franklin, under any circumstances or for any purpose, without the permission of the Mayor. This prohibition is not intended, however, to prevent negroes or colored persons from attending the usual church service, conducted by established ministers of religion. Every negro or colored person violating this law shall be imprisoned and put to work five days on the public streets.

Sect. 6. No negro or colored person shall be permitted to preach, exhort, or otherwise declaim to congregations of colored people without a special permission from the Mayor, under the penalty of a fine of ten dollars or twenty days' work on the public streets.

Sect. 7. No negro or colored person who is not in the military service shall be allowed to carry fire-arms or any kind of weapons within the limits of the town of Franklin without the special permission of his employer in writing, and approved by the Mayor. Any one thus offending shall forfeit his weapons and shall be imprisoned and made to work five days on the public streets, or pay a fine of five dollars in lieu of said work.

Sect. 8. No negro or colored person shall sell, barter, or exchange any articles of merchandise or traffic within the limits of Franklin, without permission in writing from his employer or the Mayor, under the penalty of forfeiture of the said articles and imprisonment and one day's labor, or a fine of one dollar in lieu of said work.

Sect. 9. Any negro or colored person found drunk within the limits of the town shall be imprisoned and made to labor five days on the public streets, or pay five dollars in lieu of said labor.

Sect. 10. Any negro or colored person not residing in Franklin who shall be found within its corporate limits after the hour of three o'clock P.M. on Sunday without a special written permission from his employer or the Mayor shall be arrested and imprisoned and made to work two days on the public streets, or pay two dollars in lieu of said work.

Sect. 11. All the foregoing provisions apply to negroes or colored persons of both sexes.

Sect. 12. It shall be the special duty of the town constable, under direction of the Mayor, to see that all the provisions of this ordinance are faithfully executed.

Sect. 13. Whoever in Franklin shall sell or give to any negro or colored person any intoxicating liquors, or shall exchange or barter for the same with any such negro or colored person, without special permission from the Mayor or employer of said negro or colored person, shall on conviction thereof before the Mayor or Justice of the Peace in and for the seventh ward of the parish of St. Mary, pay a fine of twenty-five dollars and costs of prosecution, and in default of the payment of said fine and costs the person thus offending shall suffer imprisonment in the parish jail for ten days.

(*Signed*) A. S. TUCKER

Mayor

R. W. McMILLAN, Clerk

APPENDIX H

The Legislature within fifteen days after its first meeting proceeded to adopt the following laws. *First*—

An Act to Provide for and Regulate Labor Contracts for Agricultural Pursuits

Sect. 1. Be it enacted by the Senate and House of Representatives of the State of Louisiana in general assembly convened, That all persons employed as laborers in agricultural pursuits shall be required, during the first ten days of the month of January of each year, to make contracts for labor for the then ensuing year, or for the year next ensuing the termination of their present contracts. All contracts for labor for agricultural purposes shall be made in writing, signed by the employer, and shall be made in the presence of a Justice of the Peace and two disinterested witnesses, in whose presence the contract shall be read to the laborer, and when assented to and signed by the latter, shall be considered as binding for the time prescribed. . . .

Sect. 8. Be it further enacted, &c., That in case of sickness of the laborer, wages for the time lost shall be deducted, and where the sickness is feigned for purposes of idleness, and also on refusal to work according to contract, double the amount of wages shall be deducted for the time lost; and also where rations have been furnished; and should the refusal to work continue beyond three days, the offender shall be reported to a Justice of the Peace, and shall be forced to labor on roads, levees, and other public works, without pay, until the offender consents to return to his labor.

Sect. 9. Be it further enacted, &c., That, when in health, the laborer shall work ten hours during the day in summer, and nine hours during the day in winter, unless otherwise stipulated in the labor contract; he shall obey all proper orders of his employer or his agent; take proper care of his work-mules, horses, oxen, stock; also of all agricultural implements; and employers shall have the right to make a reasonable

APPENDIX

deduction from the laborer's wages for injuries done to animals or agricultural implements committed to his care, or for bad or negligent work. Bad work shall not be allowed. Failing to obey reasonable orders, neglect of duty, and leaving home without permission will be deemed disobedience; impudence, swearing, or indecent language to or in the presence of the employer, his family, or agent, or quarreling and fighting with one another, shall be deemed disobedience. For any disobedience a fine of one dollar shall be imposed on and paid by the offender. For all lost time from work-hours, unless in case of sickness, the laborer shall be fined twenty-five cents per hour. For all absence from home without leave he will be fined at the rate of two dollars per day. Laborers will not be required to labor on the Sabbath unless by special contract. For all thefts of the laborer from the employer of agricultural products, hogs, sheep, poultry, or any other property of the employer, or willful destruction of property or injury, the laborer shall pay the employer double the amount of the value of the property stolen, destroyed, or injured, one-half to be paid to the employer and the other half to be placed in the general fund provided for in this section. No live stock shall be allowed to laborers without the permission of the employer. Laborers shall not receive visitors during work-hours. All difficulties arising between the employers and laborers, under this section, shall be settled by the former; if not satisfactory to the laborers, an appeal may be had to the nearest Justice of the Peace and two freeholders, citizens, one of said citizens to be selected by the employer and the other by the laborer; and all fines imposed and collected under this section shall be deducted from wages due, and shall be placed in a common fund, to be divided among the other laborers on the plantation, except as provided for above.

Sec. 10. Be it further enacted, &c., That for gross misconduct on the part of the laborer, such as insubordination, habitual laziness, frequent acts of violation of his contract or the laws of the State, he may be dismissed by his employer; nevertheless, the laborer shall have the right to resist his dismissal and to a redress of his wrongs by an appeal to a Justice of the Peace and two freeholders, citizens of the parish, one of the freeholders to be selected by himself and the other by his employer.

APPENDIX I

Second—The next act of the Legislature enacted was "to punish by fine and imprisonment any person or persons who should carry firearms on the premises or plantations of any citizen, without the consent of the owner or proprietor."

This, of course, was aimed at the freedman.

Third—Another act of the Legislature enacted provided that

"Whoever shall enter upon any plantation without the permission of the owner or agent, shall be guilty of a misdemeanor and be liable to be arrested and punished by fine in a sum not exceeding One Hundred Dollars ($100.00), or imprisoned for a term not exceeding one month, and moreover be required to give bond for good behavior during six months."

Fourth—The next act of the Legislature enacted was to define vagrancy. It provided that

"Upon the complaint of any person, that any person is a vagrant, he shall be arrested and brought before a Justice of the Peace, or other Officer, who shall determine by his confession or by competent testimony, that he is a vagrant, who shall require a Bond in such sum as the Court or Officer shall prescribe, with security for his good behavior and future industry for the period of one year, and upon his failure or refusal to give such Bond and security, the Justice of the Peace or other Officer shall issue his Warrant to the Sheriff or other Officer directing him to detain and to hire out such vagrant for a period not exceeding twelve months, or to cause him to labor on Public Works, roads, and levees under such regulations as shall be made by the Municipal Authorities, Provided: That if the accused be a person who has abandoned his employer before his contract expired, the preference shall be given to such employer of hiring the accused; and provided further, that in the City of New Orleans the accused may be committed to the workhouse for a time not exceeding six months, there to be kept at hard labor, or to be made to labor on the Public Works, roads or levees."

Fifth—Another act of this First Legislature was an Act "To provide for the punishment of persons for tampering with, persuading or enticing away, harboring, feeding or secreting laborers, servants or apprentices." This offense was punishable with fine and imprisonment. The fine was from ten to five hundred dollars and imprisonment for not less than ten days or more than one year, or both fine and imprisonment at the discretion of the Court.

Sixth—Another was an Act in relation to apprentices or industrial servants.

Seventh—Another provided that

"Any person who shall employ any laborer or apprentice who is also under contract for services for any period of time to any other person, and before such time or services shall have elapsed so as to deprive such first employer of the services of such laborer or apprentice, shall be deemed and held guilty of a misdemeanor and shall upon conviction pay a fine of not less than ten dollars or more than five hundred dollars for each and every offense, or imprisonment in the

APPENDIX

Parish jail for a period not exceeding thirty (30) days at the discretion of the Court and shall be liable for damages to the party injured."

APPENDIX J

Assumption Parish had four votes, but sent sixteen gentlemen headed by W. W. Pugh and Alfred Tate; East Baton Rouge had six votes, but sent eighteen gentlemen to cast the vote, headed by ex-Attorney-General Andrew S. Herron, Thomas Bynum, E. W. Robinson, James McCullom, and Jordan Holt, all of whom were conspicuous in the late Democratic Conventions; West Baton Rouge had two votes, but sent seven gentlemen to cast it; Bossier had four votes, but sent a large delegation headed by State Senator S. M. Thomas; Caddo had six votes, but sent twenty-five gentlemen to cast it, headed by J. M. Howell, A. H. Leonard, Samuel Armistead (colored), M. Tally, and A. D. Long.

Carroll had four votes, but sent eleven delegates; Claiborne had four votes, but sent ten delegates; De Soto had four votes, but sent thirteen delegates; East Feliciana had four votes, but sent twenty-three delegates; West Feliciana had two votes, but sent eight delegates, with Joseph A. Breaux at the head; Iberville had four votes, but sent twelve delegates with ex-Governor P. O. Hebert, C. A. Bruele and Henry Ware as leaders; Jefferson had six votes, but sent seven delegates.

Livingston had two votes, but sent forty-one delegates, headed by grand old Thomas Green Davidson; La Fourche had four votes, but sent eight delegates, headed by Judge Taylor Beattie, Louis Bush and J. W. Howell; Morehouse had two votes, but sent four delegates; Madison had two votes, but sent six delegates; St. James had four votes, but sent twenty delegates; St. Landry had eight votes, but sent sixteen delegates; St. Mary had four votes, but sent seven delegates.

Terrebonne had four votes, but sent ten delegates; Tensas had four votes, but sent eighteen delegates, headed by Judge C. C. Cordill, J. M. Gillespie and S. M. Routh; Plaquemines had two votes, but sent six delegates, headed by Effingham Lawrence and Bernard Fasterling; Point Coupee had four votes, but sent twenty-eight delegates, headed by L. B. Claiborne and General B. B. Simms. Rapides had six votes, but sent thirty-two delegates, headed by Thomas C. Manning, Louis Texado, Senator W. F. Blackman and James C. Wise.

Natchitoches had four votes, but sent forty-five delegates, headed by W. W. Jack, S. M. Hyams and Thomas C. Hunter; Ouachita had four votes, but sent eleven delegates, headed by R. W. Richardson and W. W. Farmer. Orleans Parish, First Ward, had four votes, headed

APPENDIX

by J. H. Wingfield; Second Ward, six votes, headed by Major E. A. Burke and John Fitzpatrick; Third Ward had eight votes, headed by Thomas O'Connor and James D. Houston; Fourth Ward had four votes; Fifth Ward had four votes; Sixth Ward had two votes, headed by L. E. Lemaria and Robert Brewster; Seventh Ward had four votes; Eighth Ward two votes, Ninth Ward four votes, Tenth Ward three votes; Eleventh Ward three votes, headed by Senator R. N. Ogden; Twelfth Ward three votes, headed by Robert L. Preston; Thirteenth Ward, eight votes; Fourteenth Ward, eight votes; Fifteenth Ward, two votes.

APPENDIX K
REPORT ON CREDENTIALS

Ascension (four votes)—P. O. Avraud, U. Argrave, General A. Thomas, Dr. J. C. Segarere, F. Reynaud, Bernard Lemans, Henry McCall, B. Allen, S. Taylor, V. P. Landry, W. Ballard, L. A. Bringier, E. Duffel, J. Billeison, Henry F. Duffel, Fred Duffel.

Avoyelles (four votes)—W. K. Johnson, A. D. Coco, W. M. Ewell, James Ware.

Assumption (four votes)—E. E. Lauve, John Williams, A. Bulow, A. Casinier, J. B. Whittington, W. W. Pugh, Alfred Tete, F. Pike. Alternates—E. B. Cox, D. Morris, Joseph E. Leblanc, Joseph Adams, A. Dalferes, Joe Thompson, W. A. Whitaker, P. Clark.

East Baton Rouge (six votes)—A. S. Herron, T. W. Hurst, D. M. Callihan, T. S. Brady, J. H. Lamon, E. M. Hooper, W. J. Walter, A. E. Read, P. S. Haralson, James McCullen, James Cooper, Tom Bynum, R. T. Young, Charles Weeks, J. M. Williams, Jordan Holt, T. V. Brown, E. W. Robertson.

West Baton Rouge (two votes)—Dan Hicky, R. Hebert, H. H. Hyams, H. Hebert, James L. Lobdel, N. W. Pope, H. M. Favrot.

Bossier (four votes)—S. M. Thomas, S. W. Vance, J. B. Pickett, H. W. Ogden.

Bienville (two votes)—H. Rayburn, W. Hightower. Alternates— W. A. Dewes, S. Long.

Calcasieu (two votes)—No credentials. No delegates.
Cameron (two votes)—No credentials. No delegates.
Caldwell (two votes)—No credentials. No delegates.
Catahoula (four votes)—T. C. Spencer, Wade R. Young. Alternates—J. Forsyth, J. E. Egrel.

Concordia (four votes)—D. S. Rivers, H. Stewart, John White, F. C. Witherspoon, Zeb York, F. S. Shaw. Alternates—J. C. Ferriday, Harvey Ellis, Jo Habbitt, James Warner, P. W. Chase, F. S. Shields.

APPENDIX

Caddo (six votes)—J. M. Powell, G. W. Stoner, T. Rolling, Jr., S. M. Asher, T. Byland, A. J. Pickens, R. White, W. M. Turner, S. Armistead, E. M. Johnson, F. Z. Mulhaup, W. D. Browning, M. Tally, R. J. Wright, S. Gilham, H. J. G. Battle, C. Croon, A. Flannur, M. Jones, A. H. Leonard, A. S. Vanvrelin, A. B. Lang, F. M. Sanchez, T. R. Vaughn, J. A. McCready.

Carroll (four votes)—E. J. Deloney, D. C. Jenkins, T. O. Meaux, R. J. Landon, Joseph Leddy, A. W. Roberts, T. B. Rowe, John B. Williams, J. R. Brown, T. Bieme, M. Dubose.

Claiborne (four votes)—J. C. Egan, J. H. Jordan, J. W. Todd, J. H. Simmons. Alternates—R. E. Thompson, T. Price, J. J. Duke, M. N. Bartlett, J. M. Scaife, J. S. Young.

De Soto (four votes)—John L. Cole, James T. Fisher, A. J. Caffey, R. L. Armstrong, J. L. Scales, R. F. Carr, W. P. Sample, L. H. Woodham, J. Bullenfork, S. De Soto, H. L. Custar, J. W. Stewart, J. E. Hewett.

East Feliciana (four votes)—A. G. Carter, J. T. Kilbourne, H. Marston, D. J. Wedge, H. Skipwith, Jr., Charles McVay, H. Hurstler, A. J. Norwood, J. A. Norwood, R. H. McClelland, T. J. Fauquer, A. Hazard, W. F. Conand, R. A. Cross, J. C. Thomas, A. L. East, E. E. Adams, J. H. Packwood, D. Rogelio, H. Arnold, H. Matthews, G. W. Mundy.

West Feliciana (two votes)—Eli S. Norwood, T. Leonard, J. Michel, T. T. Lawson, T. C. West, T. Butler, J. P. Newsham, W. A. Williams, S. Weil, D. Stewart, J. P. Munford, R. H. Halle, P. Butler, J. J. Barrow, J. H. Collins, Jr., L. B. Jenks, L. P. Day, J. F. Irwin, R. G. Sterling, C. M. Barrow, H. Perkins.

Franklin (two votes)—No credentials. No delegates.

Grant (two votes)—W. R. Rutland, H .V. McKain.

Iberia (two votes)—Joseph A. Breaux, John B. Marsh, J. Robertson, J. H. Levy, J. M. Avery, J. T. Wyche, H. Bussey, J. G. Soulier.

Iberville (four votes)—Gov. P. O. Hebert, G. Schlatre, A. Jumel, C. A. Brusle, D. W. Barrow, Ernest Caurier. Alternates—L. C. Connor, E. H. Boissac, Henry Ware, John H. Randolph, John H. Schauch, J. P. R. Jones.

Jackson (two votes)—No credentials. No delegates.

Jefferson (six votes)—W. Mithoff, Sr., J. C. Kahmon, S. L. Henry, L. C. Perret, W. R. Chapman, T. F. Hennings, F. C. Hester.

Lafayette (two votes)—No credentials. No delegates.

Livingston (two votes)—S. R. Terry, James Toney, S. P. Holden, George Westmoreland, A. Hoover, W. Bill, H. R. Womack, James Turner, D. Chandler, L. Spiller, L. Castle, William Hood, P. H. Spear, Henry Corkem, H. Idell, A. W. Kinchen, S. Kemp, W. S. Round,

APPENDIX

M. T. Carter, Peter Jones, Peter Cooney, P. Labourgères, O. Walker, E. Ellis, B. Wall, J. Turner, J. P. Tull, W. A. Davidson, J. F. Kane, Samuel Dickson, Ed Cooper, I. Watson, H. Hood, A. Singleton, F. Miscarr, U. F. Felder, J. Chandler, J. F. Massey, Thomas Green Davidson, William B. Round, William S. Rose.

Lafourche (four votes)—Taylor Beattie, J. D. Moore, Lou Bush, A. Weisse, J. W. Howell.

Morehouse (two votes)—D. C. Morgan, W. F. Blanchard. Alternates—George M. Sandige, J. G. Weeks.

Madison (two votes)—A. W. Crandell, William R. Stone.

St. James (four votes)—E. Scanlan, D. Webb, J. Jentil, A. L. Bourgois.

St. Landry (eight votes)—J. A. Taylor, E. T. Lewis, L. E. Prescott, L. Dupre, F. Perrodin, W. Burton, S. Hass, W. Offett, with A. R. Hawkins a substitute detained by illness.

St. Mary (four votes)—R. Macready, D. Burnick, W. J. Foster, C. Vauskiff. Alternates—G. B. Golding, G. W. Thomas, F. L. Gates, T. J. Schaffer.

St. Tammany (two votes)—A. Chevolon, G. W. Palmer, S. H. Houston.

Tangipahoa (two votes)—John Rapman, W. H. Lillard. Alternates—C. H. Mooney, A. L. Johnson, T. M. Terry.

Terrebonne (four votes)—J. Gueno, W. Beslin, A. J. Knight, J. M. Price, H. C. Minor, H. Vialian, N. S. Williams, A. Tenirot, M. R. Gibson, M. Haubichirr, F. Theazie.

Tensas (four votes)—J. M. Gillespie, S. M. Rough, L. V. Rees, C. C. Cordill. Alternates—R. Lewis, Dr. D. Newell, C. G. Nichols, Dr. F. Barnes.

Union (two votes)—No credentials. No delegates.

Vermilion (two votes)—W. Mouton, J. A. Taylor.

Vernon (two votes)—H. W. Schaneken, J. M. Smith, B. B. Lewis, E. P. Smart, G. B. Burr.

Winn (two votes)—J. J. McLearn, P. Baggadas, B. B. Schaugens, J. E. Jones.

Washington (two votes)—No credentials. No delegates.

Webster (two votes)—Isaac Murrell, T. B. Neale. Alternates—F. M. Fort, C. E. M'Donald.

Plaquemines (two votes)—E. Lawrence, E. Smith, R. D. Baldwin. Alternates—S. Mullan, J. C. Conrad, B. Fasterling.

Point Coupee (four votes)—W. Means, S. Barbin, J. J. Suthfield, J. P. Harns, M. H. Andry, J. G. Archer, A. Taylor, J. W. Denison, James Cotton, F. L. Claiborne, A. Scott, M. Thompson, S. Van Wickle, A. A. Lebeau, A. Pourcheon, J. Boudro, C. Samson, G. L. Balsy, Benjamin Jewell, L. V. Porch, S. Allain, E. Taylor, H. T.

Hereford, E. Lovell, E. Basil, J. B. Sterling, A. Raykin, S. V. McVay, L. B. Claiborne.

Richland (two votes)—J. E. Lewis, A. B. Cooper. Alternates—W. B. Oliver, W. T. Ivy.

Rapides (six votes)—T. C. Manning, W. F. Blackman, L. Texada, R. J. Bowman, T. S. Smith, J. A. Williams, W. W. Whittinger, Jr., J. W. Prescott, C. R. Hanvorth, M. Wells, H. L. Daigre, W. J. Calvet, M. Paul, M. Ryan, J. P. Poplet, Edward Neil, J. L. Walker, James C. Wise, James G. White, John S. Butler, J. G. P. Hooe, G. W. Stanford, Stephen White, T. V. Helm, E. A. Wells, J. Swan, A. G. Compton, T. G. Compton, B. Tanner, J. Levings, O. L. Robertson, J. A. Newall.

Sabines (two votes)—J. F. Smith, A. Carter, A. Lout, J. B. Vandergar, C. H. C. Brown.

Red River (two votes)—W. Sproul, E. Friend, T. E. Paxson, J. W. Sanderford. Alternates—T. D. Brown, B. W. Marston.

St. Bernard (two votes)—G. H. Flagg, C. D. Armstrong.

St. Helena (two votes)—S. D. Richardson, James Clinton, C. W. George, J. H. Pipes, J. H. Kemp.

St. John Baptist (two votes)—L. De Porter, S. Glover.

St. Martin (four votes)—C. C. Brown, A. Veazie, A. W. Ferret, A. Delahousaye.

St. Charles (two votes)—P. Harper, P. Gunia, H. L. Young, H. W. Canney, P. D. Cooks.

Natchitoches (four votes)—R. E. Hammertt, J. W. Butler, L. Perot, F. Jennings, J. D. Addison, N. Gimirvon, R. Johnson, J. A. Prudhomme, N. H. Campbell, D. Pierson, E. L. Pierson, W. H. Jack, John Sims, S. M. Hyams, S. W. Griswold, James E. Turner, J. Kile, S. O. Scruggs, A. Prudhomme, T. O. Schaillaire, C. J. C. Pucket, C. Champlim, Sr., J. M. B. Tucker, Thomas Hunter, V. Gaimie, R. S. Carter, William O. Brien, A. Earhart, R. Grant, L. Charville, W. Campbell, P. A. Morse, R. E. Burke, W. Homes, J. A. Wolfson, A. Sompayrac, J. Henry, W. A. Ponder, J. J. Key, E. Ross, A. Marronovich, J. Charleville, W. M. Levy, C. Champlin, Jr., H. E. Walmsley.

Ouachita (four votes)—R. W. Richardson, A. L. Slack, H. M. Bry, W. H. Mullan, J. H. Flannery, S. L. Moore, W. W. Farmer, Y. Mulsaup, J. F. Strouger, J. L. Hunsaker, W. W. Rischer.

Orleans—

First Ward (four votes)—James H. Wingfield, C. McRae Selph, V. J. Lambert, F. S. Washington.

Second Ward (six votes)—E. A. Burke, John A. Fitzpatrick, John McManus, John Hurley, T. B. O'Brien, Frederick Wang. Alternates—E. N. Cullum, A. Dimitri, H. H. Walsh, J. J. Lane, M. Newman, D. B. Penn.

APPENDIX

Third Ward (eight votes)—Joshua Corprew, D. Malone, D. H. Fagan, A. Fabian, T. Reiley, Thomas O'Connor, J. D. Houston, C. C. Haley (seat contested by P. Baron).

Fourth Ward (four votes)—Z. Keenan, J. W. Donnely, J. A. Magner, H. Oertling.

Fifth Ward (four votes)—E. Ramellie, E. W. Kavanaugh, J. A. Schalk, M. C. Barry.

Sixth Ward (two votes)—L. E. Lemaire, R. Brewster.

Seventh Ward (four votes)—P. Swan, B. H. Lynch, J. Asher.

Eighth Ward (two votes)—G. Delamore, J. Dillon.

Ninth Ward (four votes)—A. B. Sloanmaker, W. C. Kinsella, A. Wallace, Charles Herzberg.

Tenth Ward (three votes)—W. Redmond, L. L. Davis, T. Lilienthal.

Eleventh Ward (three votes)—R. N. Ogden, D. C. Kessler, C. A. Meyers.

Twelfth Ward (three votes)—R. L. Preston, C. J. Fox.

Thirteenth Ward (one vote)—J. A. Moran.

Fourteenth Ward (one vote)—J. A. C. B. Fish.

Fifteenth Ward, right bank (two votes)—F. Smidtky, E. Wittemore.